The Expatri

Franklin Pierce

The Expatriation of Franklin Pierce

◆

The Story of a President and the Civil War

Garry Boulard

iUniverse, Inc.
New York Lincoln Shanghai

The Expatriation of Franklin Pierce
The Story of a President and the Civil War

Copyright © 2006 by Garry Boulard

iUniverse books may be ordered through booksellers or by contacting:

iUniverse
2021 Pine Lake Road, Suite 100
Lincoln, NE 68512
www.iuniverse.com
1-800-Authors (1-800-288-4677)

ISBN-13: 978-0-595-40367-7 (pbk)
ISBN-13: 978-0-595-84742-6 (ebk)
ISBN-10: 0-595-40367-0 (pbk)
ISBN-10: 0-595-84742-0 (ebk)

Printed in the United States of America

For Frank Mercatante—a life-long inspiration

Contents

Acknowledgements

Librarians and archivists are really the ones who get history books get written; not just because they furnish materials requested by an author that can't be found in any other place, but more often than most readers know they unveil other sources of information—letters, random and remote articles in newspapers, magazines and journals, even other libraries and archives—unknown to the author, providing a gentle and reassuring assist on what is inevitably an exciting but necessarily solitary journey of discovery.

For the journey that has led me to an understanding and respectful appreciation of one of America's most obscure but yet (unfairly, I think) reviled presidents, I am indebted to Leslie Baskin, reference librarian, Memorial Hall Library, Andover, Massachusetts; Janet Bloom, archivist, the Early Americana Collection, William L. Clements Library, University of Michigan; Gail A. Carrillo, director, Polo Public Library, Polo, Illinois; Bonnie B. Coles, manuscript reference assistant, the Library of Congress; William Copeley, librarian, New Hampshire Historical Society; H. George Fletcher, assistant, photo services office, New York Public Library; Claire Gabriel, special collections librarian, Manhattanville College; Ian Graham, special collections assistant, Bowdoin College Library; Merrily Harris, librarian, W. S. Hoole Special Collections Library, University of Alabama; Evan Hocker, archivist, Center for American History, University of Texas at Austin; Sabra Ionno, assistant librarian, Harriet Beecher Stowe Center; Carl Katafiasz, reference director, Monroe County Library System, Monroe, Michigan; Deborah Kolb, reference librarian, Des Moines Public Library; Mary Loe, coordinator, special collections, Penfield Library, Oswego State University of New York; Lauren Mandel, library assistant, The Bostonian Society; Anna Lee Pauls, special collections assistant, Princeton University Library; Louise Sandberg, archivist, Lawrence Public Library, Lawrence, Massachusetts; David Smolen, special collections librarian, New Hampshire Historical Society; Patrick J. Stevens, coordinator of reference, Cornell University Library; Liz Triplett, reference librarian, Richmond Public Library; Jessica Tyree, research assistant, Southern Historical Collection, University of North Carolina at Chapel Hill; and Jessica Westphal, reference assistant, Special Collections Research Center, the University of Chicago Library.

For satisfying my endless and perhaps even obsessive interlibrary loan requests, I cannot say enough about Dee Valdez, information specialist and Ida Mazzoni, main library manager, of the Albuquerque/Bernalillo County Library System. Similarly the assistance of Monica Dorame, library specialist, who hauled out old and cumbersome volumes of the *Congressional Globe* and the *War of Rebellion: Official Records of the Union and Confederate* Armies, a 128-volume collection, from the vaults of the government documents archive at the University of New Mexico's Zimmerman Library, proved invaluable.

In New Orleans, where I lived until 2003, initial bibliographical assistance was provided by the always-helpful John Brandao, associate librarian with the Turchin Library at Tulane University's Freeman School of Business.

And finally a special word of thanks to Ana Cruz-Esparza, St. John Frizell, June Galloway, Patrick Melvin, Susan Roberts, Davis and Anamaria Iosif Ross, Sean Solowiej, John Tottenham, Molly Wales and Kathleen Zenz who either fed me, deciphered letters from the 1850s and 60s with me, helped me in my insatiable quest for microfilm or just listened to my endless stories concerning this project; and to Antonio Cruz, who created the book's cover and provided, inevitably with a smile, all of the technical support that brought a many-times computer-bewildered author to the happy end of a most satisfying project.

My debt to all of you is incalculable.

1

"He Has Satisfied No One and Disgusted All."

Washington, D.C., March 4, 1857: A slender man in black suit, wearing black gloves with black crepe wrapped around his silk hat anxiously awaits the signal from the White House doorman that his carriage has arrived.

Franklin Pierce, the doorman had once observed, "does not keep his manners for the fine folk that come here, but he gives me the compliments of the morning as grandly as he does General [Winfield] Scott." 1

Pierce, a reporter for the *Washington Post* would later recall, in his "intercourse with the citizens of Washington, was in striking contrast with the Chinese wall of etiquette erected by later administrations."

It was he and his shy First Lady, Jane Pierce, who "visited intimately families whose heads held the smaller clerkships in the departments," the reporter noted, adding that "no President ever had so entirely the heartfelt friendship of Washingtonians." 2

It was an obsession with him to treat with courtesy and respect not just those who worked for him, but virtually anyone who wandered onto the White House grounds as well. One night, as the Marine Band entertained a larger gathering on the south portico, a man whose attire suggested he was from the country, approached Pierce and quietly asked: "Mr. President, can't I go through your fine house? I've heard so much about it that I'd give a great deal to see it."

Pierce smiled and responded: "My dear sir, that is not *my* house. It's the people's house! You shall certainly go through it if you wish." 3

With that he asked a staff member to give the man a personal tour of the White House, a gift bestowed upon many the wide-eyed before and after.

Pierce greeted friends, said the diplomat Maunsell Field, "with both hands outstretched, after the manner of the French."

"He was always so amiable, so friendly in his manner, so affectionate even in his demonstrations," Field also said, "that I never could continue angry with him for forty-eight consecutive hours." 4

And his good looks didn't hurt either: upon visiting him in the White House, long-time Washington doyen Anne Royall found herself transfixed by his blue eyes, as were many, and the president's "soft and pleasing voice," which, she said, was "attuned to melody itself." Pierce's engaging manner, Royall added, "readily captivates the beholder, though he rarely smiles." 5

Presented to the American public by his handlers in 1852 as a younger, more modern version of the populist woodsman Andrew Jackson—the Democrats dubbed him "Young Hickory of the Granite State"—Pierce was in reality a man of refined tastes and interests. He read the Greek classics, sent expensive wine by the crate to friends, and sat to have his portrait preserved in oil by painters.

During his four years in the White House he enthusiastically approved and personally watched over the building of an elaborate greenhouse with a sloping glass-paned roof; the renovation of the White House garden, lush with camellias and roses; the installation of a hot-water heating system (one of the first of its kind in the country); and the creation of new ceiling decorations in gold, green and blue imitation fresco dominated by a center neoclassical sunburst of leaves.

Public receptions during the Pierce years were nearly always boisterous, crowded events, no doubt made the clumsier by the large numbers of people forced to crane their necks in order to really appreciate the beautifully detailed ceilings.

The White House chaise was equally elegant: "A handsome two-horse carriage, with driver and footman attired in plain blue dress," as described by a reporter, it boasted plate glass windows, an interior of Morocco lining, and a team of white horses whose harnesses gleamed in silver. 6

The effect of refinement was also aided by Pierce's attire, which during formal occasions never strayed from basic black. Observing him at a Diplomatic Corps reception, Benjamin Brown French, a friend of wavering loyalty, thought that the contrast between Pierce and the "glitter of gold & epaulettes on the Foreign representatives was great, and in my judgement very much in favor of *us.*"

"No man," continued French, "dresses more appropriately on all occasions than General Pierce." 7

Even John Wise, the adolescent son of Pierce's old drinking companion, Virginia Representative Henry Wise, was impressed, recalling the day that Pierce entered the carriage he and his father were riding in. "He gave me a very gracious recognition, and I, in turn, watched him intently."

The young Wise then took in Pierce's "kind, bright eyes, smooth-shaven face, sharp-pointed nose and curly hair."

But, once again, what was most remembered was Pierce's preference for black, which eventually defined almost every article of his clothing. "I had time to note his black kid gloves and black shirt buttons," Wise later remembered. 8

How much Pierce's clothing and manners were dictated by Jane remained an open question. Varina Davis, the young wife of Jefferson Davis, perhaps Pierce's closest friend in Washington and his secretary of war, was greatly amused one day as she watched Pierce pace with his hands stuffed in his pockets.

The occasion was a visit to Jefferson and Varina's country resort. Always the two couples engaged in lively conversation. This time, the subject was Nathaniel Hawthorne, which prompted Pierce to speculate about the nature of the author's genius as he walked and talked out loud, lost in thought. Suddenly Jane took a quick, disapproving look at Pierce's hidden hands, a glance that Pierce just as quickly noticed.

"No, I won't take them out of my pockets, Jennie!" Pierce exclaimed. "I am in the country and I like to feel the comfort of it." 9

At the White House, however, Pierce was sometimes surprisingly informal, or so thought Maunsell Field: "He wore a stunning dressing gown of black velvet, lined with cherry-colored silk, which some admiring lady had sent to him," recorded Field, who was astonished to observe that Pierce regularly wore the robe "not only in his private apartments, but also in the executive rooms, when he received the dignitaries of the Senate and others upon business." 10

If Field was unsettled by Pierce's informality, he would have been shocked to learn how the president sometimes wiled away his evening hours. Often, he simply walked out the front door of the White House and proceeded, by himself, down Pennsylvania Avenue.

"One could stand at Fifteenth street and mark his progress far down the street by the uplifting of hats by the citizens and businessmen," the *Washington Post* writer would recall. 11

Just weeks before the end of his term, upon learning that Varina Davis was ill and by herself with her new-born son at the Davis apartment on 14th and F streets, Pierce headed out by himself into a January blizzard with snow gusts waist-high to check on her.

When a grateful Varina later asked why he had not simply sent a White House servant or two, Pierce remarked that "they would have no personal interest to urge them on." 12

Alabama Senator Clement Clay and his outspoken wife Virginia also knew first-hand of Pierce's penchant for exploring the streets of Washington alone. One night as the couple snuggled before a blazing fire at the Ebbitt House, a favorite boarding house for Southern members of Congress, they heard a soft knock on their door. A maid responded, only to reveal what Virginia would later describe as a "tall figure, wrapped in a long storm-cloak on which the snow flakes still lay thickly."

Instructing Senator Clay to bolt the front door and "not let a soul know I am here," Pierce presented Virginia with a recent framed photo of himself while she instructed the maid to prepare what she called a "friendly egg-nog" for the President.

"Ahh, my dear friends," Pierce exclaimed as he warmed his hands at the fire, "I am so tired of the shackles of presidential life that I can scarcely endure it."

"I long for…" Pierce continued, before stopping and taking in the cozy parlor, "this!…for relaxation and privacy once more—and a chance for home." 13

So he went his own way and did what he felt like doing and often offended Washington sensibilities in the process; and now, waiting for the carriage that would transport him to his final ceremony as president, he knew that he could just as easily walk, or for that matter hop on his horse and ride, as he often did, but that his soon-to-be successor James Buchanan might be offended and relations between the two men were already frayed enough anyway.

What an outrage, Senator Clay fumed, when he later learned how long Pierce had waited for the carriage that would take him to Buchanan. But Pierce was sanguine, even joking, when he replied: "Ah, Clay, have you lived so long without knowing that all of the homage is given to the rising sun—never to the setting, however resplendent its noonday?" 14

When the carriage finally did appear, Pierce stepped into it alone. The First Lady, whose affection for Washington society had always been minimal, opted to stay behind in the book-lined residence of William Marcy, Pierce's departing secretary of state, on Vermont Avenue.

The grand dames of Washington had always been offended by Jane's indifference to them, but they explained it away by noting that the First Lady was in mourning for the last of her three sons, Benny, who died in a horrific accident just weeks before her husband became president.

But the truth of the matter was that Jane had despaired of Washington convention years before she had a socially acceptable reason to do so. As long ago as the 1830s when her ambitious husband was one of the youngest members of Congress, she could not believe that the wives of each member were expected to spend entire afternoons dropping off their calling cards at the residences of various Washington elites.

"This is a business which consumes a great deal of time and of which one gets very wearied," Jane had characteristically complained. And she was even less impressed with many of her husband's colleagues, who oftentimes took to the floors of the House or Senate for hours of frequently windy oratory. Listening with growing impatience to one particularly long speech by Representative Wise, Jane was certain of one thing: Wise was, she wrote "speaking evidently to his *own* satisfaction, to say the least." 15

The other women in the extended Pierce clan were equally irreverent. When Jane's sister, Mary Aiken, attended a White House dinner, she encountered a group of Congressmen and their wives whom she quickly sized up as "just the very last picking."

"There were only six ladies besides ourselves, and they were very common-looking people—and the men—for I can't call them gentlemen, were horrible," Aiken continued, noting that the member who sat nearest her "shoveled his food in with his knife," while another man "took a veal cutlet up in his fingers" before consuming it. 16

Such tales greatly amused the President. What the two women would say about Buchanan, who sometimes struck observers as both officious and stuffy, could only be imagined.

From the White House, the carriage carrying Pierce headed for the stately Willard Hotel at the corner of Pennsylvania Avenue and 14th street, where Buchanan invited Pierce into his open barouche. Together, the two men then rode under what was now a very bright mid-day sun back onto Pennsylvania avenue, waving at a thick crowd that lined both sides of the street.

Faces. Pierce gazed about and saw America: young boys straddling the limbs of sturdy oaks, exquisitely dressed men and women comically sharing the same uneven sidewalk space with the city's rabble; slaves and their masters, all entranced by the passing parade.

Loose dogs and horses paused, certain of their non-human brethren were less visible in the wake of an official decree from the chief of police promising to round up all "hogs and geese running at large in the city." 17

The procession of cheers grew louder as the two men neared the Capitol and the size of the crowds seemed to almost triple.

They looked directly at Pierce and smiled and waved.

How strange they should do that. Had these people not read the papers or listened to the recent Congressional debates? Were they unaware of the many nasty asides whispered in the city's salons or delivered like brimstone from the nation's pulpits?

Did they not know that he, Franklin Pierce, was the most hated man in America?

He was nothing more than a "poor, discarded, repudiated man," the blunt and physically imposing Senator Benjamin F. Wade of Ohio had recently said of Pierce. Young and fiery Representative John Sherman, also of Ohio, agreed, claiming that the ghost of Pierce's "defeated hopes haunt him at every step." Had anyone ever been as thoroughly repudiated as Franklin Pierce, Sherman asked, noting the most recent election returns. "He is about to retire defeated by his own party, by his own state, and I believe, by his own town." 18

The balding and normally reserved Senator Jacob Collamer of Vermont reduced his feelings on Pierce to a single sentence when he called him a "disappointed, ambitious man, worthy of no particular notice." 19

John P. Hale, once, many years ago, a trusted friend, now loathed Pierce: "No man in modern times has inflicted such serious and lasting injury upon his country as Franklin Pierce," Hale had written. Always capable of bringing a smile to the faces of his fellow senators with his jokes and wry observations, Hale, on the topic of Pierce, was now uncharacteristically bitter: "The President is reprehensible," Hale said from the floor of the Senate. 20

Benjamin Brown French, who shortly fell out with Pierce after he entered the White House, soon was quoting the chief justice of New Hampshire, George Kittredge, on Pierce: "In hell, they'll roast him like a herring." Pierce, Kittredge added, "has the damnest black heart that was ever placed [in] a mortal bosom." 21

French himself could only add: "We cannot get a poorer cuss than he who now disgraces the Presidential chair! Were he to come into my house, although I should probably treat him with the coldest kind of civility, my toe would feel a great inclination to perform the disagreeable duty of kicking him out!" 22

In New York, prominent businessman and attorney George Templeton Strong was convinced that Pierce, "in his approaching days of insignificance…cannot make himself more infamous than he is already by any new exhibition of baseness." 23

From Texas, Sam Houston was furious. Whenever he wrote about Pierce his usual clear penmanship was dissolved into an angry scrawl: "He is the traitor of all ages," Houston said of Pierce, claiming he had "betrayed more pledges and deceived more men than any other man that has lived." 24

At a raucous Republican banquet in Chicago, Abraham Lincoln delighted the faithful who thought he might be a national figure in the near future by likening Pierce to a "rejected lover, making merry at the wedding of his rival."

Lincoln seemed to hugely enjoy the idea that Pierce had seemingly sacrificed so much for the Democrats, in particular Southern Democrats, only to be denied a nomination for a second term by his own party. "By dragging of chestnuts from the fire for others to eat, his claws are burnt off to the gristle" said Lincoln as his audience roared, "and he is thrown aside as unfit for future use." 25

Pierce had long ago lost—indeed if he had ever possessed it—the support of the nation's intellectuals. Ralph Waldo Emerson repeatedly belittled him, astonished that the country could have elected a man such as Pierce, and personally resented the fact that Pierce enjoyed a close friendship with Nathaniel Hawthorne, the writer whom Emerson yearned to share confidences with. Petulant, Emerson described Pierce in his own journal as a "toad in amber." The young Walt Whitman, perhaps taking his signal from his intellectual elders, claimed that Pierce "eats dirt and excrement for his daily meals, likes it and tries to force it on the states." 26

Dismayed by Pierce's policies, Theodore Parker, theologian and, with Emerson, a Transcendentalist, was convinced that the president has returned to drinking. "I had intelligence of his being solemnly intoxicated on a most important occasion last May," Parker reported to a friend. "But now he is gone over, it is said, to cups, and cups only." 27

Henry Wadsworth Longfellow, who went to school with Pierce and admired him the way any young boy looks up to a more manly and confident senior student, now said nothing at all on the subject of Franklin Pierce.

But Pierce inspired perhaps the most condemnation from Lydia Maria Child, the New England poet, short story writer and abolitionist, who pronounced the President's name—as did many in New England—as "purse," and composed a poem repeatedly rhyming it with "curse." 28

Far more viciously, in her short story *The Kansas Emigrants*, Child described a young couple trying to survive in a Kansas terrorized by pro-slavery Southerners, undoubtedly friends of the President. Kate Bradford, the young protagonist of the story, laments after witnessing one Southern-led assault: "I wonder whether Frank Pierce has any children." 29

The comment, for readers, must have been shocking considering that everyone—including Child—knew that all three of Pierce's children had died in early childhood, the most recent being Benny who was crushed to death in a train accident.

But Child, like nearly all the anti-slavery activists, was on a crusade that frequently confused bitter invective for high purpose. When Calvin Stowe, the husband of Harriet Beecher Stowe, dared to defend Pierce in Child's presence, she could only stew, again making the political personal: "If I were his wife," Child said of Pierce, "I'd sue for divorce…" 30

Stinging as such comments were, the ongoing assault on Pierce by the nation's writers and thinkers had only a marginal influence on the day-to-day business of Washington. Far more damaging was the defection of James Gordon Bennett, the owner of the *New York Herald*, in 1857 the most important newspaper in the nation.

By the time Pierce had become president in 1853, Bennett had reigned supreme for more than a decade, was a millionaire many times over, lived in a splendid mansion, and was accustomed to being listened to. He had given Pierce important and enthusiastic support in 1852, and not long after the election let it drop that even though he was "far from being ambitious," he would regard being named ambassador to France, if Pierce was so inclined, as the final triumph over his critics, "the cap on the pyramid, the keystone in the arch." 31

But Pierce was not so inclined, earning him Bennett's undying scorn. Soon the favorable coverage of the president completely disappeared. In its place, Bennett sought to portray Pierce as a hapless accident, a clown, a man who was just naturally given to disappointment. In the paper's daily reporting on Pierce, he was no longer referred to as "the President," but rather as "Poor Pierce."

And now, on the very morning that Pierce was leaving the White House, Bennett's *Herald* published a stinging farewell that was soon in the hands of the very people who were cheering Pierce along Pennsylvania Avenue. "Alallelujah! We have reached the last day of Poor Pierce's administration," the *Herald* exclaimed. "At twelve o'clock this day, the worst of the United States presidents will retire into private life…he has satisfied no one and disgusted all." 32

In its sour dismissal of Pierce, the *Herald* was hardly alone. Pierce had, in fact, lost the most influential papers of New York. The passionate and cause-oriented Horace Greeley daily attacked him from his perch in the *New York Tribune*, while the *New York Times*, just emerging as a power, made it clear that it had no use for Pierce at all: "The man who enters upon the presidency an aspiring demagogue is quite certain to quit it a disappointed, soured, and resentful one." 33

In the Midwest, such papers as the *Chicago Tribune* and the *Cleveland Plain Dealer*, appealing to a western-moving readership increasingly disillusioned with the Democratic party, generally and greatly opposed him. But perhaps the most significant anti-Pierce paper in the region had become the *Detroit Tribune*, largely reflecting the views of the ascendant Republican party in that state. And even the city's Democratic organ, the *Detroit Free Press,* had soured on Pierce: "We thank God that President Pierce's term of office is coming to a close," the paper exclaimed in disgust. 34

Such opposition, however, was nothing compared to what Pierce encountered in the nation's abolitionist press, convinced that the president was pro-slavery, even though he had never uttered a word in that direction. Feeding a subscription that was almost by the hour becoming more radicalized, such newspapers as William Lloyd Garrison's the *Liberator* in Boston, the *National Era* in Washington, and the *Pennsylvania Freeman* in Philadelphia portrayed Pierce as a slave himself, in this case to Southern interests, in particular Jefferson Davis, by 1857, the most important pro-slavery voice in the nation.

When Pierce sought to defend his administration in his final state of the union message, the reaction of the *National Anti-Slavery Standard* in New York fairly well summed up the feeling of the entire abolitionist press towards him: "There can be no question now as to his moral intrepidity," it said, adding that Pierce was a "man whose personal insignificance cannot hide his going into history." 35

In their ride towards the Capitol, Pierce and Buchanan followed what for many was the most sensational display in the inaugural parade, the Liberty Car, a huge float drawn by six muscular white horses transporting the Goddess of Liberty, or at least in this case an attractive young woman dressed up to look like her. Both men could only naturally assume that the almost hysterical cheers of the young men upon catching their first glimpse of the goddess must be meant for them too.

To their rear was an equally unforgettable exhibit: a miniature ship on wheels with a dozen young boys dressed as sailors, excitedly waving flags to the ever-thickening crowd. Constructed by shipwrights at a nearby Navy yard, the float, thought a reporter for the *Baltimore American*, seemed "emblematic of national unity and power." 36

But as Pierce knew only too well, that unity was more elusive now than ever before, a vaporous dream sharply at odds with a darker and uglier reality. In Kansas, Americans were killing each other—more than 200 in 1856 alone—seeking to create a state that would either allow for slavery or prohibit it. Pierce's presidency, almost every political observer was certain, could be found in pieces strewn along the Great Plains. But it was more than that, a certain intolerance and deeply-etched division that had come to contaminate almost every intercourse; threatening to explode into violence at a moment's notice.

Pierce did not need to read the dispatches from Kansas to know that something was wrong. Right in Washington raw nerves and inflamed passions were combining to make monsters of men. In May, the tall and young Preston Brooks, a representative from South Carolina, attacked Massachusetts Senator Charles Sumner with a heavy cane in retaliation for anti-slavery remarks Sumner had made two days earlier which Brooks had interpreted, or so he later said, as a "libel on South Carolina."

After a day of drinking, Brooks entered the Senate chamber determined, he subsequently claimed, not to nearly kill Sumner, "but only to whip him." Spotting the Massachusetts senator at his desk, Brooks came at him from behind and repeatedly struck his cane hard over Sumner's head, so hard that the cane eventually broke in two pieces, in the end partially paralyzing Sumner. 37

Washingtonians were shocked by the assault, but perhaps even more troubling was the response to it. Northerners decried its sheer brutality, while Southerners seemed to feel that Sumner, whom many regarded as haughty, had it coming. The *Richmond Examiner* celebrated Brooks' defeat of what it called "an inanimate lump of incarnate cowardice." 38

In December, Sumner, after weeks of therapy, made a dramatic appearance at Boston's Fanueil Hall, waving to a packed house of ecstatic and screaming supporters, and nourishing the moment: "I seek nothing but the triumph of truth," he declared, leaving no doubt that his cause, and the suffering he had endured for it, was also theirs'. Perversely, Brooks, nine years Sumner's junior, died suddenly in January from a cold. 39

And the rancor continued: also in May William D. Wallach, the editor of the *Washington Star*, verbally accosted Major John P. Heiss, a Pierce envoy just returned from Nicaragua, after the Major declined to greet him when the two men met by accident at the Willard Hotel. Heiss, recently the subject of an unflattering profile in Wallach's paper, said that he was "not in the habit of giving his hand to a vilifier and falsifier." Astonished, Wallach cursed Heiss, only to be struck with the seasons's most deadly weapon, a cane, wielded so severely by the Major, noted a reporter for the *New York Times*, that Wallach's "blood marked the tessellated floor in numerous spots." 40

Far more deadly was a second encounter that same day at the Willard between California Congressman Philemon Herbert and one of the hotel's waiters. When told that he had arrived too late for breakfast, Herbert, who was accompanied by a friend from California, regarded the waiter as insolent and attributed that insolence to his Irish ancestry, and now demanded: "Get us some breakfast!"

When the waiter, whose name was Thomas Keating, once again tried to explain that the serving hours for breakfast had come and gone, Herbert jumped on top of him. Witnesses later said they were certain that the waiter held his own, but fists were no match against the pistol that Herbert soon pulled out from beneath his jacket, firing at least once into Keating's chest. John Edbright, another waiter, later testified that all he remembered seeing was "the blood rush out of Keating's coat," just seconds before Keating collapsed and died. 41

Herbert was shortly arrested and released on bond, his fellow congressmen paying tribute to his general character. Keating, who left behind a wife and two children, was buried two days later in a quiet ceremony.

The violence even reached, in a certain fashion, into the White House. At the end of February, Pierce hosted his final White House reception. As usual, hundreds of people—government functionaries, political insiders and simple Washington residents—turned out, crowding their way into the mansion, hoping to see Pierce and have a word with him. "Some ladies, of a provincial appearance, stood on the sofas to obtain a better view of—nothing," reported a correspondent for the *London Times*, "and several juveniles, whose heads could not reach the air, were nearly suffocated in the throng." 42

It was perhaps inevitable in such a mass of churning frustration that something would go wrong, and it did: Colonel Doddridge Lee, a clerk in the Pension Bureau, suddenly discovered his wallet was missing and loudly accused a man who was standing near him, David Hume, a businessman from Alexandria, of the theft.

Hume was astonished. "I should feel myself dishonored if I should pick the pocket of such a man as you are," he remarked.

As the crowd suddenly found something more interesting to look at than Pierce, the two men angrily turned away from each other, but not before, in the time-honored fashion, exchanging cards.

The following morning, a Saturday, Hume appeared at Lee's office and asked if he cared to repeat his accusations of the night before. The Colonel responded in the affirmative, prompting Hume to exclaim that over the course of his life he had probably "given away" more money than Lee was worth. Hume then reached for his cane to teach the Colonel a lesson. But the lesson went unlearned as Lee brandished a pistol and shot Hume in the abdomen, causing instant death. 43

"About one-half of the years of my manhood have been passed here," Pierce told a group of city officials just days before he would leave office. "And the experience of each year has only served to enhance my appreciation of the admirable qualities which characterize the permanent population of the District."

He would never forget, he said, how quiet the noisy city was on a Sunday, the day when he and Jane attended church on 14th street as part of a mixed-race congregation. And whatever the politics of the day, Pierce continued, he would always consider Washington as a "great city, pre-eminently distinguished for arts, taste, science and refinement."

His only regret, Pierce added, was that he had not done more to help build up the physical beauty of the place. Someday he would return, he promised, and then would hope to find "gushing fountains, from the great falls of the Potomac everywhere in your city springing up and sparkling in the sunlight." 44

As the parade reached the Capitol, the military opened ranks, moving to either side of Pierce and Buchanan's barouche to present arms. The two men then stepped down before being ushered into the Senate chambers by a delegation of lawmakers.

Inside, the circular gallery was filled with women, most of whom were the wives of senators, representatives, and diplomats specially invited for the ceremony and whispering with great excitement as they saw Pierce and Buchanan pause, waiting for their place in a line that included the bedecked marshal of the District of Columbia, all of the justices of the Supreme Court, and the diplomatic corp.

The procession then moved to the east portico of the Capitol, where a huge crowd had been waiting since the early morning hours in anticipation of the historic moment when the transfer of power became a reality. "The change is one of the greatest among the vicissitudes of life, albeit not visible to the eye," the same *London Times* correspondent who had nearly been suffocated at Pierce's last reception, observed.

"Mr. Pierce, in his plain suit of black, disposing of destinies and fortunes at 10 in the morning, differs in nothing externally from Mr. Pierce at 1 p.m.," the reporter continued, "but at the latter hour he is now a private citizen, and his signature would not draw a dollar from the Treasury, nor his order move a troop of Dragoons." 45

Sitting behind Buchanan and facing the large crowd, Pierce could wonder: it was four years ago exactly that he stood at the same spot, delivering his address from memory.

All of Washington then seemed entranced with him. He had been drafted by the Democrats after other, more well-known candidates had failed. That he had craftily maneuvered and planned for such an outcome was known to only a few, making his nomination seem entirely spontaneous and fresh to the nation.

His election that fall, in a year when the Democratic party enjoyed a superior organization, was almost guaranteed.

"It would be an interesting calculation to find out the number of patriots here now who were each one the first to name Gen. Pierce for the presidency," a Washington letter-writer laughed as Pierce swept into the city then. 46

That he also proceeded to craft his cabinet nearly entirely on his own, bringing into his administration powerful men from competing factions of the party, only seemed to be more proof that this young man from New Hampshire was an extraordinarily skilled politician.

And well liked, too: "He is a quiet, gentlemanlike man in appearance and manner," noted the aging Washington Irving, who was particularly delighted to learn that Pierce had given to Hawthorne the post of London counsel. Anyone who helped support a writer couldn't be all bad. 47

Pierce's inaugural address that day thrilled many. "The sentiments—the tone of the address—the earnest manner in which it was spoken—his beautiful action—his manly, erect appearance—his pale cast of countenance," said the *New York Herald*, which then seemed to almost love him, "all combined to make a deep impression in favor of General Pierce, and many asserted that this was the best inaugural address ever delivered from the spot." 48

How much had changed in just four years.

But there were still those who were devoted to him. Yet even they could not express their affection for him without making reference to his vilification. From London, Hawthorne wrote to a friend of his "sorrowful sympathy" for Pierce, adding that he hated to see him left "without one true friend, or one man who will speak a single honest word to him." 49

"Let your opponents, enemies and false friends croak as they will," a man who himself was given to controversy, Pierre Gustave Beauregard, wrote from New Orleans. "History will give you ample credit for the ability, firmness and fearlessness you have displayed in the execution of your always responsible, and at times, very trying, duties."

Maine politician and poet Josiah Pierce, no relation, remarked; "I cannot think with patience of the misrepresentation and hindrance by which weak and wicked fanatics and unprincipled slanderers have, beyond all precedent, attempted to embarrass and injure you." 51

Even when the members of his cabinet—the only cabinet in history to remain intact throughout a presidential term of office—collectively wrote a letter of tribute to Pierce, they could not resist alluding to those who condemned him: "He, therefore, who is highest in place and in functions, is, of necessity, peculiarly subject amid the prejudices and the passions of the hour to encounter blame when a better understanding of his motives and of his acts would ensure commendation." 52

But it was not until Jefferson Davis visited him on his last day in office that Pierce finally felt overwhelmed by it all. Davis had penned a personal note to him, wishing that "your days be many, your happiness great and your fame be in the minds of posterity as elevated and pure as the motives which have prompted your official action." 53

Now, as Pierce grasped Davis's outstretched hand, he remarked "I can scarcely bear the parting from you who have been strength and solace to me for four anxious years and never failed me." 54

Upon the conclusion of Buchanan's speech, the crowd politely applauded, and once again he and Pierce were back in the barouche, only this time riding towards the White House. Once there, Pierce wished Buchanan well and simply departed, for the last time, from the White House grounds.

No one knew his plans. There was talk that he might run for the Senate from New Hampshire, an idea that Hawthorne, for one, greatly approved of. "I see nothing better to be done," Hawthorne confided to Horatio Bridge, who was also an unwavering Pierce supporter. "He must have an occupation; and this would give him one, as well as a dignified and useful position." 55

Others talked of his moving South and buying a plantation in Virginia. Pierce himself hinted that he would like to farm.

The only thing that seemed certain was that Franklin Pierce, at the age of 53, was a ruined man, almost certain never to be heard from again.

CHAPTER ONE FOOTNOTES

1. William Seale, *The President's House—A History* (Washington: White House Historical Association, 1986), 323.

2. "A Popular President," *The Washington Post*, 23 September 1883, p. 4, col. 1.

3. Seale, *The President's House—A History*, 320.

4. Maunsell Field, *Memories of Many Men, And of Some Women* (New York: Harper & Brothers, 1875), 162.

5. James Pollard, *The Presidents and the Press* (New York: Macmillan Company, 1947), 287.

6. Allen Nevins, *Ordeal of the Union, Volume One, Fruits of Manifest Destiny, 1847–1857* (New York: Charles Scribner's Sons, 1947), 41.

7. Donald B. Cole, *Benjamin Brown French—Witness to a Young Republic—A Yankee's Journal, 1828–1870* (Hanover: University Press of New England, 1989), 253, from French's diary, 2 January 1855.

8. John S. Wise, *Recollections of Thirteen* Presidents (Freeport: Book for Libraries Press, 1968), 46–47.

9. Varina Davis, *Jefferson Davis—A* Memoir (Freeport: Books for Libraries Press, 1968), 559.

10. Field, *Memories of Many Men, and of Some Women*, 169.

11. "A Popular President," p. 4, col. 1.

12. Lynda Laswell Crist, *The Papers of Jefferson Davis, Volume 6, 1856–1860* (Baton Rouge: Louisiana State University Press, 1989), 103.

13. Virginia Clay-Clopton, *A Belle of the Fifties—Memoirs of Mrs. Clay of Alabama* (Tuscaloosa: University of Alabama Press, 1999), pp. 59–61.

14. Ibid., 63.

15. Norman F. Boas, *Jane M. Pierce, (1806–1863), The Pierce-Aiken Papers Supplement* (Mystic, Connecticut: Seaport Autographs, 1989), Jane Pierce to Mary Aiken, 24 December 1838, 29.

16. Ibid., Mary Aiken to Elizabeth Means Appleton, 7 April 1856, 48.

17. "To the Owners of Hogs and Geese," *Daily National Intelligencer*, 26 February 1857, p. 3, col. 5.

18. *Congressional Globe—Third Session, 34th Session* (Washington: John C. Rives, 1857), pp. 27, 53.

19. Ibid., 57

20. John P. Hale to Mrs. Hale, 3 July 1856, John P. Hale Papers, New Hampshire Historical Society; *Congressional Globe—Third Session, 34th Session*, 97.

21. Allan Nevins, *Ordeal of the Union: A House Dividing, 1852*–1857 (New York: Charles Scribner's Sons, 1947), 455–56.

22. William Brown French to H. F. French, 15 July 1856, William Brown French Papers, Library of Congress.

23. Allan Nevins, *The Diary of George Templeton Strong* (Seattle: University of Washington Press, 1952), 94, diary entry, 6 June 1856.

24. James L. Haley, *Sam Houston* (Norman: University of Oklahoma Press, 2002), 318. Of Houston's penmanship, Haley calls it "fast and sloppy and angry when discussing Pierce," but "serene and flowing" when discussing Houston's children. Sam Houston, *The Life of Sam Houston—The Hunter, Patriot and Statesman of Texas* (Philadelphia: John E. Potter and Company, 1867), pp. 271–72.

25. Page Smith, *The Nation Comes of Age—A People's History of the Antebellum Years, Volume 4* (New York: Penguin Books, 1990), pp. 1131–32.

26. Ralph H. Orth, *The Journals and Miscellaneous Notebooks of Ralph Waldo Emerson, Volume XIII, 1852–1855* (Cambridge: The Belknap Press, 1977) 369; J. R. LeMaster, *Walt Whitman—An Encyclopedia* (New York: Garland Publishing, Inc., 1998), 547.

27. Octavius Brooks Frothingham, *Theodore Parker—A Biography* (Boston: James R. Osgood, 1874), 437.

28. Louise Hall Tharp, *The Peabody Sisters of Salem* (Boston: Little, Brown and Company, 1950), 274.

29. Lydia Marie Child, *Autumnal Leaves: Tales and Sketches in Prose and Rhyme* (New York: C. S. Francis & Company, 1857), "The Kansas Emigrants" was one of the short stories written by Child appearing in this collection. The reference to Pierce appears on page 344.

30. Carolyn L. Karcher, *The First Woman in the Republic—A Cultural Biography of Lydia Maria Child* (Durham: Duke University Press, 1994), 411. Child recounted Stowe's defense of Pierce in a letter to her friend Louisa Loring, 26 October 1856.

31. James Gordon Bennett to Franklin Pierce, 15 December 1852, Franklin Pierce Papers, Series 2, Reel 1. Bennett later denied that he had ever asked Pierce for the post, but his letter refutes the claim. See also James L. Crouthamel, *Bennett's New York Herald and the Rise of the Popular Press* (Syracuse: Syracuse University Press, 1989), 64

32. "Poor Pierce," *New York Herald*, 4 March 1857, p. 4, col. 4.

33. "The President's Message," *The New York Times*, 3 December 1856, p. 4, col. 1.

34. Allan Nevins, *Ordeal of the Union, Volume Two, A House Dividing, 1852–1857* (New York: Charles Scribner's Sons, 1947), 502.

35. "The President's Message," *National Anti-Slavery Standard*, 13 December 1856, p. 2, col. 3.

36. "The Inauguration," *Baltimore American*, 5 March 1857, p. 2, col. 2. For more on the movements of Pierce and Buchanan, see "The Inaugural Ceremonies," *Daily National Intelligencer*, 5 March 1857, p. 3, col. 4.

37. Nevins, *Ordeal of the Union, Volume Two*, pp. 443–47.

38. Ibid.

39. Charles Sumner, *Charles Sumner—His Complete Works, Volume VI* (Boston: Lee and Sheppard, 1872), 38. In his newspaper, William Lloyd Garrison noted that while speakers at public receptions for Brooks nearly always mentioned Sumner by name, at the Fanueil Hall appearance, Sumner had nothing at all to say about his attacker. "How lofty and pure the sentiment," Garrison remarked in admiration. "Reception of Mr. Sumner," *The Liberator,* 7 November 1856, p. 2, col. 2.

40. "The Shooting Affray at Willard's Hotel—Examination of Mr. Herbert," *New York Times*, 10 May 1856, p. 4, col. 4.

41. Ibid.

42. "The United States," *The London Times*, 25 March 1857, p. 10, col. 4.

43. "Afflictive Occurrence," *Daily National Intelligencer*, 27 February 1857, p. 1, col. 5; see also "The Late Shooting Case in Washington," *New York Herald*, 5 March 1857, p. 8, col. 5. Both Herbert and Lee were later acquitted, prompting the *New York Times* to judge "Human life at the National Capital is not held at a high value." "The Verdict in the Herbert Case," *New York Times*, 26, July 1856, p. 1, col. 4; "Killing No Murder," *New York Times*, 31 March 1857, p. 4, col. 5.

44. "Leave-Taking at the Presidential Mansion," *Daily National Intelligencer*, 4 March 1857, p. 3, col. 5.

45. "The United States," p. 10, col. 4.

46. "Who Was the First Man?" *Daily National Intelligencer*, 16 March 1853, p. 3, col. 5.

47. Pierre M. Irving, *The Life and Letters of Washington Irving* (New York: G. P. Putnam, 1864), pp. 132–33.

48. "Inauguration of Franklin Pierce," *New York Herald*, 5 March 1853, p.1, col. 1.

49. Thomas Woodson, *Nathaniel Hawthorne—The Letters, 1857–1864* (Dayton: Ohio State University Press, 1987), Hawthorne to Horatio Bridge, 15 January 1857, pp. 8–9.

50. Pierre Gustave Beauregard to Franklin Pierce, 5 March 1857, Franklin Pierce Papers, Series 3, Reel 5.

51. Josiah Pierce to Frank Pierce, 28 January 1857, Franklin Pierce Papers, Series 3, Reel 2.

52. "Some Papers of Franklin Pierce, 1852–1862," *American Historical Review* 10, no.1,October 1904, Letter from Pierce's Cabinet to Franklin Pierce, 3 March 1857, pp.354–55.

53. Crist, *The Papers of Jefferson Davis, Volume 6, 1856–1860*, Jefferson Davis to Franklin Pierce, 2 March 1857, pp. 109–11.

54. Ibid.

55. Woodson, *Nathaniel Hawthorne—The Letters, 1857–1864* Hawthorne to Bridge, 15 January 1857, pp. 8–9.

2

A solemn, mournful silence

Between March and May 1857, William Marcy's three-story brick home on Vermont Avenue, filled with German paintings and old English literature, proved to be the perfect sanctuary for the Pierces.

There, Pierce entertained a continuing line of old administration friends, attempted to answer a growing correspondence, and made plans for returning to New Hampshire, a journey that Jane, for one, did not relish. 1

Finally in mid-May, the Pierces were set to return to Concord. Jane had two problems with their destination. The first was the weather, which was far too severe for her at least half the year. The second was far more disconcerting: Concord, the house they once shared there, everything about the city, reminded her of Bennie. She dreaded the associations.

Pierce was more optimistic. Although he had repeatedly said he had no political plans for the near future, he clearly relished the idea of returning to the state he once dominated. Yet, would the state return to him?

The signs were not promising. In September, when Pierce made a campaign visit to Concord, several hundred residents gathered at Fremont Camp and angrily voted against honoring him with a public reception. Instead, they passed a resolution saying that the "most befitting mode in which the inhabitants of Concord can receive Franklin Pierce among them is in solemn, mournful silence." 2

Such a public rebuke presaged the November returns when, for the first time in nearly three decades, New Hampshire did not vote Democratic, one more sign that Pierce's home state had turned against him.

By way of Philadelphia, the Pierces arrived in New York on May 19, staying at the Stuyvesant square home of ex-Senator Hamilton Fish, a political opponent who nonetheless considered himself Pierce's friend. Over the course of the next three days Pierce dined with Marcy, who had also left Washington, powerful New York attorney Charles O' Conor, historian George Bancroft, and Charles King, the president of Columbia University. He visited at least one art gallery in Manhattan and also stopped by the mammoth Astor Library. A correspondent for the *New York Herald*, keeping track of Pierce's movements in the city, reported that the former president "looks quite recuperated" since leaving office. 3

By May 27 the Pierces took the rail to enemy territory: Boston, the spiritual home of the abolitionist movement and site of some of the angriest anti-Pierce demonstrations in recent years. There Pierce was hosted as guest of honor at a Society of the Cincinnati meeting, and made his first public remarks for attribution since leaving the White House.

A group dedicated to preserving the memory of the Revolutionary War, as well as aiding families of veterans in need, the Society of the Cincinnati was perhaps the perfect forum for Pierce to begin a tentative return to the public arena. His father, Benjamin Pierce, had served as a lieutenant and company commander in that war and had for years sponsored similar veteran events in New Hampshire.

Throughout his boyhood, in fact, Pierce had listened in amazement to the tales of those veterans who often stopped by his father's tavern in Hillsborough, recalling to the Society the story of one veteran who, Pierce said, was "left for dead on the field," but somehow survived.

"I recollect seeing him at my father's house," Pierce continued. "He received two bullet wounds and five bayonet stabs, one shot carrying off a part of his tongue so that he could never speak plainly."

That man, Pierce said, was now dead. "They have all passed away. But their memory is left to us, and their deeds are left to us."

And those deeds, Pierce said in a pointed jab at those, both in the North and South, who were beginning to talk of secession, were all made to "protect and cherish the national honor—to cultivate union between the states."

That remark produced applause, but Pierce would not sit down without making one other observation. He noted that the widow of Captain Isaac Davis, the first man to be killed in the war, had gone for decades without a pension, and remarked "When you compare the sufferings of the men of the revolution with the sufferings of the women, I say there is no parallel."

The women of that war, Pierce reminded his audience, "were at home struggling with want, struggling with that anxiety inseparable from their condition, with no high impulse and emotion, such as bore up their husbands, sons and brothers."

"They were the heroines of the revolution, and they did as much to achieve the results of the revolution as did the men," added Pierce, who sat down to a hail of cheers. 4

Pierce's remarks were well-received in Boston as well as throughout the country. But what awaited him in New Hampshire could only be imagined.

He arrived there the same week that the *Springfield Daily Republican* ran an item about four school boys debating whether or not they wanted to stop by the local jail to look at a man accused of murder. "He's nothing but a man," one of the boys protested. "I know that, but I'd like to see him," another said. Finally, the last boy who had been quietly listening to his companions, remarked: "I wouldn't give any more to see him than Frank Pierce!" 5

It was yet one more sign of the regional hostility that awaited him. Begging off, at least for the moment, Jane decided to stay in Andover, while Pierce made short day-long forays into the state of his birth.

He visited with friends in Concord, was serenaded by a band in Manchester, and put in a losing bid for a 217-acre farm in Pemigwasset. For the better part of the summer, in fact, he retraced the events of his life, recalling, among many other things, his youth in Hillsborough, where his father served for years as sheriff and was very much a local hero.

"A nobler heart never had the honor of wearing a sword," a fellow veteran had once said of Pierce's father, recalling how the old man, when other officers were "feasting upon double rations," was always good for a free meal.

"Come in, my good fellows, and take a spoon at my soup," the General yelled out, and his men never forgot the kindness. 6

Nor did the voters of Hillsborough fail to forget how strong the General was, a strength that was sometimes masked by the simple way he talked and dressed.

One day, when he was serving in the state legislature, Benjamin Pierce retrieved from his pocket a bill he had written himself. When an opposing lawmaker read the bill, he made the point of noting that it contained several grammatical errors, perhaps wondering at that very moment how such a commoner could have made it all the way to the state house.

Taking calm measure of the man, the General responded: "My grammar and my spelling may not be so accurate, my language may not be so refined as the answer of that gentleman."

"But," the old man continued, "there is a reason for it…while that gentleman was obtaining his education at the best schools our country afforded, while he was learning to spell and write, I, a mere boy, was bearing arms in the cause of our country." 7

It went without saying that the General's bill, grammatical errors and all, shortly thereafter passed.

Elected as sheriff of Hillsborough County in 1809, Benjamin Pierce caused a sensation when he decided to pay the court costs of an aging Revolutionary War veteran who had been imprisoned for debt. "To be immured in a dungeon, standing on the very soil of liberty," the General declared, was far worse than being held on a foreign soil "by enemies and barbarians, from whom nothing better could be expected." 8

Such actions made him a wildly popular figure, so much so that some began to even envision him as a future governor of New Hampshire.

The General knew he was good at politics, but always regarded his lack of education as a hindrance. No such obstacles, however, would block his son's path: Franklin, the General decided early on, was uncommonly intelligent, a voracious reader, good with words and unfailingly courteous. With the right kind of training, there was no telling where the young boy might end up.

And to that end Franklin was sent off when he was 14 to boarding school and Bowdoin College two years after that.

The only problem was that Franklin himself wasn't so sure he wanted to follow the path that his father was laying out for him, which included studying law and eventually entering public life. His lack of enthusiasm was quickly seen in his grades: on a list of student standings, he came in dead last.

"The first half of his college career was idled or played away," a disapproving Alpheus Packard, Bowdoin professor, later said of Pierce. 9

Mortified, Franklin first thought of simply quitting the school, but decided against it after his classmates, including a young religious boy named Zenas Caldwell, urged him to stay on. "If I do so, you will see a change," Franklin promised. 10

Poor Zenas. Intense and driven, he would die of exhaustion less than two years after leaving Bowdoin. Franklin never ceased to be amazed by him, by how seriously his friend took his studies, his faith, and life in general. He could never be as religious as Zenas, but something about him made Franklin more serious too, more focused on his studies and goals in a way he had never been before. 11

It was through Zenas, in fact, that Franklin made his first salary. In January 1823, he traveled with Zenas to the remote village of Hebron, Maine where he spent several weeks teaching in a small wooden school house.

Franklin was no more certain that he wanted to become a teacher than he was about becoming a lawyer, but he was delighted with the Caldwell household, which, he noted, was "situated about 20 rods from the school house."

"The family has given me their best chamber in which there is an excellent bed, and, what I value very highly, is that I always find a good fire when I return from school," Pierce said of the Caldwell home in a letter to his brother-in-law, Colonel John McNeil.

But what undoubtedly made Franklin the most happy was his salary: he would be paid $14 for a full month of work, the first time anyone paid him for anything: "To think, however, that I am by my own exertions obtaining a little cash and at the same time gaining some useful lessons of instruction, is to me no small source of satisfaction." 12

Returning to Bowdoin, Pierce helped to form a marching unit dubbed the Bowdoin Cadets. Nathaniel Hawthorne and Henry Wadsworth Longfellow, both younger than Pierce, were two of the roughly forty students who would drill under his command. "It was remarkable how, with all the variable gentleness of his demeanor, he perfectly gave, nevertheless, the impression of a high and fearless spirit," remembered Hawthorne, who struck up a friendship with Pierce at Bowdoin that would last for the rest of his life. 13

In his last year at Bowdoin, Pierce plowed through Dugald Stewart's *Elements of the Philosophy of the Human Mind*, William Paly's *Evidence of Christianity*, and Joseph Butler's *Analogy of Religion*. But he was most intrigued by John Locke's *Essay Concerning Human Understanding*, a cumbersome, challenging work suggesting, among many other things, that human beings were born without an innate sense of morality.

The effort paid off: by the end of his last year, Franklin had improved his standing to third best in his class. But even then he may have wondered what it all meant: on July 19, his father told him that Hillsborough needed a new post master and that he had arranged for Franklin to take the job.

After all the months of dissecting and contemplating the great thinkers with his fellow students, Franklin may have been less than enthusiastic about going back home and sorting letters. But he was always respectful towards his father, responding on July 22: "I am pleased with your offer and if agreeable to you will attempt to discharge with promptness and accuracy the business of the Post-Office." 14

On graduation day, Franklin, one of several students who spoke during the ceremonies, stressed the importance of continued learning, particularly through the study of history, which he declared "destroys illiberal and unjust prejudices." 15

Hours later, he was back in Hillsborough. If, in the much distant fall of 1857, he thought at all about those first tentative days after he left college, he must have smiled with the memory: almost instantly he was dwarfed in the world of his father, now the subject of both statewide and even national attention.

On Christmas Day 1824, just three months after Franklin left Bowdoin, the old man invited the remaining county veterans of the war to his tavern, and glowed in their embrace: "We should be grateful to the Divine Being that our lives have been preserved to this advanced age," the General declared as the aging men once in his command applauded and cried. 16

The bond that held the old veterans together and the many stories they told greatly impressed Franklin, who may have found it hard to imagine how a profession as a lawyer could be similarly rewarding. Nevertheless, he agreed to pursue the vocation chosen for him, studying under a series of judges, including Samuel Howe of Northhampton, Massachusetts.

So young and so open to the world around him: Pierce left by coach in the spring of 1826, a journey he described as "exceedingly pleasant," winding as it did through a series of small towns in northern Massachusetts, towns which he thought were characterized by that "neatness so peculiar to the villages of New England."

But when the stage stopped at Worcester and two middle-aged women entered the coach, Pierce's attention was diverted: "Seeing no beauties without the coach, I turned to those within," Pierce reported to his sister Elizabeth, "& notwithstanding the grand exertion which I have to make usually to say 'it's a pleasant day' to a woman, I without difficulty entered into a brisk conversation with the old maids."

The women he judged as of the "blue-stocking order," a common phrase in the early 1800s used to gently deride women of literary pretensions. "I, of course, agreed with them in every particular (as it would be quite ungallant to do otherwise)," Pierce added, "commanding whatever thoughts would suit their tastes." 17

His stay in Northhampton was short: six months later he was back in a carriage, this time on his way to Amherst, New Hampshire, where he would study under his final tutor, Judge Edward Parker. Meanwhile Pierce's father was put up for governor in 1826. He lost. But the term was for only 12 months, allowing the old man to have a second go at it, winning in 1827.

Memories everywhere: it seemed as though there was no part of New Hampshire that did not hold some meaning for him, a piece of a distant past that he now sought to re-embrace. By August, Jane, who still resisted staying in Concord, agreed to travel with him to Portsmouth, where they would stay at the old Rockingham Hotel, a brick mansion built in the late 1700s.

Those who didn't know her, who perhaps collected their impressions only from newspaper accounts or what others whispered about her, would easily conclude that Mrs. Pierce was a morose and depressing drag on her far more fun husband. And she was, indeed, often sick, perhaps tubercular, and unable to entirely shake life's sadness.

But she could also, as Franklin knew only too well, be whimsical, if in her own quirky way.

Born Jane Means Appleton, she was the daughter of Reverend Jessie Appleton, an excessively stern man who would die young—not unlike Franklin's friend, Zenas Caldwell—exhausted by his zealotry. One of six children, Jane was also pious, but more open to the pleasant things in life. She read novels, played the piano, rode a horse and had a natural sense of wonder.

One day in boarding school, when she was supposed to be studying, she noticed the beginnings of a winter storm out the window. She wrote to her sister Frances that she could not resist the white beauty: "I have been to the door several times to eat some of the snow!" she announced with great satisfaction. 18

Because her mother descended from a wealthy family of textile merchants, Jane was socially comfortable with the New England upper crust, oftentimes—with her sisters—visiting the home of Amos Lawrence, the Boston industrialist, whose Beacon Hill mansion was said to be among the most grand. 19

Jane was also expected, as were all the daughters of New England privilege, to marry within her own social circle. Although Franklin Pierce's father was governor and Franklin would soon have his own practice in Amherst, he did not, at least according to Jane's strong-willed mother, represent promising marriage material.

The objections were many: the Pierces were well-off, but certainly not wealthy. They drank in an era when temperance was just catching the fancy of the New England elite, and they were involved in politics, a commoner's pursuit at the state and local level.

To make matters worse, the Pierces, by 1828, had made abundantly clear their all-out support for General Andrew Jackson, whose frontier populism threatened, at the very least, the emotional well-being of old-money New England. "Govr. Pierce turns out to be a <u>thorough</u> Jackson man," Daniel Webster, who often represented the rich mercantile interests of New England, reported to Henry Clay with alarm in 1827. 20

Jackson, in fact, fired Franklin's imagination as no previous national figure had done before. Hawthorne may have been right that, if given the chance, Franklin would have preferred to become a career military man. But that chance never seemed to be in the offing, prompting Franklin to finally try his own hand at public life.

It was a queer sensation to read newspapers accounts in the months after he left the White House detailing the reasons why he had been a bad president; how he was a man, they said, with virtually no apparent political or leadership skills.

If only they had seen his rise, had been around when he first embraced politics and became, in a stunningly swift manner, its master. Perhaps then they might view him differently.

In 1829 he was elected to the state legislature. Two years after, his fellow law-makers named Pierce as their Speaker. The year after that he served the first of two terms in the U.S. House, ultimately winning election to the U.S. Senate in 1836, when he was still only 32 years old.

Almost immediately even those who opposed him politically agreed that there was just something about Franklin Pierce that was irresistible, a graciousness of manner that seduced even his worst foes. At the conclusion of one particularly rancorous session of the legislature in the summer of 1831, Representative James Wilson of Keene presented a resolution lauding the young Pierce for the "able, impartial and dignified manner in which he has presided." The resolution passed unanimously. 21

The accolades easily followed him to Washington, where a correspondent taking note of Pierce's first weeks in the Senate observed "though he is a young man," Pierce is a "promising one. He is, as you know, much of a gentleman in his manners, modest in pretension, growing in his attainments, and receives here at least his full proportion of esteem and respect." 22

And the loyalty that he won from his peers would also shortly become a thing of legend. When Speaker of the U.S. House James Knox Polk heard a rumor concerning Pierce's drinking—a rumor undoubtedly stemming from the night Pierce and two other congressmen were observed drunk and involved in a brawl at a Washington theatre—he was quick to assert that "few men with whom I have been associated in Congress have possessed to a greater extent, the confidence and respect of the political friends with whom he has uniformly acted." 23

Yet, Pierce could only remember too well: despite all of his growing prominence and popularity, he always returned to his boarding house alone and lonely. Surely there was more to life than this. As early as 1828, in Hillsborough, he confided to Colonel McNeil: "I should like some society which might keep off that ennui…something to break the dull monotony, which, in such a place as this, hangs about human existence." 24

Three years later he remarked to his sister, Elizabeth: "If my whole life is a lonely one, be it so." But even the life of a permanent bachelor, Pierce reasoned, would have to be better than ending up with a wife with whom "I cannot pour forth the tribute of my whole soul, with its noblest admiration." 25

Maybe Jane had the same thoughts, wondering if Franklin, who was far more gregarious and substantially less religious than she, was really the perfect mate. At the same time she resisted the efforts of family members to introduce her to other men. "Aunt Lawrence has several gentlemen to dinner today," she reported to her mother in September 1834, "and I would gladly escape, but she says 'no,' and I must play the agreeable, if I can." 26

Whether both Franklin and Jane then realized they were in love, or at 30 and 28 years old respectively—relatively old by the standards of the day—thought they were each other's last best chances, they were married on November 19, 1834 in the Means family mansion in Amherst.

Yet almost from the start, something ominous and dark hung over the union. On February 2, 1836, in Hillsborough, she gave birth to Franklin Pierce, Jr. The happy news was reported to Franklin, who just then was in Washington, by letter from his mother-in-law. Three days later the baby died.

Relatives worried about the young couple. Jane seemed so lonely and helpless. Franklin, consumed by the almost endless demands of public life, could not be at her side when she needed him the most.

"I wish him well out of the region of those bursts of public feeling—& <u>forever</u> out of it," remarked Mary Aiken, Jane's sister.

Aiken added that her wish was not just for the well-being of her sister, but for Franklin too: "For I should deprecate the influence of such an atmosphere for any friend I have." 27

A second son, Frank Robert Pierce, was born in 1838, followed by the April 1841 birth of a third son, Benjamin "Bennie" Pierce. But again tragedy shadowed the Pierces: in the fall of 1843, "Franky," as Franklin and Jane called their oldest son, became sick.

Jane had come to greatly rely on her sister, Mary Aiken, who rushed to Concord, where the Pierces had moved. Aiken suspected the worst when the usually considerate Franklin failed to meet her at the station. Rushing to the Pierce home, Aiken was met at the front door by him. Studying his face, Mary said, "I could well guess how the case stood." Franky was dead in four days.

"This will take a heavy hold upon her," Mary said of Jane. "Mr. Pierce is bowed with anguish." 28

Yet, in a way that few outsiders could understand, Franklin and Jane, in the wake of their tragedies, grew closer together. In 1842 he promised her that he would stop drinking and also declined to run for re-election to the Senate, astonishing friends both in Washington and New Hampshire. He wanted nothing more, he said, than to be home with Jane and Bennie, supporting them by practicing law in Concord.

Pierce's allies could not believe he was serious, and continued to float his name for various public offices, none of which he showed interest in. In 1847, now-President Polk offered him the position of U.S. attorney general, and Franklin turned this prestigious position down too. "You know that Mrs. Pierce's health while at Washington was very delicate," he wrote in reply to the president.

"It is, I fear, even more so now, and the responsibilities which the proposed change would necessarily impose on her ought probably in themselves to constitute an insurmountable objection to leaving our quiet home for a public station at Washington," Pierce continued.

He would never again, he added, "be voluntarily separated from my family for any considerable length of time except at the call of my country in time of war." 29

That call came just five months later after Polk declared war on Mexico and Pierce was appointed as a brigadier general and ordered to begin forming a regiment.

It was the one assignment he could not resist, containing, as it did, the military action he always thought should be his own.

Watching Pierce and his men push out from the port of Boston, Hawthorne thought he was "in his element." In fact, the author continued, Pierce looked so good in command that it was practically impossible to doubt what would surely be his "good fortune in the field and his fortunate return." 30

Pierce served for six months, but twice he missed the thick of battle through sheer lousy luck. On the evening of August 19, Pierce's horse fell on a ledge of rocks and Pierce went over with him, his left knee twisting in the collapse. "At first I was not conscious of any serious injury, but soon became exceedingly faint," Pierce candidly admitted in a dispatch that would eventually appear in the *Boston Post*.

Pierce rallied to fight in the Battle of Churubusco the following day, only to injure his now-painful knee one more time. "I fainted and fell upon the bank in the direct range and within perfect reach of the enemy's fire," Pierce would later recall. 31

Although Pierce's men would later deny the charge, he would forever from this day forward be accused of cowardice; the victim of a whispering campaign that would reach its height in the 1852 presidential campaign when such papers as the *American and Messenger* of Manchester, New Hampshire, pointed out that the "Mexican campaign did not confer upon him the distinction of an able general," and the *Boston Evening Journal* wryly suggested that if the Democrats hoped to win with Pierce "they will not make his military service a prominent rallying cry in his favor." 32

But such aspersions were all in the future. Upon his return to Concord in January 1848, Pierce was greeted by more than 4,000 people. He told friends that he now only wanted to concentrate on his practice and family. That he was devoted to Jane and Bennie was without question. Although the boy was probably closest to his mother, often snuggling next to her at night as she read to him from the Bible, there could be no doubt of Franklin's love for him.

"I never saw more tender watchfulness exhibited by a parent," Maunsell Field remembered after he went swimming with Pierce and Bennie at Rye Beach in New Hampshire.

"He dressed and undressed the child himself," added Field, "and while the boy was in the water his attention was so engrossed by him that it was impossible to pursue any conversation." 33

From Pierce's perspective, it was a good time to retreat from the public stage given the rising emotions, particularly in New England, in opposition to slavery. When abolitionist Stephan S. Foster, speaking before the New Hampshire Anti-Slavery Society, went so far as to suggest that anti-slavery activists, if they were really serious about their cause, should march "under the banners of Mexico," because winning New Mexico and California for the U.S. would most likely only extend slavery into those areas, it signaled to Pierce and many others how radicalized the cause had become. 34

Repeatedly Pierce told anyone who listened that he was against slavery. "I wish it had no existence upon the face of the Earth," he had remarked in 1838, expressing sentiments that had not changed in the decade since. 35

But it was unconstitutional to demand that the Southern states be forced to free their slaves, Pierce said. To simply accede to the abolitionists would, instead, more than likely cause the South to secede—with their slaves intact. "One thing must be perfectly apparent to every intelligent man," Pierce had years ago written to John P. Hale. "This abolition movement must be crushed or there is an end to the Union." 36

That Pierce should feel so negatively about the abolitionists said more about him than it did them. Born and raised in New Hampshire, he had never seen a slave, at least until he moved to Washington, and was certainly not on a social basis with a black person either in his home state or the nation's capital, making it difficult for him to appreciate the personal toll that slavery took yearly on millions of black men, women and children.

But Pierce was also innately opposed to any movement that harnessed what he considered to be explosive emotions that could not be funneled through the normal legislative process. Abolitionists were dangerous. They screamed that their demands must be satisfied and, if not, the union be dissolved. For a boy who grew up listening to glorious tales of how the union was created, nothing could have sounded more irrational or been framed in a better way to almost guarantee Pierce's enmity and opposition.

Finally, Pierce always regarded himself as a man who stuck up for people who got kicked around, and by the late 1840s and early 1850s, he was convinced that no people were getting kicked around more than Southerners, who were being daily demonized in the powerful Northern press, endlessly castigated by Northern politicians, and threatened by perceived Northern military might.

That Pierce, while serving in Washington, had also become friends with a wide range of Southerners, including Jefferson Davis, James Knox Polk, and even the humorless John C. Calhoun, undoubtedly made his opinion of the abolition movement even more negative. 37

Pierce was only marginally involved in the 1848 presidential election, but as 1852 began a strange rumor was heard both in Washington and New Hampshire: if all of the other much more well-known candidates for the Democratic presidential nomination somehow failed to get the nod, Pierce would be available as an extremely dark horse.

In later years, actual and would-be Pierce supporters would disagree over the extent of his interest in the nomination. Some insisted that he only wanted to do what many state leaders across the country did at convention time, and that was to just make a symbolic showing as a favorite son.

Others, in particular New Hampshire editor Edmund Burke, claimed Pierce had been in on the planning for his candidacy from the start, and that at the convention "we exerted every energy to carry out the wishes of Gen. Pierce." 38

If Burke's charges were true, then Pierce was more manipulative than usually thought, or so contended the anti-Pierce *New Hampshire Statesman* when it dramatically declared "a more stupendous act of duplicity and intrigue was never unfolded upon this Continent." 39

But the real duplicity, if any occurred, was with Jane. Over and again Franklin promised her he was out of public life for good. He knew she dreaded politics and the kind of intrusion into her private life that would inevitably come with it.

If Pierce secretly hoped to win the nomination, he was living a lie with his wife, and, if successful, putting a frail woman at great peril.

Such machinations seem to run counter to everything that was known about Franklin Pierce. Yet he had come to enjoy politics, or at least enjoyed knowing that he was good at it, and had not actually run for elective office in more than a decade. That, plus the prospect of limiting himself forever to the provincial concerns of New Hampshire for the rest of his life may have seemed like reason enough to try for something new and much bigger.

On June 6 a small announcement appeared in the *Baltimore Sun*'s classified ads: "Wanted—A good HOME for a Negro girl from the country, slave for life. Apply at 78 Light Street, wharf (upstairs)." 40

That same day the delegates to the Baltimore convention, on the 49th ballot, nominated Franklin Pierce for president.

Riding in a carriage after visiting a cemetery in Mount Auburn, Massachusetts, the Pierces were stopped along the road by Colonel Isaac O. Barnes, an old friend, who asked Pierce: "Who do you suppose has got the nomination?"

Pierce, who had been waiting for several days to hear the results before deciding to go on an outing with Jane, said he could not say. Barnes, who had just learned the news in Boston, then announced: "It is no other person than yourself."

Pierce was shocked. "Impossible, Col. Barnes. It cannot be!" 41

At that very moment, upon hearing the very worst news she could imagine, Jane passed out.

Did those memories, now after it was all over and his presidency had been roundly declared such a disaster, haunt Franklin Pierce?

He kept his thoughts to himself. But he was glad to see that Jane was back with him again in New Hampshire, staying in Portsmouth. In early September 1857 a columnist for the *Portsmouth Morning Chronicle* noted that Franklin was enjoying himself in the small town and that Jane's health "is better here than it has been for a long time," giving hope this might serve as a "great inducement for them to abide with us." 42

Yet sometimes Franklin revealed more than he intended, even within the confines of a public address. Appearing before the annual state agricultural fair on October 9, Pierce advised his listeners "whatever the young men may do, let those who are surrounded by the ties of family and who have a homestead to live upon, stay where they are. They will find no better." 43Maybe if he had to do it all over again, he would have never left New Hampshire, never gone to Washington to accept the most important job in the world, never have tried to keep the country together, desperately trying to keep united southern and northern flanks almost destined to come apart.

During the same week that Pierce spoke to the farmers of New Hampshire and enjoyed a good response, his name was cheered in Mississippi after Jefferson Davis, now back in the U.S. Senate, lauded Pierce as president for "fixing his eye on the Constitution and disregarding all selfish considerations." Davis then reminded his audience that unlike many presidents, Pierce remained a lightning rod of opposition even though he was no longer in the White House. The abolitionists, said Davis, "with unmitigated hate, [have] pursued him in his retirement to private life." 44

His loyalty to Pierce never wavering, Davis, several weeks earlier had single-handedly defeated a move by Democrats meeting in Jackson to censure Pierce for wavering in the face of abolitionism, a move that Davis told Pierce by letter "years of friendship and an intimate knowledge of your opinions authorized me to denounce." 45

But that Pierce could generate hostility just by his presence alone was once again demonstrated when he visited Boston in late October. The British author Charles Mackay was also visiting Boston and in possession of a letter of introduction to Pierce written by Hawthorne.

Upon meeting the former president, Mackay secured an invitation for both men to visit the Boston Club, then the city's most prestigious social club. Once there, Mackay was astonished to observe the city's finest snub Pierce.

Not one of the gentlemen, recalled Mackay "made any attempt to obtain an introduction to Mr. Pierce, whom they suffered to enter the room unwelcomed, and almost unobserved, and some few were rude enough to turn their backs upon him."

Mackay was incredulous: was this how Americans treated their former commanders-in-chief? Pierce was gracious under the circumstances but left the club early. Just then an elderly member of the club, whom Mackay described as looking sour and "ultra-puritanical," approached him and demanded to know the identity of his recently-departed companion.

"It is possible that you did not know him," Mackay replied. "It was Mr. Franklin Pierce, formerly President of the United States."

"Never saw the fellow before," the man replied indignantly, "never wish to see him again!" 46

In mid-November, the Pierces sought to put it all behind them. By rail and boat they traveled to Norfolk, Virginia, where, on December 5th they boarded the steam frigate *Powhatan* set to sail to the Madeira Islands off the coast of Portugal.

For now, the former president of the U.S. would observe the coming crisis in his own country from a distant foreign shore.

CHAPTER TWO FOOTNOTES

1. Marcy bought the pleasant Vermont avenue property during his first year as Pierce's secretary of state. Working often in the home's library, he was surrounded, noted a reporter, with "Shakespeare, Milton's prose or poetry, Bacon's Essays, or Sir Thomas Brown's *Urne-Buriall*" and was comfortably conversant with them all. Ivor Debenham Spencer, *The Victor and the Spoils—A Life of William L. Marcy* (Providence: Brown University Press, 1959), 3; "Late Secretary Of State—Anecdotes, &c," *Daily National Intelligencer*, 7, July 1857, p. 2, col. 3.

2. "Refusal of Citizens of Concord to Receive President Pierce," *New York Times*, 25 September 1856, p. 2, col. 3.

3. "City Intelligence," *New York Herald*, 20 May 1857, p. 10, col. 1; "City Intelligence," *New York Herald*, 22 May 1857, p. 8, col. 2.

4. "Speech of Ex-President Pierce," *New York Times*, 1 June 1857, p. 5, col. 4.

5. "A Lower Deep," *Springfield Daily Republican*, 6 June 1857, p. 4, col. 5.

6. "The Soldier's Story," *New Hampshire Patriot and State Gazette*, 13 March 1826, p. 2, col. 5.

7. Untitled article, *New Hampshire Patriot and State Gazette*, 6 March 1826, p. 2, col. 5.

8. "General Pierce," *New Hampshire Patriot and State Gazette*, 6 March 1826, p. 2, col. 2.

9. Nehemiah Cleaveland, *History of Bowdoin College* (Boston: Twayne Publishers, 1977), pp. 281–87. Pierce was not the only one having fun at college. Nathaniel Hawthorne admitted to his sister: "I generally pass the time very tolerably, by dint of playing cards," while Henry Wadsworth Longfellow, perhaps more discreet than Hawthorne, would only say "The students have considerably more leisure than I expected." Thomas Woodson, *Nathaniel Hawthorne—The Letters, 1813–1843* (Dayton: Ohio State University Press, 1984), Hawthorne to his sister, Elizabeth Hawthorne, 28 October 1821, pp. 159–60; Andrew Hilen, *The Letters of Henry Wadsworth Longfellow Volume*

I, 1814–1836 (Cambridge: The Bellknap Press, 1966), Longfellow to Zilpah and Stephen Longfellow, 22 September 1822, pp. 334–34.

10. Cleaveland, *History of Bowdoin*, pp. 281–87.

11. Caldwell was not the only young Bowdoin graduate to die early: of the 91 boys enrolled in the school in the fall of 1820, nearly twenty would die during young manhood. Although some of the fatalities were due to illnesses peculiar to the early 19th century, such as pleurisy, tuberculosis, and consumption, others seemed to simply wither way, suggesting that an excessive New England Calvinism combined with an intense rivalry among the graduates was a murderous disease of its own making. Typical of the tragedies is Ebenezer Deane, a member of Pierce's class, who died in 1848, a probable suicide. The official history of Bowdoin says only that "his sky became overcast and the fair promise of his morning was never fulfilled." Cleaveland, *History of Bowdoin*, pp. 225, 249, 261, 277–78.

12. Franklin Pierce to John McNeil, 10 January 1823, Franklin Pierce Papers, Series 3, Reel 3.

13. Nathaniel Hawthorne, *The Life of Franklin Pierce* (New York: Chelsea House, 1983), pp. 14–15.

14. Franklin Pierce to Benjamin Pierce, 22 July 1824, Franklin Pierce Papers, Series 3, Reel 3.

15. "The Influence of Circumstances on the Intellectual Character," by Franklin Pierce, 1 September 1824, Franklin Pierce Papers, Collections of the Manuscript Division, Library of Congress.

16. "The True Fire of the Flint," *Niles' Weekly Register*, 22 January 1825, p. 522, article reprinted from the *New Hampshire Patriot*.

17. Franklin Pierce to Elizabeth McNeil, May [no exact date given] 1826, Franklin Pierce Papers, Series 3, Reel 3.

18. Norman F. Boas, *Jane M. Pierce (1806–1863)—The Pierce-Aiken Papers* (New London, Connecticut: New London Printers, 1983), 64, Jane Appleton to Frances Appleton, 31 January 1822.

19. For more on Amos Lawrence, see Barry A. Crouch, *In Search of Union: Amos A. Lawrence and the Coming of the Civil War* (Ph'd dissertation, University of New Mexico, 1970). Although Lawrence and Pierce would come to have diametrically opposed views of the abolition movement, Lawrence could not help but be charmed by the future president, noting in his own diary in 1852 that "Pierce has good talents, good manners, generosity and courage,"; diary entry from 13 June 1852 quoted on 123 of Crouch's work.

20. Charles M Wiltse, *The Papers of Daniel Webster, Correspondence, Volume 2, 1825–1829* (Hanover: University Press of New England, 1976), 232, Daniel Webster to Henry Clay, 24 July 1827.

21. Untitled, *New Hampshire Patriot and State Gazette*, 4 July 1831, p. 2, col. 5.

22. "Our Washington Correspondent," *Amherst Farmers' Cabinet*, 4 March 1836, p. 2, col. 4.

23. Herbert Weaver, *Correspondence of James K. Polk, Volume III, 1835–1836* (Nashville: Vanderbilt University Press, 1975), 670, James Knox Polk to James B. Thornton, 22 June 1836. Pierce was more observer than participant in the confrontation that took place at the theatre between his drinking companion Representative Edward Hannegan, an Indiana Democrat, and an Army lieutenant who challenged the congressman to a duel, see Peter A. Wallner, *Franklin Pierce—New Hampshire's Favorite Son* (Concord: Plaidswede Publishing, 2004), 62.

24. Franklin Pierce to John McNeil, 11 November 1828, Franklin Pierce Papers, Series 3, Reel 3.

25. Franklin Pierce to Elizabeth McNeil, December [no exact date given] 1831, Franklin Pierce Papers, Series 3, Reel 3.

26. Boas, *Jane M. Pierce (1806–1863)—The Pierce-Aiken Papers*, pp. 65–66, Jane Means Appleton to Elizabeth Appleton, September [no exact date given] 1834.

27. Ibid.; 32, Mary M. Aiken to Elizabeth Aiken, 22 February 1836.

28. Ibid.; 32–33, Mary M. Aiken to John Aiken, no date given, but probably written in mid-November 1843.

29. Franklin Pierce to James Knox Polk, 6 September 1846, Franklin Pierce Papers, Series 3, Reel 4. While not accepting a public post, Pierce remained busy in New Hampshire politics, drumming up—behind the scenes—support for his friends and doing all he could to defeat his enemies, which, by 1846, very clearly included John P. Hale, who had emerged as a major advocate of the abolitionist cause. See Franklin Pierce to Horatio Bridge, 20 February 1846, Horatio Bridge Papers, Bowdoin College Library.

30. Hawthorne, *The Life of Franklin Pierce*, pp. 67–68.

31. "Letter from Gen. Pierce," *Niles' National Register*, 2 October 1847, p.74, col. 2.

32. "The Surrebutter—State Capital Reporter," *American and Messenger*, 17 July 1852, p. 2, col. 2; untitled article, *Boston Evening Journal*, 7 June 1851, p. 2, col. 1. In his memoirs, Ulysses S. Grant, who would serve as a first lieutenant in the war, said of Pierce twice losing consciousness: "This circumstance gave rise to exceedingly unfair and unjust criticisms of him when he became a candidate for the Presidency. Whatever General Pierce's qualifications may have been for the Presidency, he was a gentleman and a man of courage." In a more recent account, John S. D. Eisenhower argues that the "implication of weakness on Pierce's part is totally unfair…Pierce's mistake was in being too conscientious. He had looked weak while trying to stay on duty." Ulysses S. Grant, *Personal Memoris of U. S. Grant* (Old Saybrook, CT: Konecky & Konecky, 1992), 89; John S. D. Eisenhower, *Agent of Destiny—The Life and Times of General Winfield Scott* (New York: The Free Press, 1992), pp. 328–29. For a different contemporary perspective on Pierce's service, see Leslie Chase to Franklin Pierce, 10 August 1847, Franklin Pierce Papers, Series 1, Reel 1.

33. Mausell B. Field, *Memories of Many Men—And of Some Women* (New York: Harper & Brothers, 1875), 160.

34. Merton L. Dillon, *The Abolitionists—The Growth of a Dissenting Minority* (DeKalb: Northern Illinois University Press, 1974), 163.

35. Franklin Pierce to Reverend D. W. Burroughs, Document number 2634, [no exact date given] 1838, Gilder Lehrman Insititute of American History. Pierce additionally told Burroughs, an active abolitionist and editor, that the "violent course of the Abolitionists at the North has postponed the emanci-

pation of the coloured population in Maryland, Kentukcy & Virginia Many & many a long year."

36. Wallner, *Franklin Pierce—New Hampshire's Favorite Son*, 67.

37. Pierce's friendship with Calhoun had a rocky early moment when the South Carolina senator attacked him for misrepresenting the strength of the abolitionist movement in New Hampshire. It was a silly assault, and Calhoun later admitted it by apologizing to Pierce in person. In later years, after Pierce had made it clear through his many votes in the Senate that he was far more with Calhoun than against him, he would be characterized by at least one Calhoun correspondent as "our excellent friend." Clyde N. Wilson, *The Papers of John C. Calhoun, Volume XXII, 1845–1846*, (Columbia: University of South Carolina Press, 1995, pp. 592–93, Marcus Morton to John C. Calhoun, 16 February 1846.

38. "Important Disclosure," *New Hampshire Statesman*, 29 October 1853, p. 2, col. 3.

39. Ibid.

40. "Wants," ad column, *Baltimore Sun*, 6 June 1852, p. 3, col. 2.

41. "How Gen. Pierce Was Informed Of His Nomination," *Baltimore Sun*, 9 June 1852, p. 1, col. 3.

42. Untitled article, *Portsmouth Morning Chronicle*, 11 September 1857, p. 3, col. 1.

43. "Speech of Ex-President Pierce, at the New Hampshire Agricultural Fair, Oct. 9th, 1857," Franklin Pierce Papers, Series 2, Reel 3.

44. Lynda Lasswell Crist, *The Papers of Jefferson Davis, Volume 6, 1856–1860*, (Baton Rouge: Louisiana State University Press, 1989), 143.

45. Ibid,; pp 131–32, Jefferson Davis to Franklin Pierce, 23 July 1857.

46. Thomas Woodson, *Nathaniel Hawthorne—The Letters, 1857–1864* (Dayton: Ohio State University Press, 1887), pp. 108–09, Nathaniel Hawthorne to Franklin Pierce, 24 September 1857; Charles Mackay, *Through the Long*

Day—or Memorials of a Literary Life During Half a Century (London: W. H. Allen & Co., 1887), pp. 158–61.

3

In the Absence of Plans

By the time the Pierces left American territorial waters, the new president was already sinking.

James Buchanan had won the White House largely because the Democrats continued to enjoy a huge organizational advantage in the country and he seemed more sympathetic to a Northern electorate that could no longer stomach Pierce.

But just five months after Buchanan took office, almost any American with a savings account was shocked by the sudden failure of the Ohio Life Insurance Company. That such a one-time solid company could go belly-up confirmed for many their worst fears about financial institutions in general, leading to bank runs across the country, which, in turn, precipitated a severe recession that would last for all of Buchanan's term.

Meanwhile, Kansas seemed no more governable under the new president than it had been under Pierce. A governor appointed by Buchanan had angrily resigned, blasted the president in the press, and, in leaving, deprived the territory of the administrative and law and order presence it so desperately needed. Violence, once again, was on the rise.

And also once again, the Democrats began to peck at each other, proving that Pierce's inability to keep a huge and unwieldy party together was no aberration. Perhaps no detractor was louder or more important than Stephen Douglas, who said he was outraged over patronage issues and Buchanan's Kansas policies, but really was concerned more about positioning himself for president in 1860.

Now, Douglas told friends, he was determined to do everything he could to make life miserable for the already-suffering Buchanan. "By God, sir, I made James Buchanan," the hardly wilting Illinois Democrat declared in November 1857, "and by God, I will unmake him!" 1

Pierce could be excused if he secretly enjoyed, a least a little, the swift decline in Buchanan's fortunes. It took more than a year, he could recall with pride, indeed it was nearly two years, before the Pierce presidency seemed to be in any real trouble.

True, when his name was first revealed to the voters of America, his nomination was seen in some quarters as a kind of joke, largely because Pierce really was so unknown on the national stage. Even the delegates to the very same convention that had just nominated him were heard by one reporter to ask "Who is Pierce?" and even more troubling, "What has he done?" 2

The wildly popular Major Jack Downing, a fictional character invented by humorist Seba Smith, who appeared in dozens of newspapers, reported the news of Pierce's nomination to his uncle Joshua, who asked in astonishment: "Are you sure there is such a person, or did somebody play a hoax on the Baltimore Convention."

"Yes," Downing replied to his fictional uncle with some irony: "I'm as sure of it as I am that there is such a person as Uncle Joshua Downing." 3

But just five months later no one was asking who Franklin Pierce was. The Democrats ran a near-flawless campaign that exploited Pierce's modernism, military record and good looks. "His portrait is everywhere," Nathaniel Hawthorne marveled, "and in all sorts of styles—on wood, steel and copper, on horseback, on foot, in uniform, in citizen's dress, in iron medallions, in little brass medals and on handkerchiefs." 4

On election night, Pierce won a stunning victory, "almost beyond precedent in our political history," thought the New Orleans *Daily Picayune*. 5

He swept New England, the Middle Atlantic states, most of the growing Great Lakes states and virtually all of the South to win the largest popular vote up to that time in history. His electoral margin, meanwhile, was a thumping 254 to 42. "Never was a president of the United States elected under more gratifying circumstances, or by a more overwhelming popular vote," judged the *Boston Transcript*. 6

Pierce would enter the White House, declared the *New York Times*, which had opposed him in the campaign, "with a more general degree of kindly feeling from all sections and all parties than has been usual in some years past." 7

"His majority is large," conceded Massachusetts Senator Charles Sumner, who would eventually prove to be one of Pierce's greatest foes, "but composed of most discordant materials, & his first difficulty will be to harmonize those in his Cabinet." 8

Actually, the first difficulty was hiding from hungry office-seekers who now turned to Pierce to butter their bread. There were thousands of them, and for that reason Pierce decided to stay away from Washington as long as possible, a decision that angered party elders in the nation's capitol who also wanted to influence him.

Only momentarily frustrated, they came to see him instead: "Thousands of men have gone to Concord," a reporter for the *London Times* noted. A Democratic insider revealed: "Some go alone, some with letters, some without," adding that Pierce was "dogged from city to city and from village to village; from his office to his house, from his house to his barn and from his barn to his kitchen." 9

Yet despite all the clamor, Pierce managed to form a cabinet composed of some of the nation's most strong-willed and powerful men: William Marcy of New York as secretary of state; James Guthrie of Kentucky as secretary of the treasury; Michigan's Robert McClelland as interior secretary; James C. Dobbin as postmaster general; and Caleb Cushing of Massachusetts as attorney general.

But Pierce was most beguiled by Jefferson Davis, whom he hoped to snare as his secretary of war. Through letters and intermediaries, Pierce pursued him: "I have no right to put you to trouble and could not think of asking you to leave your home unless you can do it without anxiety," Pierce wrote to Davis in the early days of 1853. 10

Davis had happily spoken for Pierce in Mississippi during the presidential election. But he had resigned from the U.S. Senate in 1851, lost a long-shot bid for the governorship of his state and was now content—or so he said—to remain at his Brierfield estate with Varina and their new son Samuel. 11

Pierce, however, when he put his mind to it, could be enormously persuasive. And what he couldn't get one way he would try another. He talked Buchanan into accepting the post as ambassador to Great Britain, even though Buchanan wanted anything but. Pierce yearned to have Buchanan as part of his team, but not in a prominent way because he also viewed Buchanan as a potential rival for 1856. Shrewdly floating the offer through the press, Pierce made it almost impossible for Buchanan to refuse without committing "serious offense," Buchanan admitted, "and without danger of an open rupture with the administration." 12

A Buchanan biographer would later note of Pierce's nomination of Buchanan: "He had given him a mission foredoomed to failure, robbed him of his patronage, and put a gag in his mouth. Had anyone ever been so taken to the market?" 13

Pierce also showed that he knew how to work his way around his own cabinet members when he wanted something. Picking the controversial Dan Sickles, a New York wheeler-dealer, as Buchanan's assistant would rouse the opposition of Marcy who would normally have the final say over the commission. So, Pierce instead made certain that only the assistant secretary of state signed the papers necessary to hire Sickles. 14

Facing what could be a highly hazardous challenge of putting a new associate justice on the U.S. Supreme Court, Pierce, to an extent, even manipulated the other associate justices of the high bench when he agreed to hear their recommendations for the seat.

When they suggested the brilliant and young 41-year-old John A. Campbell of Alabama, Pierce swiftly nominated him and enjoyed a significant and easy political victory several days later when the Senate confirmed Campbell on a unanimous voice vote. 15

On that same day, Pierce won additional good will from the American public when his nomination of Hawthorne as U.S. consul in Liverpool also easily won approval from the by-now impressed senators.

But such political parlor games would not work with Davis who was nothing if not forthright. Fortunately the two men soon rediscovered that they were in basic agreement not just on the obvious issues of abolitionism and states' rights, but also on the need to modernize the nation's military and expand the country's borders.

The country could only thrive, Davis believed, through that expansion, and after agreeing to join the cabinet, he enthusiastically dispatched—with Pierce's full backing—survey teams that would lay out the routes for the future transcontinental railroad.

To get to the Western reaches, said Davis, Americans must "skip the mountains, tunnel them, or pass them by any means known to civil engineering." Together, Pierce and Davis supported the acquisition of a 45,000-square mile swath of land in the southwest that would eventually become New Mexico and Arizona, and tried unsuccessfully to annex Cuba, either by buying or invading it. 16

When Matthew Perry, a U.S. Naval officer who called himself an admiral, arrived in Japan in the summer of 1853 with a fleet of vessels designed to intimidate that country into establishing diplomatic relations—Perry said he only wanted to "bring a singular and isolated people into the family of civilized nations"—Pierce and Davis began to think that America's frontiers were growing beyond their imagination. 17

Perhaps the emotional highpoint of the young Pierce administration came in that same summer when the president agreed to an unprecedented tour of the east cost that would include officially opening the grand Crystal Palace in New York City.

In Baltimore, Wilmington, Philadelphia, Newark and New York, Pierce—with Davis in tow—greeted thousands of well-wishers, people who had never before seen a president in person. Not everyone was completely supportive of the journey. "We question the taste of his making street addresses to the multitude. It is enough for the lesser lights to shine there," proclaimed the *Daily National Intelligencer* on the same day that Pierce spoke to a huge crowd of laborers in Wilmington's town square. 18

Unfortunately, away from the restraining influence of Jane, Pierce also drank throughout the trip. He gulped down what one reporter described as a "slight refreshment" at Barnum's City Hotel in Baltimore, tasted the best wine in stock at the Merchant's Hotel in Philadelphia, swallowed a brandy at Mass & Villamon's Saloon in Manhattan, and sat down to a huge table at the elegant Metropolitan Hotel, also in New York, where the wine and champagne flowed, as did the cognac sauce that blanketed his plum pudding. 19

Pierce drank so much, in fact, that when he first arrived in New York to a boisterous reception of more than 10,000 people at the Castle Garden, a reporter noticed that he looked "very pale and occasionally placed his hand to his temple as if suffering from a headache." Democratic insider John Forney, on board the president's caravan, was shocked by Pierce's behavior. "I deeply, deeply, deplore his habits," Forney said. "He drinks deep." 20

At the Castle Garden, Pierce was presented with a black stallion that he would ride down Broadway to the Crystal Palace. New Yorkers expecting to see their president waving to them from an open carriage—Davis took that ride—were startled and began to cheer. "He appeared to much advantage on horseback," Buchanan had noted two days before when Pierce also rode in Philadelphia. 21

When a sudden rainstorm stopped much of the parade, prompting hundreds of onlookers to dash underneath nearby awnings, Pierce continued to ride, even rejecting the offer of an umbrella. "I am not sugar! I shall not melt!" Pierce declared. 22

At the Palace, Pierce reminded a crowd of more than 20,000 that "we live in a utilitarian age," where science was now just as important as agriculture, manufacturing and the arts in promoting "our domestic comforts and our universal prosperity." 23

As soon as Pierce concluded his remarks, a local choir broke into a rousing rendition of Handel's "Messiah." 9

It seemed like a good time to leave. By carriage, Pierce was taken to the exclusive Astor House where a huge shield with silver letters announced: "General Frank Pierce, President of the United States." 24

But inside the hotel, enemies of Pierce were plotting his ruin. Upset over a tangle of patronage issues, disappointed in what was increasingly viewed as a "Southern-leaning" presidency—many now claimed Davis was the real power in the White House—and divided, as ever, over the issue of slavery and abolition, New York Democrats were about to split into two angry, warring factions. They caucused at the Astor House to air their grievances, but to little obvious effect. Yet the ultimate decision to mount two separate Democratic campaigns in the fall 1853 elections meant that the party would lose almost every state office in New York. Pro-Pierce candidates, during that same month, won in New Jersey, Maryland, Louisiana and Mississippi.

Surveying what he viewed to be the declining fortunes of the president, Charles Edwards Lester, the New York correspondent for the *London Times,* was happy. He had tried and failed to win public office in the Pierce administration and now retaliated by writing only the worst things about the president. As early as the late summer of 1853, Lester was telling his readers that Pierce's desire to have every region and thought represented in his cabinet gave "satisfaction to no section, faction or interest." 10

As Lester saw it, Pierce was doomed, revealing himself as a "weak, irresolute and vacillating man." 25

In reality, Pierce's fortunes at the end of 1853 were much brighter than Lester could admit. He clearly excited voters, as his trip up and down the East coast demonstrated, and he won over—if even for the moment—the New York press, which had tended to view him suspiciously. A correspondent for the *New York Times* prominently declared that Pierce was not only "one of the most amiable, sociable, frank and freest of gentlemen it has been my fortune to meet," but also "the most literally democratic of all public men." 26

But four days after New Year's Day 1854, everything changed when Stephen Douglas reported a bill out of the Senate Committee on Territories that he chaired calling for the creation of the territories Kansas and Nebraska.

In a rapidly growing country that had added five states in just the last ten years alone, Douglas' legislation would have been under normal circumstances duly received and calmly contemplated by his fellow lawmakers as only the latest reflection of the nation's need for more room to accommodate a thriving westward expansion. But in a nation that was also traumatized by the existence of slavery and warily supportive of the Compromise of 1850, which, generally speaking, recognized free states to the North and slave states to the South, the Douglas bill was dynamite because it contained no provision prohibiting slavery, allowing instead for settlers in those territories to decide the question for themselves.

Douglas predicted that his measure would "raise a hell of a storm," and he was right. Almost instantly northern and some border state lawmakers, emboldened by a re-energized abolitionist movement in their states, took to the floor of both the Senate and House, promising a vigorous opposition. 27

Michigan's Lewis Cass, almost always a Democratic loyalist, said the measure was "fraught with infinite evil," and was not even sure he could support it. Sam Houston of Texas, never short for words, described the measure as a disaster, arguing that it would fire a new debate over slavery that would "convulse the country from Maine to the Rio Grande." 28

Watching the opposition grow, Benjamin Brown French remarked "There never was so great a political blunder committed." 29

As early as January 30, in fact, the proposal was in such serious trouble that Massachusetts Congressman Nathaniel Banks could report that the "Nebraska Bill [has] met terrific opposition & will fail." 30

But then Douglas got a great idea, meeting with Jefferson Davis and asking a crucial question: how could he line up Pierce behind the bill?

Listening calmly as Douglas explained the purpose of his measure—to organize the vast river country west of Missouri and Iowa as the first step towards establishing a transcontinental railroad—Davis suggested they pay an impromptu visit to Pierce in the White House. 12

The only problem was that it was Sunday and Pierce, no doubt because of Jane, usually refrained from doing business on that day. But he did cordially receive Davis, who told him that Douglas and several other senators were waiting to speak with him.

"He thereupon met the gentlemen, patiently listened to the reading of the bill and their explanations of it," remembered Davis, who was relieved to hear Pierce say he thought the measure was based on "sound constitutional principles." 31

That Douglas felt that Pierce's support for his bill was important was evidence that the president's influence with Congress was regarded as significant. That Davis was the intermediary would soon be cited as proof that the secretary of war had some sort of mystical hold over the president.

But in fact, Pierce needed little persuasion to back the bill. Like Douglas and Davis he was an enthusiast of the proposed transcontinental railroad and saw Douglas' measure as a means of bringing that transportation closer to reality. Unfortunately, also like Douglas and Davis, Pierce seriously misjudged the mood of the people, having no idea that the re-emergence of the slavery issue would prove to be so painful and explosive to so many Americans.

"The old questions between political parties are at rest," declared Senator Salmon P. Chase of Ohio, who took to the floor of the Senate in February to deliver an emotional address in which he predicted that from here on in only slavery would matter as a national issue. Undoubtedly referring to Pierce, Davis and Douglas, Chase continued: "It will light up a fire in the country which may, perhaps, consume those who kindle it." 32

William Seward of New York was similarly apoplectic, warning "We are on the eve of the consummation of a great national transaction—a transaction which will close a cycle in the history of our country." 33

From New England, Harriet Beecher Stowe, now a literary lion with the enormous commercial success of her book, *Uncle Tom's Cabin,* helped to organize a petition that would be signed by more than 3,000 clergymen begging Congress "in the name of Almighty God" to reject the bill. Ralph Waldo Emerson urged that "every true hearted American abroad ought to come home & defend freedom here," while Henry Wadsworth Longfellow encouraged Massachusetts Senator Charles Sumner in his attacks on the measure, which he characterized as an "abomination." 34

"For my own part," Longfellow said of the Douglas bill, "I put it on a level with cheating at cards." 35

Sumner, however, was uncommonly philosophical about the measure, calling it "at once, the worst and the best bill on which Congress ever acted."

Continued Sumner: "The worst bill inasmuch as it is a present victory of slavery. The best bill, for it annuls all past compromises with slavery, and makes all future compromises impossible." 36

Both Pierce and Davis lobbied incessantly with wavering congressmen for the bill, which finally passed the House on May 22 by a vote of 113 to 100. Eight days later, Pierce, viewing the bill's passage as his first major legislative victory, signed it into law.

But the president had paid a terrible price for his victory. French had predicted as much two months before when he wrote "the power of the President over Congress is such that he can control the vote of the Senate and perhaps the House…but he cannot control the *people* of the Free states; and *that* he will ere long discover." 37

Massachusetts Congressman Samuel Clarke Pomeroy felt the same way, telling Pierce that "this measure which has passed is not the triumph you suppose. It does not end, but only commences hostilities." 38

When the handsome and long-time Democratic insider Francis P. Blair and his daughter Lizzie rode horses one day in Washington, they saw Pierce, who was also on horseback, and made a point of not looking at him. Pierce, "from the expression on his face," Lizzie later wrote, "observed the incivility." Blair, meanwhile, would soon throw himself over to the cause of helping to organize the new Republicans, so upset was he with Pierce. 39

Former Pierce supporters felt betrayed not only because the Douglas bill threatened to extend slavery, but also because the president, with his support of that bill, had stirred anew passions thought to be dormant on the subject. The whole controversy had somehow made him unattractive to those who liked him before. From Boston, Amos Adams Lawrence was astonished to hear his stepmother, a woman of Irish-Scotch ancestry who had previously "never been willing to listen to anything derogatory to Mr. Pierce," now announce "the fact is Pierce is too small a man for the place." 40

Meanwhile the abolitionists were reawakened to a whole new range of thinking, going well beyond simple protest. William Lloyd Garrison wondered what was to become of a country so willing to go against the "laws of God and the rights of universal man," while Wendell Phillips began to explore anarchy's potential. 41

"Pierce and Douglas," said Horace Greeley, no doubt correctly, "have made more Abolitionists in three months than Garrison and Phillips could have made in half a century." 42

And then on May 24, the very night that the House passed the Douglas bill, a black man named Anthony Burns was arrested in Boston, sparking a series of events that would personalize in the most vivid manner not only the brutality of the slave system, but the perception of Pierce as its most conspicuous apologist.

There had been escape slaves captured in the North before, and almost always their travails made some sort of national news. But what made the case of Anthony Burns so sensational was that he fled to the very city that served as the epicenter of the abolitionist movement.

"Ratify in the streets of Boston tomorrow that Anthony Burns has no master but God," thundered abolitionist Phillips to a large and angry crowd meeting at Boston's Faneuil Hall two nights after Burn's arrest. Here was the chance for Phillips to give action to his belief in anarchy, noting that an immoral law demanded citizens of conscience to defy it; indeed, to pretend that it did not even exist. "There is now no law in Massachusetts," said Phillips, "and when law ceases, the people may act in their own sovereignty." 43

Other speakers that night were even more incendiary. The net result was a chaotic call to action seeing a large segment of the audience rush to the nearby courthouse where Burns was being held. A group of black men, breaking away from the others, lifted a battering ram against one of the thick wooden doors of the building, but were stunned and beaten back by guards wielding clubs and swords. In the melee, one of the guards was killed.

Both Pierce and Attorney General Cushing had anticipated such events in Boston, with Cushing trying to give his fellow Massachusetts Democrats a real feel for the president's personal feelings when he told them that Pierce had long ago determined that abolitionism, "under whatever guise or form it may present itself, shall be crushed out, so far as this administration is concerned." 44

The message was clear, or at least should have been: Pierce would react fiercely to any abolitionist civil action in Boston which he judged to be unlawful. Yet he was still not certain if he had the power to enforce the Fugitive Slave Act through the use of federal troops. Cushing, undoubtedly aware of Pierce's doubts, quickly presented him with a brief citing the legal precedents for such action. Satisfied, Pierce sent a telegram to Watson Freeman, the U.S. Marshall in Boston who had earlier told him that he already had federal troops guarding the courthouse: "Your conduct is approved. The law must be executed." 45

When, three days later, U.S. district attorney Benjamin F. Hallet asked if Washington would help defray the costs for hiring an additional city militia, Pierce was equally decisive, wiring back: "Incur any expense deemed necessary by the Marshall and yourself for city military, or otherwise, to insure the execution of the law." 46

Jefferson Davis, expecting the worst, additionally ordered the Army's adjutant general, Colonel Samuel Cooper, to Boston, making available the use of even more troops if so needed.

The outcome of the hearing determining Burns' fate was probably inevitable, despite a late attempt on the part of the abolitionists, who always said they were opposed to engaging in the commerce of human beings, to purchase his freedom.

On June 2, Burns was ordered returned to Virginia and his owner. Amos Adams Lawrence, now also radicalized, watched Burns as he was escorted to a revenue cutter dispatched by Pierce that would take him back South. "He was on foot, dressed in a new black suit; he looked well and bore himself very handsomely," recorded Lawrence. 47

But the Burns affair did not end with his departure. Longfellow expressed well the explosive outrage felt throughout Boston and much of New England when he took note of a "fiery leaven" that was "at work in the hearts of men here."

Lawrence, sure that at least the "boiling heart of the Negro excitement," was, for the moment, quelled, nevertheless remained convinced that the bottom of the pot was "hot yet." 48

How hot was seen in the November 1854 mid-term elections, which proved a disaster for Pierce: the Democrats lost most of New England, the Middle Atlantic states, and the Great Lakes states—everywhere, in fact, in the North.

Several months later when the Democrats held on to Virginia, Pierce thought the worst must be over, telling Douglas that the victory "put a new face upon the prospects of the Democratic party." In a reference to the newly ascendant Know-Nothing party, which got a lot of mileage out of excoriating foreigners, Pierce reminded Douglas that it was the Democratic party, "which carries no dark lanterns." 49

Yet even in the South Pierce would find himself in trouble, largely because many Southerners felt that the Kansas-Nebraska act, which had so excited feelings in the North against them, would never have become a reality had it not been for his backing. In Louisiana, both of the state's senators, John Slidell and Judah P. Benjamin, had washed their hands of him. Slidell, noting the declining fortunes of the Democrats, blamed it all on Pierce, or what he called "the personal unpopularity or rather want of consideration & influence of the administration." 50

House leader Alexander Stephens, who had almost single-handedly guided the Kansas-Nebraska bill through the lower chamber, described Pierce as "the miserable little creature in the White House," and his policy towards Kansas and Nebraska as one of "fickleness, folly and vacillation." 51

Yet even as his congressional position grew more precarious, Pierce became more assertive. When House leaders in December of 1855 deadlocked over the choice of a new Speaker, making it impossible—at least according to tradition—to receive the president's official message, Pierce broke with that tradition and sent it to them anyway. Georgia Congressman Howell Cobb, for one, was impressed: "The credit is given to the President for the boldness of the move," he said. 52

And when Congress adjourned in the summer of 1856 without acting on a military appropriations bill, an angry Pierce, remarking that "the public peace is seriously threatened," called it back into session, eventually securing the legislation's passage. 53

But by then it was too late for Pierce, and he knew it. "I shall not be nominated," he confided to his sister-in-law Mary Aiken just days before the Democratic convention.

"You would be surprised to know with how much indifference I contemplate the result so far as it is calculated to affect me personally," he added. 54

The comet that had exploded across the nation's sky in 1852 had now nearly entirely burned itself out for years later.

Onboard the *Powhatan* in late 1857, Pierce watched the country that had turned against him recede into the distance.

"It is not the fault of anybody if we do not have a pleasant and prosperous voyage," Jane wrote hopefully. Perhaps trying not to think too much, Pierce was preoccupied leafing through a copy of a just-published work by the Reverend David Livingstone concerning his missionary work in South Africa as well as a book on Madeira given to him by an admiring Naval officer. The executive officer of the *Powhatan*, Lieutenant James D. Johnston, later noted that Pierce so charmed the vessel's officers with his "ease and affability," that, if given the chance, "every one of them would have voted for his restoration to the elevated position he had so recently filled." 55

For the next six months, the Pierces would know a kind of quiet tranquility that had never before existed in their turbulent marriage. Arriving at Madeira, Piece often walked by himself into the island's tiny villages by day. At night, he and Jane listened to symphony and opera recitals performed by local musicians and singers.

Oftentimes in the afternoon, they studied French together. "I enjoy seeing him so interested," Jane would note with evident bemusement of her husband's willingness to learn a new language: "He has begun [and] seems (in the true spirit of the conquerer) determined to master it." 56

Regularly they rode horses down dusty roads or into thick forests. Jane, perhaps rediscovering the sense of wonder she once owned before everything went wrong, was in awe of the splendor about her, of the "scenery unlike anything I had ever seen," she described it. 57

"I never saw so magnificent a rainbow as the one this evening, they occur daily here," she wrote to Mary Aiken on January 9. Two months later she observed a deadly storm and recorded: "It was most magnificent in its fury, and terrific in its violence." 58

If Pierce was worried about being forgotten, his friends tried to reassure him otherwise. George Dallas, now the minister to Great Britain, sent him a package of American newspapers. Caleb Cushing told him that the only thing keeping Buchanan going was the "particular friends of the last administration" who were now working in the White House. Jefferson Davis felt the country was rudderless without Pierce at the helm. "There is certainly little to make the present pleas-

ing," Davis told Pierce in early April, "or to give the patriot hope for the future."
59

Always in letters to and from Pierce, in newspaper accounts and in casual con-
versations was talk about his future. He was still only 54 years old, and had good
reason to believe that if only the Democrats had given him the nod he would
have been re-elected.

But he also knew that, at least for the time being, his name had become a met-
aphor for everything that had gone wrong in America. To his former secretary
Sidney Webster, he bluntly remarked: "I would have you say nothing about my
future plans, for I have really formed none." 60

In late July, the Pierces traveled from Lyons to Geneva. Everywhere they went
they were greeted by foreign dignitaries, consuls and the inevitably faceless and
nameless people who attach themselves to a man who has been president. They
dined in Paris, walked through castles at Chillow, and were guests in a duke's palace at Magadino.

But what may have touched Jane the most was meeting a young boy in
Geneva, the son of a deceased U.S. general whose wife introduced herself to the
Pierces: "A beautiful boy of 13…the sight of such goes straight to my heart," Jane
wrote of the encounter. "I love (at once) every sweet looking boy I meet." 61

She would never, ever forget Bennie, whose fading smile and unknown potential was with her always.

Perhaps it was also almost impossible to forget the way in which her young
son had died.

It had started out as a gray and cold New England morning in January, during
the first week of the new year, 1853. The Pierces had attended the funeral of
Amos Lawrence in Boston, who had died suddenly at the age of 66 on New
Year's Day, and were now boarding a single passenger rail car in Andover that
would return them to Concord. The car was filled with commuters. Passing by a
coal-burning stove used for heat, Franklin and Jane found a seat near the front,
with Bennie—slender and blonde—sitting behind them. As the heavy train
heaved forward, the Reverend Arthur B. Fuller gazed out the window and made a
mental note of the grassy bank supporting the tracks and how icy it was.

Suddenly a huge wooden axle beneath the train cracked, causing the car to
veer wildly out of control. The movement prompted the iron coupling connect-
ing the baggage car to the passenger car to break loose, allowing the second vehi-
cle to pivot and fall off the embankment, breaking into pieces "like a cigar box,"
as one passenger later put it. 62

In less than a minute a heap of splintered wood and broken glass was all that was left of the car, and even that was partially consumed by a fire that broke out when the oilcloth that hung from the car's ceiling made contact with the stove.

"We are alive!" a man, half-hysterical and covered in blood, yelled as he climbed out from the debris and saw that most of the other passengers were not seriously injured. But that was before anyone saw the dead, limp body of Bennie, whose skull was crushed under the weight of the mass, his head partially severed. 63

Franklin ran over to his son and held him in his arms. The Rev. Fuller, observing Jane as she suddenly realized what had happened, later remarked that her face registered an agony that "passes beyond description." 64

Mary and John Aiken opened their nearby farmhouse to the injured passengers. As the dark afternoon turned to night, Franklin and Jane sat by themselves alone with Bennie's body in an empty room.

"What grief in this world, and may we even say in another, can equal that of Mr. and Mrs. Pierce," asked Amos Adams Lawrence, who himself was in the mourning over the passing of his father. 65 Letters of condolence to the Pierces were embarrassing confirmations that sometimes words do fail: "Poor Little Benny!" lamented Josephine Brodhead, wife of John Brodhead, comptroller of the U.S. Treasury. "He was a dear and amiable boy and I loved him." 66

"I used to feel bad in looking forward to his future because there were peculiar temptations growing out of the heights of your fortunes," Francis Upham, a religious author, told Pierce, rather oddly.

"But from all earthly harm he is now shielded in heaven." 67

Meanwhile the nation worried about Jane. To an amazing degree journalists dared to broach the subject of her mental stability in the wake of the accident: "The blow is a cruel one to the parents," editorialized the New Orleans *Daily Picayune,* adding "it is one which Mrs. Pierce will not be apt to recover from." 68

Those who knew Jane personally thought the same thing. "Our grief is all the greater that we can do so little; alas, nothing to assuage her anguish," historian George P. Bancroft told Pierce. 69

In his grief, Pierce was silent, revealing himself only to Jefferson Davis when he referred to the "terrible catastrophe upon the railroad," and openly speculated: "How I shall be able to summon up my manhood and gather up my energies for the duties before me is hard for me to see." 70

Uniquely, after seeing Bennie's empty bedroom back in Concord, Jane wrote a letter to her dead son, telling him how much she would give to "recall all that was unreasonable—or hasty—or mistaken in my conduct towards you."

"I know not how to go on without you," she added, "you were my comfort, dear—far more than I thought." 71

Yet somehow she did go on, if only barely. Although she avoided social functions during the first year of her husband's presidency, Jane felt strong enough to make her official Washington debut to a greatly sympathetic city at the White House New Year's Ball in 1855.

And to the surprise of everyone, whenever Jane encountered a child in the White House, it was a happy moment: "I was very much touched to observe her interest in little boys," recorded Anne E. Hall, a distant relative visiting the White House. "I should have feared it would be so painful to her to see them, & that she would have shrunk from friends."

Instead, continued Hall, no such child could "escape her eye & her kindly attention if within her reach." 72

And perhaps no child delighted her as much as Samuel Davis, the son of Jefferson and Varina Davis. Dubbed "Le man," by his father, Samuel shortly became the center of attention not only of his parents, both for the Pierces, as well, who frequently visited the Davis residence in Washington.

But young life was fleeting in an era in which the word "pediatrics" did not even exist. In the early summer of 1854, Samuel became ill, possibly with the measles. Holding on for more than two weeks, he died on June 13, not yet two years old.

Pierce went to the funeral. Jane, unwilling and perhaps even unable to say goodbye to one more child about to be lowered into the earth, remained behind in the White House. 73

Now in late September 1858, Jane read a letter from Mary Aiken describing a picture she had of Bennie. Jane knew the image well: "Does it not seem to say, as he does in my dreams, 'I'm nicely, Mother, just as well as I want to be.'" 74

It had been more than five years since Bennie's death, but for his mother he was alive every day.

By the late winter of 1859 Nathaniel Hawthorne was dining with his family in Rome when he heard a voice that sounded familiar. Walking into his parlor he encountered Franklin Pierce. "I was rejoiced to see him," Hawthorne later wrote, "though a little saddened to see the marks of care and coming age, in many a whitening hair, and many a furrow."

Even worse, Hawthorne felt that something "seemed to have passed away" in Pierce, "without leaving any trace." 75

In the days to come, the two old friends would spend countless hours walking along the streets of Rome, and Hawthorne soon found, on the contrary, that

Pierce was as buoyant as ever. "The more I see him, the more I get him back, just such as he was in our youth," marveled Hawthorne. 7627One day Pierce told Hawthorne that there was talk of running him for president again in 1860. Buchanan, by the spring of 1859, was almost as unpopular as Pierce had ever been, and voices from both the North and the South were saying that it was almost inevitable that the country would be divided in two—and soon.

At least Pierce, the last "Northern man with Southern principles," might just be able to keep the two regions talking to each other, and beyond that, bound as a union.

That Democrats were beginning to think of Pierce was relayed to him by Jefferson Davis in January of the new year who reported: "Your old friends in Mississippi have not forgotten you and are ready to show their appreciation of you on the first occasion."

Continued Davis: "Many said to me that your renomination for the Presidency was their first wish and best hope." 77

To Hawthorne, Pierce said he was not interested in running again. Wryly, Hawthorne wrote: "No doubt, he is perfectly sincere; no doubt, too, he would again be a candidate, if a pretty unanimous voice of the party should demand it." 78

Trying to complete work on a new book and distracted by the illness of his daughter Una from malaria, Hawthorne was an anxious, troubled man in the spring of 1859. Pierce's sudden reappearance in Hawthorne's life, thought his wife, Sophia, was a God-send: "No one else could have supplied his place." 79

Pierce also regularly sat by the bedside of Una, and vowed that he and Jane would not leave Rome until the girl recovered. "He really did us good," Hawthorne would later write, "and I shall always love him the better for the recollection of these dark days." 80

By June the Hawthornes had left Rome for London. It was then that Franklin and Jane began to move in the direction of at last returning to America, entirely uncertain of the reception that awaited them in a country on the verge of coming apart.

CHAPTER THREE NOTES

1. Robert W. Johannsen, *Stephen A. Douglas* (New York: Oxford University Press, 1973) p. 585.

2. "Reception of the Nominations," *New York Tribune*, 6 June 1852, p. 9, col. 3.

3. Seba Smith, *My Thirty Years Out of the Senate, by Major Jack Downing* (New York: Oaksmith & Company, 1859), pp. 283–91; see also Milton and Patricia Rickels, *Seba Smith* (Boston: Twayne Publishers, 1977), the authors say that after Pierce won the nomination Smith produced a series of "witty strokes on the theme of Pierce as a leader without a past, without principles, and without purpose—in short, as a non-person." 129–31.

4. Thomas Woodson, *Nathaniel Hawthorne—The Letters, 1843–1853* (Dayton: Ohio State University Press, 1985), 604–07; Nathaniel Hawthorne to Horatio Bridge, 13 October 1852

5. "The Election," *Daily Picayune*, 3 November 1852, p. 1, col. 4.

6. "Before and Since the Election," *Richmond Express*, 11 November 1852, p. 1, col. 2; a reprint of the *Boston Transcript* column.

7. "The Political Future," *New York Times*, 4 November 1852, p. 4, col. 1.

8. Beverly Wilson Palmer, *The Selected Letters of Charles Sumner* (Boston: Northeastern University Press, 1990), p. 378, Charles Sumner to Lord Wharncliffe, 19 December 1852.

9. "The United States," *London Times,* 28 December 1852, p. 5, col. 3; "Trials of a President," *Daily National Intelligencer*, 22 November 1852, p. 3, col. 4.

10. Franklin Pierce to Jefferson Davis, 12 January 1853, Series 2, Reel 2, Franklin Pierce Papers.

11. For a brief chronology on Pierce's efforts to recruit Davis see, Lynda Lasswell Crist, *The Papers of Jefferson Davis, Volume 5, 1853–1855* (Baton Rouge: Louisiana State University Press, 1985), 3–5, Albert G. Brown to Jefferson Davis, 1 January 1853.

12. John Bassett Moore, *The Works of James Buchanan, Volume IX, 1853–1855* (Philadelphia: J. B. Lippincott, 1909). Buchanan's notes to himself, 11 July 1853, p. 24.

13. Philip Shriver Klein, *President James Buchanan—A Biography* (University Park, Pennsylvania: Pennsylvania State University Press, 1962), p. 226.

14. W. A. Swanberg, *Sickles The Incredible* (New York: Charles Scribner's Sons, 1956), p. 89.

15. It was a measure of the general esteem for Campbell that he was supported by both associate justices John Catron and Benjamin Curtis, two men who held radically different ideas on many constitutional issues. Catron, for example, was doubtful that the government could ever prohibit slavery, while Curtis believed that the states had the power to provide a legal definition of slavery. Henry G. Connor, *John Archibald Campbell—Associate Justice of the United States Supreme Court, 1853–1861* (Boston: Houghton Mifflin Company, 1920), p. 15. See also "Latest Intelligence," *New York Times*, 23 March 1853, p. l, col. 2.

16. Crist, *The Papers of Jefferson Davis, Volume 5, 1853–1855*, p. 31, Davis address delivered in Philadelphia, 12 July 1853.

17. Page Smith, *The Nation Comes of Age—A People's History of the Ante-Bellum Years, Volume 4* (New York: Penguin Books, 1981), 1050–53.

18. Untitled editorial, *Daily National Intelligencer*, 13 July 1853, p. 3, col. 1.

19. "The President's Trip to New York," *New York Herald*, 12 July 1853, p. 1, col. 1; "The Reception at Castle Garden," *New York Herald*, 15 July 1853, p. 1, col. 2; "The Great Exhibition," *New York Times*, 16 July 1853, p. 1, col. 1.

20. "Arrival of the President," *New York Herald*, 15 July 1853, p. 1, col. 1; Roy Franklin Nichols, *Franklin Pierce—Young Hickory of the Granite Hills*, (Newtown, CT: American Political Biography Press, 1998), 283–84.

21. John Bassett Moore, *The Works of James Buchanan, Volume IX, 1853–1855* (Philadelphia: J. B. Lippincott Company, 1909), 22; Buchanan's notes to himself, 11 July 1853.

22. "The Reception at Castle Garden," p. 1, col. 2.

23. Ibid.; Pierce's remarks at the Crystal Palace were perfunctory in keeping with the occasion. His speech at the Castle Garden was far longer and one that he had worked on extensively, although it, too, was general in nature. "Memoranda—New York," 15 July 1863, end of Series 3, Reel 6, Franklin Pierce Papers.

24. "The Reception at Castle Garden," p. 1, col. 2.

25. "The New York Exhibition," *London Times*, 18 August 1853, p. 4, col. 5. (?)

26. "Washington," *New York Times*, 19 July 1853, p. 4, col. 4.

27. Carl Sandburg, *Abraham Lincoln—The Prairie Years and the War Years* (San Diego: A Harvest Book: 1982) p. 117.

28. Willard Carl Klunder, *Lewis Cass and the Politics of Moderation* (Kent, Ohio: Kent State University Press, 1996), p. 266; John Hoyt Williams, *Sam Houston—The Life and Times of the Liberator of Texas, an Authentic Hero* (New York: Touchstone Books, 1993), 288–91.

29. Donald B. Cole, *Benjamin Brown French—Witness to the Young Republic, A Yankee's Journal, 1828–1870* (Hanover: University Press of New England, 1989), 249–50, from diary dated 5 March 1854.

30. Nathaniel P. Banks to Whiting Griswold, 30 January 1854, Whiting Griswold Papers, Manuscript Division, Library of Congress. See also Banks to Griswold, February 6, 15 and 18, in the same collection.

31. Jefferson Davis, *The Rise and Fall of the Confederate Government, Volume I* (New York: Appleton & Company, 1881), p. 28.

32. *Congressional Globe—First Session, 33rd Congress, Appendix* (Washington: John C. Rives, 1854), 3 February 1854, p. 134,

33. *Congressional Globe—First Session, 33rd Congress, Part II* (Washington: John C. Rives, 1854), 25 May 1854, p. 520.

34. *Right of Petition, New England Clergymen, First Session, 33rd Congress, 1853–1854* (Washington: Buell & Blanchard, 1854); Albert J. Frank, *The Trials of*

Anthony Burns—Freedom and Slavery in Emerson's Boston (Cambridge: Harvard University Press, 1998), 12–13; Eleanor M. Tilton, *The Letters of Ralph Waldo Emerson* (New York: Columbia University Press, 1991) 404–05, Ralph Waldo Emerson to Charles Loring Brace, 26 June 1854; Andrew Hilen, *The Letters of Henry Wadsworth Longfellow, Volume III, 1844–1856* (Cambridge: The Belknap Press, 1972), p. 417, Henry Wadsworth Longfellow to Charles Sumner, 22 February 1854.

35. Hilen, *The Letters of Henry Wadsworth Longfellow, Volume III, 1844–1856*, p. 417, Henry Wadsworth Longfellow to Charles Sumner, 22 February 1854.

36. Oscar Sherwin, *Prophet of Liberty—The Life and Times of Wendell Phillips* (New York: Bookman Associates, 1958), p. 314.

37. Cole, *Benjamin Brown French—Witness to the Young Republic, A Yankee's Journal, 1828–1870*, 249–50, from diary dated 5 March 1854.

38. Edgar Langsdorf, "S. C. Pomeroy and the New England Emigrant Aid Company, 1854–1858," *Kansas Historical Quarterly*, Volume VII, Number 3, August 1938, p. 231.

39. Elizabeth Blair to Samuel Phillip Lee, 22 and 23 May 1856, Blair-Lee Papers, Rare Books and Special Collections, Princeton University Library.

40. Barry A. Crouch, *In Search of Union: Amos A. Lawrence and the Coming of the Civil War* (Ph'd, University of New Mexico, 1970), p. 132.

41. John L. Thomas, *The Liberator—William Lloyd Garrison—A Biography* (Boston: Little, Brown and Company, 1963), p. 382

42. Sherwin, *Prophet of Liberty—The Life and Times of Wendell Phillips*, p. 316. For a chronology of the Kansas-Nebraska bill in Congress, see Robert R. Russell, "The Issues in the Congressional Struggle Over the Kansas-Nebraska Bill, 1854," *The Journal of Southern History*, Volume 29, Number Two, May 1963, 187–210.

43. "The Boston Riot," *New York Times*, 29 May 1854, p. 1, col. 6.

44. Jane H. Pease and William H. Pease, *The Fugitive Slave Law and Anthony Burns: A Problem in Law Enforcement* (Philadelphia: J. B. Lippincott Company, 1975), p. 27.

45. "The Fugitive Slave Case," *The Liberator*, 9 June 1854, p. 91, col. 5. David R. Maginnes, "The Case of the Court House Rioters in the Rendition of the Fugitive Slave Anthony Burns," *The Journal of Negro History*, Volume LVI, Number One, January 1971, 31–42.

46. Ibid.

47. Crouch, *In Search of Union: Amos A. Lawrence and the Coming of the Civil War*, p. 140.

48. Hilen, *The Letters of Henry Wadsworth Longfellow, Volume III, 1844–1856*, 434–35, Henry Wadworth Longfellow to Francis Lieber, 1 June 1854.

49. Franklin Pierce to Stephen A. Douglas, 28 May 1855, Stephen A. Douglas Papers, Special Collections Research Center, University of Chicago Library.

50. Irving Katz, *August Belmont—A Political Biography* (New York: Columbia University Press, 1968), p. 51.

51. Alexander H. Stephens to Linton Stephens, 19 August 1856, Alexander H. Stephens Papers, Special Collections, Manhattanville College Library; Nichols, *Franklin Piece—Young Hickory of the Granite Hills*, p. 452.

52. Nichols, *Franklin Pierce—Young Hickory of the Granite Hills*, 436–37.

53. "Proclamation of the President, calling an Extra Session of Congress," *New York Times*, 19 August 1856, p. 1, col. 1.

54. Norman F. Boas, *Jane M. Pierce (1806–1863)—The Pierce-Aiken Papers* (New London, CT: New London Printers, 1983), 61–63.

55. Boas, *Jane M. Pierce (1806–1863)—The Pierce-Aiken Papers*, 71–72, Jane Pierce to Mary Aiken, no date given, but probably late December 1857; James D. Johnston, *China and Japan: Being a Narrative of the Cruise of the U.S. Steam-Frigate Powhatan* (Philadelphia: Charles DeSilver Publishers, 1861), 16. Noting that Pierce often visited the ward-room of the vessel, Johnston added that he and his fellow officers were "charmed with the ease

and affability with which he [Pierce] at once adapted himself to the new style of association into which he had suddenly been thrown."

56. Boas, *Jane M. Pierce (1806–1863)—The Pierce-Aiken Papers,* p. 73, Jane Pierce to Mary Aiken, 9 January 1858.

57. Ibid.; 72–73, Jane Pierce to Mary Aiken, 29 December 1857.

58. Ibid.; p. 75, Jane Pierce to Mary Aiken, 9 March 1858.

59. George Dallas to Franklin Pierce, 5 January 1858; Caleb Cushing to Franklin Pierce, 9 April 1858; both Series 3, Reel 5, Franklin Pierce Papers; Lynda Lasswell Crist, *The Papers of Jefferson Davis, Volume 6, 1856–1860* (Baton Rouge: Louisiana State University Press, 1989), 172–73, 4 April 1858, Jefferson Davis to Franklin Pierce.

60. Norman F. Boas, *Jane M. Pierce (1806–1863)—The Pierce-Aiken Papers Supplement* (Mystic: Connecticut: Seaport Autographs, 1989), p. 40, Sidney Webster to Mary Aiken, 6 March 1858.

61. Boas, *Jane M. Pierce (1806–1863)—The Pierce-Aiken Papers,* 76–77, an excerpt from Jane's diary, 6 August 1858.

62. "The Railroad Accident—Latest Particulars," *New York Tribune,* 9 January 1853, p. 5, col. 2.

63. "Further Particulars of the Accident on the Boston and Maine Railroad—Letter of Rev. Mr. Fuller," *New York Times,* 10 January 1853, p. 2, col. 4. In his account of the accident, Pierce biographer Peter A. Wallner notes that exactly what killed Bennie remains uncertain. He suggests the young boy's head may have been struck by debris from a broken seat or that he "got caught between the superstructure of the car and the side of a seat as the car turned over." In his own memoirs, Sidney Webster, Pierce's secretary during the White House years, says Bennie "fell with his head near where the side of the car joins the bottom, and the side and bottom, springing apart for an instant in the strain, closed back again upon the head and crushed it." Peter A. Wallner, *Franklin Pierce—New Hampshire's Favorite Son* (Concord: Plaidswede Publishing, 2004), p.293; Sidney Webster, *Franklin Pierce and his Administration* (New York: D. Appleton and Company, 1892), 30–31.

64. Ibid.

65. Crouch, *In Search of Union: Amos A. Lawrence and the Coming of the Civil War*, 125–26.

66. Josephine Brodhead to Franklin Pierce, 7 January 1853, Series 3, Reel 5, Franklin Pierce Papers.

67. Francis Upham to Franklin Pierce, 7 January 1853, Series 3, Reel 5, Franklin Pierce Papers.

68. "Death of Gen. Pierce's Son," *Daily Picayune*, 10 January 1853, p. 2, col. 3.

69. George Bancroft to Franklin Pierce, 7 January 1853, Series 2, Reel 1, Franklin Pierce Papers.

70. Franklin Pierce to Jefferson Davis, 12 January 1853, Series 2, Reel 2, Franklin Pierce Papers.

71. Jane Pierce to Bennie Pierce, 23 January 1853, Franklin Pierce Papers, New Hampshire Historical Society.

72. Norman F. Boas, *Jane M. Pierce (1806–1863)—The Pierce-Aiken Papers Supplement* p.17, Anne E. Hall to E.M.G. Hall, 23 February 1855.

73. Crist, *The Papers of Jefferson Davis, Volume 5, 1853–1855*, p. 11. Varina Davis later noted that Jane greatly loved Samuel, and "constantly sent or called for him to drive with her," p.73, footnote to letter from William B. Howell to Jefferson Davis, 19 June 1854.

74. Boas, *Jane M. Pierce (1806–1863), The Pierce-Aiken Papers*, p. 78, Jane Pierce to Mary Aiken, 24 September 1858.

75. Thomas Woodson, *Nathaniel Hawthorne—The French and Italian Notebooks* (Dayton: Ohio State University Press, 1980), 507–08, Hawthorne diary entry, 11 March 1859.

76. Ibid., p. 508, Hawthorne diary entry, 15 March 1859. Pierce felt the same about Hawthorne, telling Horatio Bridge, "He is entirely unchanged in heart and genius." Franklin Pierce to Horatio Bridge, 11 September 1859, Horatio Bridge Papers, Bowdoin College Library.

77. Jefferson Davis to Franklin Pierce, 17 January 1859, Series 3, Reel 5, Franklin Pierce Papers.

78. Woodson, *Nathaniel Hawthorne—The French and Italian Notebooks*, 507–08, Hawthorne diary entry, 11 March 1859.

79. Brenda Wineapple, *Hawthorne—A Life* (New York: Random House Trade Paperbacks, 2003), p. 315.

80. Woodson, *Nathaniel Hawthorne—The French and Italian Notebooks*, p. 518, Hawthorne diary entry, 19 April 1859. In this same entry, Hawthorne notes that Pierce was "evidently happier than I have known him since our college days," and speculates that achieving the "highest success that public life could give him," (the presidency) had given his old friend an air of satisfaction and contentment that he had not possessed before.

4

Darkness and Blood

On the night of June 16, 1858, while the Pierces were still in Madeira, a tall man with coarse black hair, large hands and a disarming sense of humor, rose in the marble hall of the Illinois House of Representatives and reminded an extremely attentive audience that it had been more than four years since passage of the Kansas-Nebraska Act, an act that was initiated, he said, "with the avowed object, and confident promise, of putting an end to slavery agitation."

But since passage of that act, said the man, reading carefully from a text he had worked on for days, "that agitation has not only not ceased, but has constantly augmented."

"In my opinion, it will not cease until a crisis shall have been reached and passed," he continued, before quoting from the New Testament: "A house divided against itself cannot stand." 1

Abraham Lincoln in the summer of 1858 was 49 years old and the possessor of a face that John G. Nicolay, his private secretary, said "moved through a thousand delicate gradations of line and contour, light and shade, sparkle of the eye and curve of the lip," before coming together to form a countenance that flowed from "grave to gay, and back again, from the rollicking jollity of laughter to that far-away look." 2

Having only served for 8 years in the Illinois state legislature and one term in the U.S. House, Lincoln remained a relatively unknown public figure in the summer of 1858. But as the new Republican nominee for the U.S. Senate, he stood on the precipice of what would prove to be a national fame of legendary proportions.

In a series of free-flowing, open-air debates with his opponent—the always-lively incumbent Democratic Senator Stephen A. Douglas—Lincoln in the great campaign of 1858 tried to tie the opposition party to Franklin Pierce, whom he was certain remained unpopular with his state's voters, or at least the emerging Republican base Lincoln would need to be competitive. Finally Douglas, to a hail of both cheers and catcalls, was forced to defend the former president as a "man of integrity and honor." 3

But the Lincoln-Douglas debates, covered by an insatiable national press, were not about Franklin Pierce. The former president simply served as an easy punching bag for Lincoln, who was ardently trying to make the point that the Democrats as a party were through. Rather, the debates were focused almost entirely on the question of slavery, making Illinois, judged the *New York Times*, "from this time forward, until the Senatorial question shall be decided, the most interesting political battleground in the Union." 4

The Illinois contest also finally made slavery the only issue in American political life, hardening positions and attitudes throughout both the North and South in response, and once again giving rise to talk of secession from those at both extremes who now declared that the country could no longer live peaceably with itself.

Oddly, for all the sensation he caused, Lincoln was no abolitionist. "I have no purpose directly or indirectly to interfere with the institution of slavery in the states where it exists," Lincoln reminded a raucous gathering of farmers in Ottawa, Illinois on August 21. "I believe I have no lawful right to do so, and I have no inclination to do so." 5

Nor could Lincoln by any reasonable measure be regarded at this point in his career as a friend to black Americans. In 1854, when he first attacked the Kansas-Nebraska Act, he said that if given the power to settle by himself the slavery issue, his first impulse would have been to free all of the slaves, yes, but then to "send them to Liberia." 6

"I have no disposition to introduce political and social equality between the white and black races," Lincoln now told Illinois voters, adding that he remained "in favor of the race to which I belong having the superior position." 7

He had even professed himself to be a friend of the South, or at least—again, unlike the abolitionists—to understand their needs. "I have no prejudice against the Southern people," Lincoln declared, in one of his many nicely-composed phrases. "They are just what we would be in their situation. If slavery did not exist amongst them, they would not introduce it. If it did now exist amongst us, we should not instantly give it up." 8

What made Lincoln such a sudden and real figure of hatred across the South was his realistic view, as he stated frankly in his House Divided speech, that one way or the other the country would soon have to decide what it wanted to be: "This government cannot endure half slave and half free," he said, adding "I do not expect the Union to be dissolved—I do not expect the house to fall—but I do expect it will cease to be divided. It will become all one thing, or all the other." 9

Even though Lincoln's proposition may have seemed both reasonable and balanced, at least to his fans in the North, Southerners angrily responded to his "all one thing or all the other" idea, primarily because it suggested the *possibility* that an institution they had come to feel enormously defensive about could one day no longer exist.

Ironically, the issue of slavery would prove to be far more politically dangerous for Douglas than for Lincoln. Lincoln's base was overwhelmingly in the North and his Republican backers easily perceived a successful national future as long as he kept that base intact. Douglas, on the other hand, as a Democrat, could never expect to become president without the backing of most of the South, and he seemed to have risked a considerable portion of the region when he acknowledged, after considerable heckling from Lincoln, that a "local legislature could indeed exclude slavery simply by refusing to enact such laws." 10

Although Lincoln would lose the 1858 election, he emerged from the contest a national figure and top contender for the 1860 Republican presidential nomination, helped, no doubt, by the publication of his debates with Douglas, more than 30,000 copies of which were quickly sold by the spring of 1859.

From the South, enjoying a similar kind of growing prominence, also fed by an active national press, Jefferson Davis had emerged by 1858 as the most prominent spokesman for the region, or as the *New York Herald* called him, "the Mephistophiles of the South." 11

Elected to the U.S. Senate in 1856, while still serving as Pierce's secretary of war, Davis quickly, through the force of his personality and undeniable power of his intellect, became the leader of the chamber's Southern bloc, never missing an opportunity to not only defend his native region from attacks real and perceived, but also to promote what he envisioned as a "Southern nation state," that would be economically and even to a degree politically free of the more powerful North.

As Davis saw it, the South needed to rethink itself as a separate country without really becoming one. Part of the U.S., it could build up its physical infrastructure, expand its economy and provide a public education for its children complete with textbooks "placed in the hands of our children" that would "indoctrinate their minds with sound impressions and views." 12

It went without saying that teachers who failed to sign on to this particular vision should be let go, Davis continued, noting that they "do us irremediable evil" by corrupting what he called "the rising generation."

Like Lincoln, Davis in 1859 was seen as a possible contender for the presidency in 1860, and was determined to press the South's advantage in that campaign, as he most dramatically demonstrated when he introduced a series of resolutions designed to ward off abolitionist legislation. Any attempts to do away with slavery where it existed, proclaimed Davis, were both "in violation of the Constitution [and] insulting to the states so interfered with."

Furthermore, Davis asserted, the abolitionist notion that run-away slaves could be assisted was a legal heresy: such slaves could only be properly viewed as "hostile in character, subversive of the Constitution, and revolutionary in their effect." 13

Americans who contemplated the public affairs of their nation, daily reading the lengthy columns of congressional debates, presidential proclamations, and candidate letters published in the vast majority of the country's press, could view the respective positions of men like Lincoln and Davis as interesting intellectual exercises in political philosophy, exercises that incited oftentimes passionate debate in the local town square, but usually little more than that.

But all of that changed during the third week of October 1859 when John Brown, a militant abolitionist, seized control of a quiet federal arsenal in the small town of Harpers Ferry, Virginia, perched on a soft bluff above the Potomac River.

It would later be learned that Brown, who had spectacularly launched a raid on a pro-slavery settlement in Kansas in the spring of 1856 that saw five men hacked to death, had received financial and moral support from Northern abolitionists who were increasingly attracted to the use of guerilla warfare in their battle against the slave states.

Brown's goal this time was typically bold and impractical: to free all of the slaves of Virginia through a mass mutiny that would have undoubtedly resulted in the deaths of their owners. The time for talking, he said, having long since expired.

"Moral suasion is hopeless," Brown decided.

"I don't think that the people of the slave states will ever consider the subject of slavery in its true light until some other argument is resorted to than moral suasion," Brown added. 14

That meant action. At Harper's Ferry, Brown led a disciplined band of 18 white and black men who helped him round up and hold as hostage some sixty local citizens, not all of them slaveholders.

For more than a day, Brown's men hunkered down, unsure of their next step. But a detachment of marines under the order of Colonel Robert E. Lee soon overwhelmed them. Ten of Brown's followers, including his two sons, were killed.

In captivity, Brown was unflinching and eerily calm. Realizing that he would probably be executed—he was hanged on December 2 after a week-long trial—did little to upset his equanimity.

"You are guilty of a great wrong against God and humanity," Brown serenely told a delegation of incredulous politicians who came by to interrogate him in his Charleston, Virginia jail cell. "I say that without wishing to be offensive."

"It would be perfectly right for anyone to interfere with you," Brown continued, "so far as to free those you willfully and wickedly hold in bondage. I do not say this insultingly." 15

There were many things that alarmed the South about Brown's attack. Certainly the idea that someone could come along and inspire a slave insurrection was scary. But just as bad was the fact that Brown clearly had the backing of some Northerners, surely concrete proof that the abolitionists now would stop at nothing in their struggle to free the slaves and punish those who owned them.

This was, of course, the very thing that Franklin Pierce, who had castigated the Brown raid as a "violation of all law, human and divine," had repeatedly predicted could happen if just one person should take to heart the growing militant rhetoric of the abolitionists. 16

Arriving in the U.S. on August 29 from London with Jane, Pierce could immediately tell that the country was more angry and divided than ever before.

And he took the first opportunity that came to him to try and quiet things down, remarking to a group of locals who had gathered to welcome him in Nashua, New Hampshire on September 2 that "as we have grown older" there was a greater need for "mutual forgiveness and forbearance," and that all Americans, no matter what their political opinions, shared what he called "a common country."

"Passions and prejudices and narrow views fall before that great, broad patriotism which, thank God, does move all our hearts when we are away from our homes," Pierce added. 17

If those who listened to Pierce's first address stateside thought perhaps that he had been out of the country too long, or was simply out of touch, living in a distant past as he talked about an America that seemed more reminiscent of the 1820s, a communication he composed three months later to a pro-Union rally at Boston's Fanueil Hall proved he was entirely of the moment, and more than willing to forcefully become engaged in the hottest controversy of the day.

"It is to be remembered that those who boldly approve and applaud the acts of treason and murder perpetrated within the limits of Virginia are not the most dangerous enemies of the Constitution," Pierce wrote in a letter that was read out loud to the crowd.

It was really those who "habitually appeal to sectional prejudices and passions by denouncing the institutions and people of the South," continued Pierce, who posed the greatest threat to Constitutional order.

They are the ones, Pierce added, "who are hurrying us upon swift destruction." 18

Pierce's message was received with loud applause. But he was hardly done with a topic that greatly excited him. On December 17, he sent a separate letter to a similar group, this one gathering in New York, and wondered how calmer heads would prevail in a season dominated by extremism "from the pulpit, the platform or the press."

"We cannot go on in this way," Pierce bluntly remarked. "The present status cannot be maintained. The condition of affairs must, of necessity, soon become a great deal better or a great deal worse." 19

He was full of foreboding, as were many. Arriving in New York with Jane during the week of Christmas, Pierce described for his brother a desultory scene: "I am sorry to say that in my intercourse with residents of this city or with people casually here, I have found nothing to quiet apprehensions with regard to the serious dangers which threaten the Union," he confided to Henry Pierce.

Strained business relations between the North and the South portended economic disaster for the entire country, he predicted, but particularly for New England. And as economic ties frayed and separated, surely those that were political would follow.

It only stood to reason that Pierce would be more than happy to lend his weight to pro-Union meetings, which he described as "well so far as they go and for the present." But he was quick to add, with a renewed sense of urgency, that unless political power was wrestled from the hands of the abolitionists, "the letters which have been written and the resolutions which have been passed will not be worth the paper on which they have been printed." 20

For now, Pierce was willing to do what he could through the pro-Union movement, which was largely a collection of mostly Northern Democrats and prominently included Caleb Cushing, former attorney general in Pierce's cabinet, and the famed orator and former Massachusetts senator Edward Everett.

On New Year's Eve, Pierce sent yet another message to a pro-Union gathering, this one in Bangor, Maine, and admitted that while there had been talk of secession in the South, "it will be well not to forget that bitter language, hard epithets, criminations and recriminations between us at the North satisfy no man's judgment, reach no man's conscience, and can be productive only of evil." 21

The effect of Pierce's sudden re-emergence on the national scene was telling. Old friends and those newly devoted to him soon began to see him as the logical Democratic presidential nominee for 1860. Just days after the Pierces returned to the U.S., Jefferson Davis, once again, told Pierce that his support in the South for a return bid to the White House remained firm. In Mississippi, said Davis, "I am sure you are preferred above all others." 22

When Cushing was named as the chairman for the upcoming Democratic convention, which would be held in Charleston, South Carolina, observers only naturally concluded that this would be a decided factor in Pierce's favor, if he decided, as he did in 1852, to mount a late-blooming effort should the other more obvious contenders—in this case primarily Stephen A. Douglas and a host of lesser candidates—fail.

That, at least, is how Cushing himself saw it when he told Sidney Webster that his chairmanship was being regarded "as a movement of the Pierce men—not merely with contingent or possible reference to Gen'l Pierce himself, but rather in regard to that general interest." 23

By late January, a Washington political correspondent for the *New York Times* reported that the "friends of Gen. Pierce are flocking to this City in great numbers, pipelaying for the Charleston nomination." 24

But the truth of the matter was that even a draft movement, to be successful, needed minimally the oblique participation of the would-be candidate, and in this case such participation was pointedly missing.

To a Massachusetts supporter who urged him to run, Pierce candidly responded that he regarded his public career as being over, "and have not a single lingering desire that it should be otherwise."

"This and more my friends at the North fully understand," Pierce continued, adding: "they know it would annoy me if I believed that my name could come before the Charleston Convention under any possible combination of circumstances." 25

Instead, Pierce, doubtful that Douglas could win, thought Davis should run, and told his old friend as much on January 7, 1860 when he said that New England Democrats "are looking for 'the Coming Man,'" whom he described as "one who is raised by all the elements of his character above the atmosphere ordinarily breathed by politicians." 26

Davis, however, was also reluctant, and repeatedly told friends and reporters that he only wanted to serve out his senatorial term and see elected to the White House a Northern Democrat sympathetic to the South's issues and challenges.

That task became manifestly more difficult when Douglas finally emerged as the Democratic nominee after the convention met twice, prompting a large delegation of Southerners to hastily form a break-away party and nominate as their standard-bearer John C. Breckinridge, recently vice-president under Buchanan.

Dramatically, during the same spring of 1860, the delegates to the young Republican party threw over Senator William Seward of New York, the presumed favorite for their nomination, in favor of Lincoln, causing instant alarm across the South—although why Seward, even more an abolitionist, seemed less a threat was not remarked upon.

"We ought to beat them," former Connecticut Governor Thomas H. Seymour told Pierce on May 19, "but madness rules the hour and no one can tell what is to be our future." Alexander H. Stephens, foreseeing what he thought would by the cataclysmic results of a Lincoln victory, was much more certain: "In less than twelve months we shall be in the midst of a bloody war. What is to become of us then God only knows." 27

Pierce was asking the same questions, but, for once, from a different perspective, as he criticized Democratic activists for allowing the party to be split in two. Was devotion to the "integrity of the Union," he asked, really about to be sacrificed to the "blind control of passion, of which we have already had too much?" 28

Davis was perplexed as well, criticizing Douglas, whom he described as a "grog-drinking, electioneering Demagogue," for staying in the 1860 race even though his chances to win with the Democrats divided seemed hopeless. "It must be," Davis told Pierce, "that we have been doomed to destruction." 29

That destruction arrived on election day, November 6, which saw Lincoln win only 40 percent of the popular vote, but a large majority in the electoral college.

The division that Pierce had worried about among the Democrats was seen in the fact that between them, Douglas and Breckinridge won a strong 47 percent of the vote, hardly an affirmation that the country was pro-abolition, anti-South, or interested in embracing policies markedly different from the conservative North/pro-South administrations as represented by Pierce and Buchanan.

But none of that mattered now as the nation, and in particular, the South, tried to absorb what had happened. For Southern extremists, it could only mean one thing: secession. On the day after the election, the *Charleston Mercury*, owned by secession enthusiast Robert Barnwell Rhett, Jr., declared: "The tea has been thrown over board, the revolution of 1860 has been initiated." 30

Davis, who had throughout 1860 voiced his concerns over the effect a Lincoln victory would have on his native South, now told Rhett "If the secession of So. Ca should be followed by an attempt to coerce her back into the Union, that act of usurpation, folly and wickedness would enlist every true Southern man for her defence." 31

Davis wrote his remarks to Rhett in a letter from the quiet of his Mississippi Brierfield plantation. Just then, some two hundred miles to the south in New Orleans, things were a bit noisier as Stephen A. Douglas arrived in the city.

Buoyed by cheering crowds and the very public support of the always controversial Pierre Soule, former U.S. Senator, Douglas was asked by local businessmen if he could give them his thoughts on what everyone now regarded as the coming crisis.

In response Douglas wrote a letter that would shortly gain a wide circulation urging calm and remarking that "the election of Mr. Lincoln, in my humble opinion, presents no just cause, no reasonable excuse for disunion." 32

Douglas' remarks in many ways reinforced the prevailing attitudes of the New Orleans business sector.

Although Louisiana had voted for the pro-South Breckinridge and Lincoln's name never appeared on the ballot there, many traders and investors were nervous about all of the talk about secession.

Their caution was given voice in the New Orleans *Daily Picayune* which professed to foster hope that the North and the South could still "create a mutual understanding, strengthened in some binding form of guarantees, which shall define terms of peace by which we may live together." 33

But the secessionist movement, nurtured by years of grievances, was by now too strong across the South to be suddenly halted. Those who wanted to leave the U.S. may not have ever made up a real majority of the population, but secession was supported by a majority of the delegates who attended specially-called conventions in the states of the Deep South, and in the end they were the only ones who mattered.

For Pierce, it was all too much. He could not fathom even the prospect of disunion. "Can it be that this flag, with all the stars in their places, is no longer to float at home, abroad, and always as an emblem of our *united* power, common freedom, and unchallenged security?"

"Can it be," he continued, obviously overwhelmed by the thought, "that it is to go down in darkness, if not in blood, before we have completed a single century of our independent national existence?" 34

Benjamin Brown French, one-time Pierce confidante, weighed the same imponderables. "'Secession'-'Disunion'-'Southern Confederacy'-'Monarchy'-are now the leading words in the Southern states, especially in So. Carolina," Brown recorded in his diary on December 9.

"No one knows what a day may bring forth, & the great result—whether happy or dread—is known only to that Providence who rules." 35

The next day Cushing, reflecting perfectly the views of his old boss, remarked to a Boston audience: "Gentlemen, revolution is upon us, and we are on the high road to anarchy and civil war."

Like Pierce, Cushing had no doubt as to who should bear the blame for current conditions: "The evil is agitation of slavery here in Massachusetts and the other Northern states," he declared bluntly, "and the remedy is for the Republicans to leave off that agitation." 36

Senator Charles Sumner, the abolitionists' long-time advocate, only naturally viewed the crisis from a different perspective when he commented "the existing hallucination of the slave masters is such that I doubt if this calamity can be avoided. They seem to rush upon their destiny." 37

But Sumner, at least, worried about war, and for all of his conflicts with his Southern colleagues, did not relish seeing the country split in two. Other abolitionists were less troubled. After South Carolina, Mississippi, Alabama, Florida, Georgia and Louisiana had all seceded, Henry Wadsworth Longfellow remarked to Sumner "Tragic as secession is, it also has its ludicrous sides," adding that the six seceding states reminded him of "Six paupers leaving the Union Workhouse."

"It is worthwhile to advertise them, and pursue them?" Longfellow asked. 38

Poet Lydia Maria Child, whose hatred for slavery had been transmuted into a general hatred for the South, thought not. "My *own* soul utters but *one* prayer," Child wrote, "and that is that we may be effectively separated from *all* the Slave States." Only by so doing, Child added, could America "present to the world a fair experiment of a free Republic." 39

Harriet Beecher Stowe was happy, too; happy that Lincoln had won, that the South was leaving and that war seemed at last near, although she wondered if there could be such a thing as a "Christian Soldier." Wendell Phillips, meanwhile, could hardly contain his joy. "All my grown up years," he told an abolitionist gathering in Connecticut, "have been devoted to creating just such a crisis as that which is now upon us." 40

But even as the sky darkened and the air was filled with the cries of warriors, there were those who continued to hope for some sort of as of yet unseen "third way." Some of them turned to Pierce, hoping he could somehow mediate passions.

Supreme Court Associate Justice John A. Campbell, whom Pierce had appointed to the bench, now wondered if the former president would be willing to head up a negotiation effort with the South. Amos Adams Lawrence asked for the same thing, prompting Pierce to reply that he had "never been able to see how a successful appeal could be made to the South," if the North was not first willing to account for its own errors, which he, again, attributed entirely to the abolitionists. 41

By the time Pierce responded to Lawrence, five Senators from the South, including most prominently Davis, officially withdrew from the upper chamber and declared their fealty to a new nation, the Southern Confederacy.

The speech of the normally jocular Judah P. Benjamin was particularly dramatic as the Louisiana senator told his Northern colleagues: "You can never subjugate us; you can never convert the free sons of the soil into vassals, paying tribute to your power."

As the packed Senate galleries listed in awe, Benjamin added: "And you never, never can degrade them to the level of an inferior and servile race. Never! Never!" 42

The exit of Davis was less clamorous, but of far more deadly consequences. He had long been against secession and as the unofficial leader of the Southern bloc in the Senate, was the man that even most Northerners knew by name and reputation.

His defection truly meant that the South was now certain to go its own way.

Before leaving Washington by train with Varina, Davis penned a heart-felt note to Pierce in which he began: "I have often and sadly turned my thoughts to you during the troublous times through which we have been passing."

He was leaving the Senate, and indeed the U.S., Davis said, because he at long last had no choice. He added that "civil war has only horror for me, but whatever circumstances demand shall be met as a duty and I trust be so discharged that you will not be ashamed of our former connection or cease to be my friend." 43

There was little chance of that. Pierce's devotion to Davis was complete. Bound by their joint service in war, political philosophy, personal tragedy and years in the White House, which both agreed—together with the rest of the cabinet—seemed more like a brotherhood, Pierce and Davis shared a friendship that was exceedingly rare in politics and altogether unusual in the experience of most middle-aged men.

Not even a war, which would inevitably and sadly see Pierce and Davis on opposite sides, could severe their bond.

When Davis also sent to Pierce his Brierfield mailing address, he was telling the former president that he expected to maintain that friendship, even if it now transcended the boundaries of two nations. There could be no doubt that Pierce felt the same way in response, although living in New England, in the region most inclined to view the South as a monolithic evil, he would have to now be more careful when it came to advertising his friendship with Davis.

From the perspective of New Hampshire, Jefferson Davis was now the enemy, a reviled and hated man. Just for the sake of his own personal safety, silence—for Pierce—would be the better part of valor.

Two months later Davis would be elected as the first president of the Confederacy and officially sworn in on February. By then young men in new uniforms had been seen marching through the streets of almost every major Northern and Southern city.

Abolitionists in the North were astonished to suddenly see their cause so totally ignored. The war would have "nothing to do with the damn niggers," a Union enthusiast told the husband of Maria Lydia Child. She now woefully realized: "The war was to preserve the Union." 44

What was dubbed the "Peace Conference," headed up by former president John Tyler, met that same month to stave off war, and failed, with the delegates quickly realizing that neither region now showed much interest in compromise. There seemed to be, on the contrary, almost an eagerness for the war to begin, an itching desire to go to battle and let the best man win.

Yet the idea that someone who wasn't Abraham Lincoln or Jefferson Davis might be able to do something, tantalized many, including Pierce.

On the night of April 16, he sat down to write a letter. The war had now begun. Just four days before, South Carolina, under the direction of Pierce's old friend, General P.G.T. Beauregard, fired on Fort Sumter, prompting a Union commander there to surrender on April 13.

Now Pierce wrote to former President Martin Van Buren and wondered: "Is there any human power which can avert the conflict of arms now apparently near at hand, between the two sections of the Union."

"There is no time for effective assemblages of the people—no time for conventions or protracted discussion," Pierce continued.

He noted that the country now had five living former presidents, which, with the correspondents, included Tyler, James Buchanan, and Millard Fillmore, and suggested that they all meet soon in Philadelphia, a city of noted symbolism "where the Constitution was framed."

How Lincoln was supposed to respond to such an unusual conclave, one which, as Pierce envisioned it, would supersede his diplomatic prerogatives, went unsaid.

"Might not their consultation, if it should result in concurrence of judgment, reach the Administration and the country with some degree of power," Pierce asked.

Noting that Van Buren was the country's most senior former president, Pierce added: "No man can with propriety summons such a meeting but yourself." 45

Van Buren, however, declined to take the bait, noting first that Pierce was wrong in assuming that he was "entitled to precedence in such matters on account of my being senior ex-president," and then wondering what, if anything, such a conference could accomplish.

Not for nothing was he known as the "Little Magician": Van Buren instead suggested that Pierce, who obviously nourished what he called "more hopeful expectations," should be the one to head up such an effort, and vowed that if Pierce did so and still required his participation, "I will accept the invitation without hesitation." 46

It was there that Pierce let the matter drop, undoubtedly realizing that any conference he might lead would immediately arouse the suspicions of Northerners who already felt he was too close to the South.

The next day, Pierce found himself facing a large crowd of people waving American flags and cheering the arrival of war. If they expected a buoyant cry to action, they were soon disappointed. Instead, looking down on the faces of both the young and the old from the balcony of the Eagle Hotel in Concord, Pierce pondered the unreality of it all.

"Can I, if I would, feel other than the proudest sadness when I see that those who so often stood shoulder to shoulder in the face of foreign foes," were now in "imminent danger of standing face to face as the foes of each other." 47

Just five days before Lincoln had issued a call for 75,000 volunteers. In response, Davis asked for 32,000, and would see that number exceeded by nearly four thousand as the month neared its end.

Surveying what he thought was a world gone mad, Pierce was left cold by the bellicose militarism of both the North and South. But he lived in the North, and it was there that he everyday heard vows of revenge and hatred and the kind of demand for uniformity that mark every nation marching into battle. He soon began to wonder if the right of dissent in Lincoln's America would soon prove to be the most important casualty of this strange war.

"The loss of property, so far as I am concerned, is nothing," Pierce bluntly told an old friend, Bishop Carlton Chase of Claremont, New Hampshire, on May 6.

"But the loss of my country—the overthrow of what I esteem the last hope of civil liberty," Pierce continued, "is fearful." 48

Just how fearful Pierce would soon discover as he prepared to leave for a trip to Michigan and what would prove to be the gravest political crisis of his life.

CHAPTER FOUR FOOTNOTES

1. "Speech of Hon. Abraham Lincoln," *Chicago Tribune*, 19 June 1858, p. 2, col. 4.

2. Carl Sandburg, *Abraham Lincoln—The Prairie Years and the War Years* (San Diego: A Harvest Book, 1982), pp. 401–02.

3. Harold Holzer, *The Lincoln-Douglas Debates—The First Complete Unexpurgated Text* (New York: HarperPerennial, 1993), 125.

4. "Senator Douglas at Chicago," *New York Times*, 13 July 1858, p. 4, col. 3.

5. Holzer, *The Lincoln-Douglas Debates,* 63.

6. Ibid., 61.

7. Ibid., 63.

8. Ibid., 61.

9. "Speech of Hon. Abraham Lincoln."

10. Holzer, *The Lincoln-Douglas Debates*, 88.

11. William C. Davis, *Jefferson Davis—The Man and His Hour* (New York: HarperPerennial, 1991), 258.

12. Lynda Lasswell Crist, *The Papers of Jefferson Davis, Volume 6, 1856–1860* (Baton Rouge: Louisiana State University Press, 1989), 157–62; excerpts from a speech given in Jackson, Mississippi, 4 November 1857.

13. *Congressional Globe, First Session, 36th Congress* (Washington: John C. Rives Publishing, 1860), 658–59 and 935.

14. "The Abolition Invasion," *Richmond Dispatch*, 22 October 1859, p. 1, col. 2.

15. Ibid.

16. Roy Franklin Nichols, *Franklin Pierce—Young Hickory of the Granite Hills* (Newton, Connecticut: American Political Biography Press, 1998), 510.

17. "Ex-President Pierce at Home," *New York Times*, 6 September 1859, p. 2, col. 3.

18. Franklin Pierce to Faneuil Hall Union Meeting, 2 December 1859, Franklin Pierce Papers, Series 3, Reel 2; "Sympathy with the South," *New York Times*, 9 December 1859, p. 8, col. 1.

19. Franklin Pierce to Committee of the New York Union Meeting, 17 December 1859, Franklin Pierce Papers, Series 3, Reel 2.

20. Franklin Pierce to Henry Pierce, 21 December 1859, Franklin Pierce Papers, Series 3, Reel 2.

21. Franklin Pierce to Bangor Union Meeting, 22 December 1859, Franklin Pierce Papers, Series 3, Reel 2.

22. Jefferson Davis to Franklin Pierce, Franklin Pierce Papers, 2 September 1859, Franklin Pierce Papers, Series 3, Reel 2.

23. Claude M. Feuss, *The Life of Caleb Cushing—Volume II* (Hamden, Connecticut: Archon Books, 1965), 243–44, Caleb Cushing to Sidney Webster, 20 September 1859.

24. "From Washington," *New York Times*, 31 January 1860, p. 1, col. 1.

25. "Some Papers of Franklin Pierce, 1852–1862," *American Historical Review*, Volume 10, Number One, October 1904, 361; Franklin Pierce to Eli Shorter, 22 September 1859.

26. Franklin Pierce to Jefferson Davis, 7 January 1860, Franklin Pierce Papers, Series 3, Reel 2.

27. Thomas H. Seymour to Franklin Pierce, 19 May 1860, Franklin Pierce Papers, Series 3, Reel 2; Bruce Catton, *The Coming Fury, Volume One* (New York: Doubleday & Company, 1961), 46–47.

28. Franklin Pierce to Benjamin Franklin Hallett, 29 June 1860, Franklin Pierce Papers, Series 3, Reel 2.

29. Jefferson Davis to Franklin Pierce, 23 November 1860, Franklin Pierce Papers, Series 3, Reel 2.

30. "The News of Lincoln's Election," *Charleston Mercury,* 8 November 1860, p. 1, col. 2.

31. Crist, *The Papers of Jefferson Davis, Volume 6, 1856–1860,* 368–71; Jefferson Davis to Robert Barnwell Rhett, Jr., 10 November 1860.

32. Robert W. Johannsen, *The Letters of Stephen A. Douglas* (Urbana: University of Illinois Press, 1961), 499–503, Stephen A. Douglas to Ninety-six New Orleans Citizens, 13 November 1860.

33. "South Carolina—The Future," *Daily Picayune,* 13 November 1860, p. 1, col. 6.

34. "Ex-President Pierce on the Political Crisis," *New York Times,* 3 December 1860, p.1, col. 4.

35. Donald B. Cole, *Benjamin Brown French—Witness to the Young Republic, A Yankee's Journal, 1828–1870* (Hanover: University Press of New England, 1989), 337; entry from French diary, 9 December 1860.

36. Feuss, *The Life of Caleb Cushing,* 272.

37. Beverly Wilson Palmer, *The Selected Letters of Charles Sumner, Volume Two* (Boston: Northeastern University Press, 1990), 38–39; Charles Sumner to the Dutchess of Argyll, 14 December 1860.

38. Andrew Hilen, *The Letters of Henry Wadsworth Longfellow, Volume IV, 1857–1865* (Cambridge: The Belknap Press, 1972), 212; Henry Wadsworth Longfellow to Charles Sumner, 29 January 1861.

39. Deborah Pickman Clifford, *Crusader for Freedom—A Life of Lydia Maria Child* (Boston: Beacon Press, 1992), 254.

40. Edward Wagenknecht, *Harriet Beecher Stowe—The Known and the Unknown* (New York: Oxford University Press, 1965, 188; Irving H. Bartlett, *Wendell Phillips—Brahmin Radical* (Westport: Greenwood Press, 1961), 234. Phillips, against all evidence, was convinced that if the South became its own nation it would somehow abolish slavery on its own through a combination of economic coercion from the North and pressure from the slaves themselves. "Soon every breeze that sweeps over Carolina will bring to our ears the music of self-repentance," Phillips remarked.

41. John A. Campbell to Franklin Pierce, 19 December 1860; Franklin Pierce to John A. Campbell, 7 January 1861, Franklin Pierce Papers, Series 3, Reel 2; Franklin Pierce to John A. Campbell, 24 December 1860, John A. Campbell to Franklin Pierce, 29 December 1860, Campbell Family Papers Collection, Southern Historical Collection, University of North Carolina at Chapel Hill; Franklin Pierce to Amos Adams Lawrence, 27 January 1861; Franklin Pierce Papers, Series 3, Reel 2.

42. *Congressional Globe, 2nd Session, 36th Congress* (Washington: John C. Rives Publishing, 1861), 212–17, 487, 720–21. In his farewell address, Davis, who had frequently clashed angrily with his Senate colleagues, now remarked "I am sure I feel no hostility to you Senators from the North," adding that as he prepared to return to the South, "I carry with me no hostile remembrance."

43. Jefferson Davis to Franklin Pierce, 20 January 1861, Franklin Pierce Papers, Series 3, Reel 2.

44. Carolyn L. Karcher, *The First Woman of the Republic—A Cultural Biography of Lydia Maria Child* (Durham: Duke University Press, 1994), 446.

45. Franklin Pierce to Martin Van Buren, 16 April 1861, Martin Van Buren Papers, Series 2, Reel 34.

46. Martin Van Buren to Franklin Pierce, 20 April 1861, Martin Van Buren Papers, Series 2, Reel 34.

47. "Ex-President Pierce on the Crisis," *New York Times*, 23 April 1861.

48. Franklin Pierce to Bishop Carlton Chase, 6 May 1861, Franklin Pierce Papers, Series 3, Reel 2.

5

The Avant-Courier of the Rebellion

Early on the morning of May 25, several hours before sunrise, a squad of federal troops arrived at the modest home of John Merryman in Haysfield, Maryland.

Responding to the orders of Major General George Cadwalader, the soldiers, wasting little time on pleasantries, announced they were there to arrest Merryman and quickly hustled the surprised man, who had been sound asleep, to nearby Fort McHenry, outside of Baltimore.

When a lawyer for Merryman later that day appeared before U.S. Supreme Court Chief Justice Roger B. Taney—who was serving as a circuit judge while the higher court was out of session—the chief justice ordered an absent Cadwalader to appear and bring with him, as Taney put it, "the body of John Merryman." 1

Cadwalader, in response, heard about Taney's order through an aide and promptly wrote out a statement of defiance, explaining first that because Merryman, a Confederate sympathizer, was suspected of aiding and abetting the Rebel cause, he thought it was entirely proper that he should be arrested.

In addition, said a staffer the following day who read a statement from Cadwalader in Taney's court room, "He has further to inform you that he is duly authorized by the President of the United States in such cases to suspend the writ of habeas corpus for public safety." 2

It was hard to say whether Taney, 84, ill and tired after more than three decades on the bench, was more angry or astonished by this news. But his response was immediate, declaring that Cadwalader was in contempt of court.

Word in Baltimore—where Union General Benjamin F. Butler had greatly excited everyone several days earlier by moving up to 1,000 troops into the city—quickly spread of the upcoming showdown, resulting in a packed courtroom on May 27 listening as an obviously frustrated U.S. marshal said that his attempt to retrieve Cadwalader had failed because soldiers at Fort McHenry blocked the way.

The ante was upped.

Taney then issued a written decision declaring that Lincoln "under the Constitution and laws of the United States," could not suspend the writ of habeas corpus on his own, nor "authorize any military officer to do so."

In what would become one of the most famous civil liberties arguments of the Civil War, Taney additionally warned that if such a fundamental right as the writ of habeas corpus could be suspended no American would be living under a government of law.

On the contrary, the chief justice continued, every citizen would hold "life, liberty and property at the will and pleasure of the army officer in whose military district he may happen to be found."

At the same time, and with no small amount of horror, Taney realized that because, for the moment, Lincoln had the entire military behind him, it was entirely possible for the President of the United States to actually ignore a court order from the Chief Justice of the United States Supreme Court without fear of retribution.

Defeated for the moment, Taney said he could only put into writing "the reasons under which I have acted," as he called upon Lincoln, "to perform his constitutional duty to enforce the laws; in other words, to enforce the process of this court." 3

But Lincoln wasn't listening. On April 27, in an unprecedented act, he had suspended the writ of habeas corpus from an area beginning in Philadelphia to the north and ending in Washington to the south, telling Winfield Scott, the commanding general of the Army of the U.S., "You are engaged in repressing an insurrection against the laws of the United States."

Eventually, through a series of proclamations, that suspension would be spread across the entire country.

If Scott, on his own in the field, should find it necessary at any point to suspend the writ of habeas corpus, continued Lincoln, "You personally or through the officer in command at the point where resistance occurs are authorized to suspend that writ." 4

For jurists, the Merryman case contained a number of theoretical ironies, perhaps the most obvious of which was the defendant's desire to seek protection behind the very government and constitution he obviously preferred to destroy.

But Lincoln's stand was equally curious as he discarded one of the most cherished rights of a government and constitution he sought to defend.

Upon reading of the Merryman case, Franklin Pierce quickly dashed off a communication to Taney expressing his astonishment over Lincoln's stand and support for the chief justice. In response, Taney—it would later be said that Lincoln was even contemplating having him arrested—expressed thanks for the former president's words, remarking: "My duty was plain—and that duty required me to meet the question directly and firmly, without evasion—whatever the consequences to myself." 5

Lincoln's usurpation of power that was clearly not delegated to him by the constitution would have many ramifications: throughout the summer and fall of 1861 thousands of citizens, some guilty of nothing more than criticizing the president, were rounded up and thrown behind bars, usually charged with treason or sedition.

They were writers, political activists, judges, and lawmakers. But in many other cases they were nothing more than simple American citizens.

At the same time Washington, in its zeal to suppress dissent, regarded the press as a particularly attractive target with such papers as the *New York Daily News* and the German *National Zeitung* forced to cease publication after the federal government denied them their postal privileges.

In just a one-week period in September, the editor of a Long Island newspaper was arrested and charged with treason; a New York grand jury voted in favor of arresting the editors of three other papers on the same charge; and federal marshals in Connecticut seized one hundred copies of the *New York Daily News*.

During that same troubling seven days the mayor of Baltimore, George William Brown—an old Pierce friend—was hauled in for remarking, in an intercepted letter: "I recognize in the action of the Government of the United States in the matter in question [the Civil War] nothing but the assertion of superior force." 6

After spending most of the summer in New Hampshire with Jane, who had long been opposed to slavery and was, unlike her husband, not so sure that Lincoln was doing the wrong thing, Pierce, by himself, traveled to Michigan in early September where he visited Robert McClelland, his former Secretary of the Interior, and Lewis Cass, the undisputed spiritual leader of the Michigan Democratic party.

Both men were steadfast and even at times loud critics of the Civil War.

Crossing the Michigan border on September 7, Pierce had little idea of the trouble he was about to encounter in a state that had been dramatically transformed by the war.

Once solidly Democratic, Michigan in the 1850s was increasingly the new home to the same kind of New England abolitionists and reformers whom Pierce had come to so eschew in New Hampshire. Almost instinctively given to causes, they gave active support to the Underground Railroad, temperance and the Republican party, early formation of which took place in Jackson, Michigan in 1855.

Although Pierce had carried Michigan by more than 12,000 votes in 1852, that may have well as been a century ago politically as the new Republicans swung the state over to their column in 1856 and gave Lincoln a substantial 23,000-vote plurality (out of 150,000 cast) in 1860.

Instrumental in the sweeping Republican takeover of Michigan was the booming voice of the *Detroit Tribune*, whose influence stretched across the state and daily editorialized in a way that could only be described as excessively pro-Lincoln and anti-South.

It was, in fact, in a day when the line between the press and politics was thinly drawn and sometimes non-existent, inside the very editorial offices of the *Tribune* where officials from the old Whig and Free Soil parties one day came together in an effort to break bread under the new Republican banner.

That first meeting was unsuccessful, but eventually the two groups did unite, "irrespective of old party organizations," an excited Joseph Warren, editor of the *Tribune*, happily proclaimed, realizing instantly the political possibilities. 7

Equally happy was Detroit dry goods merchant and millionaire Zachariah Chandler, elected to the U.S. Senate in 1856, and loudly pro-war, convinced as he was that only by completely beating and thoroughly humiliating the South could the country ever come back together.

"No concession, no compromise—ay, give us strife, even to blood—before a yielding to the demands of traitorous insolence," he cried, in what was a fairly characteristic outburst, as the war began. 8

Anyone who joined the Rebel cause, Chandler proclaimed on another occasion, had "no right to life, liberty, property or the pursuit of happiness," and must be crushed. 9

Bombastic, Chandler was quite capable of backing up his incendiary language with action: arriving by carriage with fellow Radical Republican Ben Wade of Ohio to witness first-hand what he assumed would be a swift victory for the North at Bull Run, he got the surprise of his life when he instead observed a Yankee rout, with soldiers from the North running away from the Rebels.

Angrily Chandler jumped onto the path with his pistol drawn, trying to halt the tide, but to little avail. Undaunted, that night he reported on what he had seen to Lincoln, demanding up to half a million more federal troops for battle in order to show the Confederates "that the government is not discouraged a whit, but is just beginning to get mad." 10

In Washington, Chandler was regarded as something of a comical figure largely because everything he did had come to seem so predictable. This made him good for jokes that he did not appreciate. When Chandler dramatically declared he would join the Comanche Nation if the North permitted the South to secede, Texas Senator Louis T. Wigfall, unable to resist, responded "God forbid! I hope not. They [the Comanches] have already suffered much from their contact with the whites." 11

Everyone but Chandler laughed in response.

But within Michigan, at least by 1861, no one was laughing, at least not to Chandler's face: in an attempt to keep this unpredictable force at his side, Lincoln had agreed to give Chandler control over almost all federal patronage in the state. Soon even those who had complained about the senator's long and often windy speeches found that everything he said was interesting.

On the opposite end of the political spectrum in Michigan—and with substantially less power in 1861—was Robert McClelland, former secretary of the interior under Pierce, who shared with the former president the opinion that the North was the primary cause for the Civil War mainly because it had adopted an aggressive, confrontational strategy with the slave states.

"There is no question about the South having great cause of complaining," McClelland told a correspondent several days after Lincoln's election as he wondered whether or not the South would actually secede. 12

Like others in the exceptionally close Pierce cabinet, McClelland had remained loyal to his fellow former department heads, particularly the man who would become the first president of the Confederacy, remarking that Jefferson Davis "is sometimes rash and impetuous, but he knows more in a minute than Lincoln does in a year." 13

Now a lawyer living in Detroit, McClelland tended to do business and socialize with a diminished group of mostly Democratic politicians who thought that the Civil War was wrong, the abolitionists irresponsible, and the South maligned.

On the night of Sunday, September 8, Pierce stayed at McClelland's house and may have met informally with McClelland's friends, including Colonel T. F. Broadhead, who had served under Pierce in the Mexican-American war.

Although accounts of what happened that night would later vary, one thing was certain: Pierce and McClelland were being watched.

Bunched together under the term "Peace Democrats" just then coming into currency because they had openly criticized Lincoln, they were among the growing number of statesmen and political leaders that some regarded as both suspicious and dangerous, and probably worth keeping tabs on.

This was the dark underside of Lincoln's America.

Accordingly, J.A. Roys, a Detroit bookseller, would shortly send a letter to Secretary of State Seward telling him that on the night of September 8 he observed Pierce, Broadhead and another man whose identity he could not verify, walking together along Fort Street in downtown Detroit.

It was, the correspondent reminded Seward, the very same day that Washington Mayor James G. Berret had been arrested and charged with treason for declining to take an oath of loyalty to the U.S. And perhaps because of that event, Pierce's comments made sense and sounded ominous to Roys: "They must stop that sort of thing or there will be fighting at the North, and we shall have to send for you to come back, Colonel Broadhead," Pierce supposedly remarked.

What exactly Pierce meant by the comment, Roys could not be certain, but that did not stop him from adding: "Either from being aware of my presence or some other reason, the conversation changed without any response that I heard and was in another tone while I passed by and out of hearing."

But to add gravity to his suspicions Roys said that he had recently heard a conversation with a man who had "lost a minor office under the Government"—undoubtedly a Democrat—and was told of plans to "establish a provisional government and make some conservative man [Pierce?] President in place of Lincoln."

Finally tying all of the information together, Roys concluded: "These incidents may be of little consequence unless there are other reasons for suspecting an organization hostile to the Government to which the ex-President is lending his position and influence." 14

Pierce left Michigan on September 10, delivered a brief address in Lafayette, Indiana, where he admitted that he was devoting most of his journey to observing for himself "the attractions and advantages of a portion of the Great West," and then traveled to Louisville, Kentucky, where he stopped in on another member of his cabinet, James Guthrie, the former secretary of the treasury. 15

It was only after visiting with Guthrie that Pierce, by rail, decided to return to New England, his brief journey to a part of the country he had only read about before, over and presumably forgotten.

Until September 25, when the *Detroit Tribune* lobed an incredible charge.

Taking note of Pierce's travels, the paper said Pierce's real reason for coming to Michigan, Indiana, and Kentucky was to "get up an organized treasonable opposition to the efforts of the Government to crush out rebellion in the Northern States."

"He goes through State after State the avant-courier of the rebellion to stir up sympathy for the rebel traitors in arms."

The *Tribune* then contended that while in Detroit, Pierce had met with a "select circle who are known to be doubtful in their loyalty," before concluding: "Our opinion is that Franklin Pierce is a prowling traitor spy." 16

For regular readers of the *Tribune* and any number of Northern Republican newspapers, the reference to a "select circle" (also called a "secret circle," by the *Tribune*), could only mean one thing: the Knights of the Golden Circle, a subversive organization dedicated to the triumph of the Confederacy, the extension of slavery, and Lincoln's ruin.

The influence of the Golden Circle, the extremely pro-Lincoln *Chicago Tribune* would soon warn, "is all over the North, a potent agent for evil, directed and controlled by the men who have plunged the country into war." 17

This may have simply been a case of hysteria, but if it was, it was a malady that would also prove to be remarkably infectious, particularly in Michigan : "We have information from a reliable source that the organization already exists in Flint city," warned the *Flint Citizen* in great alarm, while the *St. Joseph Weekly Traveler* in St. Joseph, Michigan, presented a neat formulation for proving someone was a member of the seditious group. If they said they weren't, they were: "The pleadings, disavowals and bluffing of *the initiated* will amount to but little," the paper declared, reminding readers that members of the group were sworn to secrecy "as a *condition precedent* to *full* membership." 18

Whether or not the men who decided on the editorial content of these papers really believed that the Golden Circle existed and was an actual threat to the national well-being, was never said. But one thing was certain: it was effective politics. Fearing Democratic gains in the upcoming mid-term congressional elections in 1862, many Lincoln Republicans desperately *wanted* there to be a Golden Circle in the hope that its shadowy presence would scare enough people into supporting pro-administration candidates.

Ironically, Jefferson Davis, too, had high hopes for the Golden Circle. Receiving a message that the group could offer the Confederacy up to 30,000 new recruits, all in the North, was powerful stuff. A Davis biographer would later conclude that the president of the Confederacy found reports of the Golden Circle's popularity "tantalizing," marveling over the notion of an "organized, armed and anxious" membership willing to mutiny against Lincoln. 19

The only problem for both the foes and supporters of the Golden Circle was that by and large the group did not really exist. The brainchild of a traveling con artist named George Bickley, the Golden Circle was never more than a revolt on paper, a reason for Bickley to shake down gullible Confederate sympathizers, and an excuse for unscrupulous Republican newspapers to demand blind support for Lincoln's assault on civil liberties.

Perhaps nothing more would have come of the *Detroit Tribune*'s reference to a connection between Pierce and the Golden Circle had it not been for an excitable man by the name of Dr. Guy Hopkins, an ardent Democrat and strong supporter of Pierce, who had read the paper's broadside against the former president and decided to avenge the honor of his hero.

From his residence in North Branch, Michigan, Hopkins composed a strange letter, bathed in what he imagined would be the code language members of the Golden Circle might use. Through a circuitous process, the letter made its way to the offices of the *Tribune*—which was Hopkins' goal all along. The surprise of the Republican editors, who probably knew the Circle did not really exist, upon reading Hopkins' correspondence, can only be imagined.

Exhibiting, at least for the moment, surprising caution, they then turned the letter over to a federal marshal.

Several days later in Washington, a slender man whose narrow face and thin lips masked a generally affable personality, was handed a three-page document. What he read greatly shocked him.

"The work, sir, goes bravely on…I feel greatly strengthened in the belief that when the hour comes to erect our glorious standard, an overwhelming force will spring up at the first trumpet call."

"Presidt. P-----in his passage has drawn many brave and influential men to the League," the document continued, adding, several sentences later, "He is cautious but in common with others is gradually preparing the minds of the people for a great change."

The letter-writer also said that "Presidt.P-----" had expressed a fear that "any attempt to draft men will produce a premature outbreak. I think his fear is well founded." 20

Secretary of State Seward knew enough about subversive organizations—or at least thought that he did—to instantly appreciate the dynamite in his hands: a letter from a Golden Circle insider not only proving, at last, that the group existed, but clearly implicating the dreaded Franklin Pierce as an activist supporter.

Hopkins' fake coded correspondence had been sent to Seward by William H. Barse, a federal marshal in Detroit, who helpfully attempted to unscramble it. The message had been addressed to "R.M.C., Esq.,"—obviously McClelland, said Barnes. "M------d" meant Maryland; "Ft. M-----" was Fort Monroe; and "Presidt.P" could only be President Pierce.

Next to the name of a man referred to as "H, the Mormon elder," Barse wrote: "Don't know, am on his track."

Barse ended his correspondence with Seward on a high note: "It is hoped that I may come across some more papers that will throw light upon the subject," he added, before asking if Seward could underwrite all of this detective work. 21

Seward had no response to Barse's plea for money. But it may have been because he had other things on his mind.

Trying to hold together a government that had been, often unsuccessfully, at war for only five months, and daily hearing all kinds of reports of subversive activity in the North, Seward was susceptible to the very worst kind of news and gossip. That he did not particularly like Pierce, and was obviously angered by the former president's public criticisms of the administration, only made things worse.

And he wasn't the only one. On September 2, Henry McFarland, the editor of the anti-Pierce *New Hampshire Statesman*, had sent a letter to Lincoln warning that Pierce's mission in Michigan "is not one friendly to the government…if the government has any way to observe his motions, I hope it will do so." 22

But Lincoln, who always seemed to have a level head, was not nearly as alarmed as Seward. In response he betrayed bemusement: "I think it is well that P. [Pierce] is away from the N.H. people," wrote Lincoln. "He will do less harm anywhere else; and *when* he has gone, his neighbors will understand him better." 23

Seward himself heard from an anonymous source two weeks later, on September 17, who reported: "The object of the present is to appraise you that Franklin Pierce and Clement March, now a senator of the state of New Hampshire, are traitors and are aiding and abetting secretly and covertly the leaders of the Southern rebellion." 24

Through Barse, Seward ordered the immediate arrest of Hopkins and two other men he believed to be involved with the Knights of the Golden Circle. Doing as ordered, Barse rounded up Hopkins and then told Seward: "I think he is as great a scamp as goes unhung." 25

Disposing of Hopkins had been easy. But what to do about Pierce was far more problematic. From his jail cell at Fort Lafayette outside New York City, Hopkins realized the incredible trouble he was in, and began to try and set things straight by attempting to clear the air in a way that should have absolved Pierce of any suspicion.

On November 29, Hopkins wrote to Seward, telling him that his coded Golden Circle letter had never been intended as anything more than a "practical joke upon the Detroit press."

Hopkins went on to explain that he had single-handedly wrote the letter himself, hoping it would eventually come into the hands of the *Detroit Tribune* where the partisan editors would be unable to resist the temptation to play it big on their pages…

And when that happened, Hopkins would reveal himself as the man behind the hoax and the laugh would be on the Republicans.

It was clearly the kind of joke that must have seemed a lot funnier at conception.

Nonetheless, Hopkins reaffirmed that the only purpose of the letter had been to "produce lots of fun," a goal that now seemed sadly elusive.

Before closing, Hopkins added, in an obviously reference to Pierce and McClelland, that his greatest regret was "casting suspicion on good and loyal men."

"I beg and pray that whatever penalty is attached to this act may be confined to the only party guilty, and that nothing in it be allowed to reflect upon anyone else whom it may seem to hint at." 26

If Hopkins hoped his letter would give Seward pause, he failed. On the contrary the Secretary now seemed greatly certain that somehow or other all of the strange things he had been hearing about Pierce must mean something.

Disregarding logic in favor of prejudice, Seward on December 20 wrote a quick, harsh note to the former president, addressing him only as "sir," and attaching a copy of the coded Hopkins letter, from which, he said, "it would appear that you were a member of a secret league, the object of which is to overthrow the Government."

"Any explanation upon the subject which you may offer," Seward concluded, "would be acceptable." 27

Was it possible? Could Seward really have been so brazen? Had he momentarily—as the undeniable pressures of his job mounted—taken leave of his senses?

Everything about the letter was wrong. Its tone, its abrasiveness, the way Seward appeared to have already convicted Pierce and now demanded that the former president merely provide answers which probably would not be satisfactory anyway.

But even worse was the moment in which Seward's letter arrived: not everyone who had been arrested since Lincoln suspended the writ of habeas corpus was a traitor. Many went down simply because they honestly opposed the Civil War, or because they were foolish enough to express admiration for Jefferson Davis or publicly doubted whether or not the federal government had a right to suppress the Southern rebellion.

But that was enough to get anyone arrested in 1861.

And clearly neither Lincoln nor Seward had any problem with throwing people in jail. They had been doing it by the thousands since the war began.

What was to stop them from doing it to Franklin Pierce, surely a man they reviled in the first place? And wouldn't the site of the former president and very prominent war critic being taken away in chains not only be proof of how serious the administration was about suppressing dissent, but also a rather delicious political retribution to boot?

If Pierce thought he was about to be arrested, he would have only been human.

Amazed, he passed Seward's letter around to several friends, all of whom found the correspondence outrageous. On Christmas Even, Pierce was in Andover with Jane and barely able to contain his rage as he wrote in response: "It is not easy to conceive how any person could give credence to or entertain for a moment the idea that I am now or have ever been connected with a secret league the object of which was or is the overthrow of the Government of my country."

Characterizing the coded Hopkins letter as "incoherent and meaningless," Pierce made it clear: "As there is not the slightest ground for any reference to me in the connection indicated, I take it for granted that your inference is wholly erroneous, and that neither I nor anything which I ever said or did was in the mind of the writer."

The insinuation was so unreal, Pierce continued, that he was inclined not to respond at all. But he knew how things worked in Washington, and he wanted his response to become a part of the State Department's permanent files, determined not to leave any "ambiguity on the record." 28

Seward must have been astounded to read Pierce's reply. Here was a man who would fight back, and even worse, he had the financial resources, legal acumen and public pulpit to do so.

Six days later, writing from his Washington office, Seward—this time upgrading his previous salutation of "sir" to "dear sir,"—acknowledged to Pierce that his letter of December 20th "has given you offense."

He continued: "I regret it and apologize for it." Then in the time-honored tradition of every bureaucrat on every hot seat, he blamed the entire matter on an underling in his department, whom he said was the real author of the letter.

Seward additionally promised Pierce that he had placed the ex-president's Christmas Eve response in the State Department's permanent files in order to "render you a service."

If the obtuseness of Seward's reply was not enough, he added a postscript explaining that the word "Sir" had been employed in the original letter, rather than using the last public title Pierce held before becoming president, which was common practice, because that was the way Daniel Webster did it: "I have invariably left off all titles of address as being the most respectful." 29

This was a lie. In fact, Seward almost always used titles, especially when writing to both former and current public officials. The governor of Maine, Israel Washburn, was "His Excellency," as was Thomas H. Hicks, the governor of Maryland; Vice-president Hannibal Hamlin was the "Hon. Hannibal Hamlin," and Lincoln was always "Mr. President." 30

Obviously Seward either thought Pierce was not worthy of anything above the appellation of "sir," or purposely employed that title to insult him.

Back at his home in Concord, seven days in 1862, Pierce responded to Seward a final time.

Although, at 60, Seward was three years his senior, Pierce now seemed the secretary's elder; a wiser and more mature retired statesman sadly forced by events to chastise an undisciplined junior officer for his impetuosity.

Pierce began by turning the final sentence in Seward's last letter against him: "It could hardly have surprised you to learn that I failed to discover in your official note to me a desire to render me a service," he began.

On the contrary, thought Pierce, Seward had seemed determined to do precisely the opposite, with a "note of rebuke" which might be more appropriately addressed, thought Pierce, to a "delinquent clerk."

The problem, Pierce said, was and remained that the full record of the charges against him had never been disclosed—who said what about whom—and whether or not Hopkins had ever officially implicated or cleared him. (Incredibly, Seward had failed to send Pierce the Hopkins letter which very much cleared him).

"I think you will, upon reflection, arrive at the conclusion that the whole ground upon which the allegation is reported should as a simple act of justice been placed before me."

As to the tone of Seward's letter and his curious decision to address Pierce as only "sir," the former president coldly set things straight: "It was not the manner of your official note as you seem to suppose, nor any form of address which awakened on my part a deep sense of wrong. These, whatever they may have been, were not worthy of serious note."

"The substance was what I intended as courteously as I could but very distinctly to repel." 31

Seward had clearly been bested and offered no further explanations on the matter. But Pierce remained upset, not just from the odd exchange with the Secretary, but also now with a very personal illustration of the administration's cavalier approach to civil liberties in general.

When Senator James Albert Pearce of Maryland noted that his fellow senators were demanding an inquiry into Lincoln's suspension of habeas corpus, Pierce encouraged him, offering that "no recent measure has been fraught with more mischief," than this particular presidential policy, with its "consequent arrests and imprisonments in violation of the provisions of the Constitution."

"The earlier the system is effectively checked," Pierce continued, "the better it will be for the government and the country as well as for the subjects of oppression."

The former president also told Pearce that he thought his recent encounter with Seward "serves to illustrate in a striking manner the slight grounds, or rather the groundless suspicions upon which in these times citizens are loathe to suffer in reputation if not in loss of liberty." 32

Yet despite his alarm over the course the country was taking under Lincoln, Pierce could never wean himself of a love for the United States itself. Polishing off a bottle of rum with Nathaniel Hawthorne in late January, Pierce remained convinced that the American experiment could still work: "He is bigoted to the Union," Hawthorne said of Pierce, "and sees nothing but ruin without it." 33

Meanwhile back in Michigan, McClelland, noting that the Pierce-Seward letters were still a private correspondence between the two men, urged the former president to make them public: "The correspondence should be brought to life," McClelland argued, if for no other reason than to expose "the contemptible knavery of this political mountebank [Seward]." 34

Pierce, however, seemed willing to let the matter drop, content that he had forced Seward into retreat. The news that the federal government on February 22 was dropping treason charges against Hopkins, resulting in his release from Fort Lafayette, seemed only to be another reason to suppose that this strange episode had now come to an end.

That Pierce rarely took things personally was once again evident on March 4 when he took pen in hand to write a confidential letter to Lincoln. On February 20, "Willie" Lincoln, the 11 year-old son of the president, had died nearly a week after catching a cold.

The young boy's death saddened Pierce, who undoubtedly was reminded of another child's death on another winter day nearly a decade ago.

Candidly, Pierce told Lincoln that the news of his son's death "brought back the crushing sorrow which befell me just before I went to Washington in 1853."

Briefly reminding the president of the war that divided them, Pierce wrote: "Even in this hour, so full of danger to our country, and of trial and anxiety to all good men, your thoughts will be of your cherished boy who will nestle at your heart until you meet him in that new life when tears and toils and conflict will be unknown."

Ending the letter, Pierce added: "With the Pierces' and my own best wishes and truest sympathy for Mrs. Lincoln and yourself, I am truly your friend, Franklin Pierce." 35

Abraham Lincoln had never had any use for Franklin Pierce. He had opposed him and made fun of him throughout his career. But Lincoln was also a man with an enormous capacity for understanding. Although there is no record of a response from Lincoln, it can be assumed that he was touched by the former president's concern, and, overwhelmed with his private loss and duties as commander in chief, did not have the time to respond.

If Lincoln failed to acknowledge Pierce's note for any other reason, it suggests a smallness of character that has eluded virtually every Lincoln scholar.

But if Pierce was capable of removing the personal from the political, certainly not all of his opponents were. And that was very much true of the Republicans in Michigan and elsewhere who remained convinced that the issue of the Knights of the Golden Circle was just too good to let go of so soon. And, for the moment, there was no better way to do so than by once again linking the name of the former Democratic president with the imaginary group.

Only two weeks after Pierce's letter to Lincoln, the *Detroit Tribune* publicly rehashed it's charges against the former president. But this time, the eastern press paid more attention, in particular the *Boston Evening Journal*, the same paper that had once accused Pierce of cowardice during the Mexican-American war.

A Boston Democrat, George Stark, sent a copy of the *Journal* article to Pierce, and, like McClelland, frankly told the former president it was time to fight back, if only to confront these "foul and systematic aspersions upon your personal and political character." The renewed slander, Stark added, "afford ample and honorable reason for the publication of your Seward correspondence upon the same subject." 36

From New York, Pierce's former secretary, Sidney Webster, said the same thing, noting that such Democratic luminaries as former president Martin Van Buren and former and soon-to-be New York Governor Horatio Seymour thought Pierce should demand that all materials relating to the Hopkins hoax be made public, in particular the correspondence that made Seward appear so wanting.

Webster also thought that Pierce should compose one more letter to Seward, this one a point-by-point chronology of the charges made against him and his responses, all of which would also be made public. "I think you can, as lawyers say, 'sum up the case' in a letter to Seward better than any newspaper editorial can or will," advised Webster. 37

Two days later, Pierce was at last ready to act.

Writing to California Senator Milton Latham, an old friend, he asked if he would be willing to demand from the Senate floor that the Seward-Pierce letters be entered into the public record.

"It will strike you, I am sure, both upon public and personal grounds, that such imputations should not be permitted thus to circulate unchallenged, especially when an answer to them, at least as far as I am concerned, have been for months upon the files of the first Department of the Government," Pierce told Latham. 38

In choosing the California senator to carry his spear, Pierce could not have chosen more wisely. A strapping man with a bright red beard and hair, Latham was a contentious Democrat and wily political strategist.

In fact, Latham's very membership in the Senate was a testament to his skills: he had been elected as governor of California in 1859 but served only five days, calling the legislature into session and getting his friends to vote for him to fill a recent vacancy in the U.S. Senate, which was the office had had desired all along.

In the Senate, Latham was skeptical, but not unreasonably so, of Lincoln's handling of the war, and after the mass walkout of Southern Democrats in 1861, was very much a confident voice in the sudden Democratic minority.

Now, on March 28, Latham introduced the letter Pierce had sent him, as well as the *Boston Evening Journal* article, and asked simply that the full correspondence between Seward and Piece be made a part of the official public record.

"I deem it nothing more than proper," Latham said bluntly, "not only to this distinguished individual, but to the country, that the truth in relation to this charge should be known, and if a malignant and base calumny, that it should be branded as such." 39

A "malignant and base calumny": that was good and caught the ear of many reporters who filed dispatches on Latham's request that afternoon.

Caught off guard, Senate Republicans were not sure what to do. But Zachariah Chandler tried to regain the offensive, arguing that he had a copy of the original fake Hopkins letter that had started all of the trouble in his possession "but it is at my room, and I have not got it with me at this time."

What exactly Chandler hoped to prove with a correspondence that had since been discredited by almost all parties, was not made clear. It may have been that, lacking for the moment any other props or material, he too wanted to somehow just keep the issue going and damn Franklin Pierce's sullied reputation.

If the Senate was intent upon airing the Seward-Pierce correspondence, the Michigan Senator continued, then they should also think about opening a much larger investigation into the Knights of the Golden Circle, a group Chandler once again described as "treasonable and infamous," not to mention "wide-spread" in terms of its influence…

In a sentence that displayed a curious perception of what is and isn't funny, Chandler added: "This man Hopkins acknowledged the writing of the letter, but undertook to call it a joke. Well, sir, it was a pretty serious joke."

Then, somewhat mysteriously, Chandler concluded: "I have, perhaps, more information than it is necessary for me to divulge at this time in reference to the matter." 40

But Latham was too wily for Chandler, calmly asserting that he only wanted to ascertain whether or not Franklin Pierce was associated with an organization that went by the name of the Knights of the Golden Circle. "It is due to him, and it is due to the country, that it should be known whether such is the fact; and that is simply the object of my resolution." 41

Point made, Latham then agreed that he would be more than willing to have the Senate launch an investigation into the Knights of the Golden Circle, something that Chandler—undoubtedly knowing the organization was only good for fund-raising and vote-getting purposes—made no comment on at all.

Almost immediately Seward and the Republicans realized they had overplayed their hand. Press comment overwhelmingly favored Pierce, led by the *New York Times*, which predicted that once the Seward-Pierce correspondence was published it will "show how utterly false was this charge" against the former president. "This will result in the complete vindication of Ex-President Pierce," said the *Philadelphia Press*, edited by John Forney, not always a Pierce supporter. The *Albany Argus*, summing up what had obviously been a well-orchestrated Republican campaign to humiliate Pierce, remarked that the letters would obviously reveal "the baseness and malignancy of the party spirit which has brought this evil upon the country with other calamities and degradation." 42

But if things were not bad enough for Seward in this matter, the Secretary of State only made things worse when he at last authorized release of his correspondence with Pierce, but very pointedly failed to include Pierce's angry letter of January 7.

It was then that Latham called Seward's bluff.

"I find that one of the material letters, so regarded by Mr. Pierce's friends, is omitted in the return made by the Secretary of State," Latham said in a manner that made it seem like Seward had probably just left out the letter by accident.

Trying to be helpful, Latham then announced that he had no choice but to "avail myself of the privilege which I hold here as a speaker," by reading for himself the Pierce letter—out loud, to all of his colleagues.

It took Latham nearly five minutes to do so, during which time the members from the other side of the aisle—in particular Chandler—fell into a conspicuous silence.

Upon conclusion, Latham remarked: "This letter and the printed correspondence will show the country how great a calumny has been uttered against one of our most distinguished citizens."

"I am now done with this subject." 43

Latham, and by inference, Pierce, had clearly scored a smashing triumph. And even his greatest enemies were forced to admit it was so, although the way in which the *New York Herald* acknowledged the fact showed what can happen when grapes turn decidedly sour: "Poor Pierce, in this matter, has enveloped himself in the first positive blaze of glory by which he has ever been surrounded. He did nothing in the Mexican-American war, and nothing while he was President, to satisfy anybody that there was such good stuff in him." 44

Pierce's supporters, however, rejoiced, and meant it: "In common with every just man in the land, I am indignant at the insult and outrage offered to you by Seward," former Ohio Congressman Clement Vallandigham, himself about to endure the same flames of patriotic indignation, wrote to Pierce on April 11. "But it has resulted in his disgrace and your vindication." 45

He was only one man against a large government in the middle of a war. But by demanding that his accusers step forward from the shadows and prove their charges, Franklin Pierce suddenly represented the plight of many more who were locked away in forbidden places and lacked his prominence, fortitude, and friends.

His vindication was swift and passing. His alienation would shortly prove to be much more enduring.

CHAPTER FIVE FOOTNOTES

1. Edward McPherson, *The Political History of the United States During the Great Rebellion* (Boston: Philp & Solomons, 1865), 134–58 "Reports from Baltimore," *New York Herald*, 26 May 1861, p. 1, col. 5.

2. Ibid.; "The News," *Baltimore American*, 28 May 1861, p. 1, col. 1; "Important Legal Case Growing Out of the War," *New York Herald*, 28 May 1861, p. 1, col. 4.

3. McPherson, *The Political History of the United States During the Great Rebellion*, 154–58.

4. Ibid.

5. Roger B. Taney to Franklin Pierce, 12 June 1861, Franklin Pierce Papers, Series 3, Reel 6.

6. "Treason on Long Island," 9 September 1861, p. 6, col. 4; "Presentment of Newspapers by the Grand Jury of Westchester County," 9 September 1861, 9. 8, col.3; "Seizure of One Hundred Copies the N.Y. Daily News," 14 September 1861, p. 5, col. 2; and "A Blow at Baltimore Rebels," 14 September 1861; p. 5, col. 4; all in the *New York Tribune.*

7. William E. Gienapp, *The Origins of the Republican Party, 1852–1856* (New York: Oxford University Press, 1987), 104–05

8. Mary Karl George, *Zachariah Chandler—A Political Biography* (East Lansing: Michigan State University Press, 1969), 38; *Congressional Globe, 36th Congress, 2nd Session, Part Two* (Washington: John C. Rives, 1861), 1372.

9. *Congressional Globe—37th Congress, 2nd Session* (Washington: John C. Rives, 1861), 11.

10. Stephen B. Oates, *With Malice Toward None—The Life of Abraham Lincoln* (New York: New American Library, 1977), 275–77.

11. *Congressional Globe, 36th Congress, 2nd Session* (Washington: John C. Rives, 1861), 1370–72.

12. Frederick D. Williams, "Robert McClelland and the Secession Crisis," *Michigan History*, Volume XLIII, (1959), 156.

13. Ibid.; 163.

14. *The War of Rebellion: A Compilation of the Official Records of the Union and Confederate Armies,* (Washington: Government Printing Office, 1897), 1256–56. Frank L. Klement, "Franklin Pierce and the Treason Charges of 1861–1862," *The Historian,* Volume XLVII, Number 4, August 1961, 439. No historian has done as much to explain the political significance of the Knights of the Golden Circle as Klement. See also his article, "The Hopkins Hoax and the Golden Circle Rumors in Michigan: 1861–1862," *Michigan History*, Volume XLVII, (1963), 1–4; and book, *Dark Lanterns—Secret Political Societies, Conspiracies and Treason Trials in the Civil War* (Baton Rouge: Louisiana State University Press, 1984), 7–33.

15. "A Speech by Ex-President Pierce," *New York Times*, 7 September 1861, p. 2, col. 2.

16. *The War of Rebellion*, 1256.

17. "Knights of the Golden Circle," *Chicago Tribune*, 3 April 1862, p. 1, col. 1.

18. "Ex-President Pierce's Appeal to the U.S. Senate," *St. Joseph Weekly Traveler,* 9 April 1962, p. 1, col. 5. The quotes from the *Flint Citizen* are referred to in this article.

19. William C. Davis, *Jefferson Davis—The Man and His Hour* (New York: HarperPerennial, 1991), 543–44.

20. *The War of Rebellion*, 1248–49. More than 140 years later, Pierce would be maligned by authors Warren Getler and Bob Brewer in a book arguing that the Knights of the Golden Circle really did exist. Offering no evidence to back up their charge or even a reason for their thinking, the authors characterize Pierce as "pro-KGC," even though he never uttered a public word about the group, attended one of their meetings, or subscribed to their goals; Warren Getler and Bob Brewer, *Shadow of the Sentinel—One Man's Quest To Find The Hidden Treasures of the Confederacy* (New York: Simon & Schuster, 2003), 179.

21. Ibid., 1247–48.

22. Roy P. Basler, *The Collected Works of Abraham Lincoln, IV* (New Brunswick, New Jersey: Rutgers University Press, 1953), 505.

23. Ibid.

24. *The War of Rebellion*, 1246.

25. Ibid., 1249.

26. Ibid., 1250–51.

27. William H. Seward to Franklin Pierce, 20 December 1861, Franklin Pierce Papers, Series 3, Reel 1.

28. Franklin Pierce to William H. Seward, 7 January 1862, Franklin Pierce Papers, Series 3, Reel 1.

29. *The War of Rebellion*, 1260–61.

30. *The Political History of the United States of America During the Great Rebellion*, see Seward's letters to Washburn, dated 4 October 1861 and Hicks, dated 22 April 1841; 154, 345.

31. Franklin Pierce to William H. Seward, 7 January 1862, Franklin Pierce Papers, Series 3, Reel 1.

32. Franklin Pierce to James Albert Pearce, 15 January 1862, Franklin Pierce Papers, Series 3, Reel 1.

33. Thomas Woodson, *Nathaniel Hawthorne—The Letters, 1857–1864* (Dayton: Ohio State University Press, 1987), Nathaniel Hawthorne to Horatio Bridge, 13 February 1862, 427–428.

34. Robert McClelland to Franklin Pierce, 15 January 1862, Franklin Pierce Papers, Series 3, Reel 4.

35. Franklin Pierce to Abraham Lincoln, 4 March 1862, Abraham Lincoln Papers, February 16-March 14, 1862, Series 3, Reel 33.

36. George Stark to Franklin Pierce, 24 March 1862, Franklin Pierce Papers, Series 3, Reel 4.

37. Sidney Webster to Franklin Pierce, 22 March 1862, Franklin Pierce Papers, Series 3, Reel 4.

38. Franklin Pierce to Milton Latham, 24 March 1862, Franklin Pierce Papers, Series 3, Reel 4.

39. *Congressional Globe, 37th Congress*, (Washington: John C. Rives: 1862), 1370–71.

40. Ibid.; 1371.

41. Ibid.

42. "Gen. Pierce," *New Hampshire Patriot*, 2 April 1862, p. 2, col. 1; quotations from both the *New York Times* and *Atlas Argus* appear in this article.

43. *Congressional Globe, 37th Congress*, 1489–90.

44. "Poor Pierce Triumphant At Last," *New York Herald*, 5 April 1862, p. 4, col. 3.

45. "Franklin Pierce and the Treason Charges of 1861–1862," 447–48. At least three Seward biographers have been critical of the Secretary's role in attacking Pierce. Frederic Bancroft, in one of the first surveys of Seward's career, said the Secretary's charge against Pierce "illustrates more than one phase of the exercise of arbitrary power"; Glyndon G. Van Deusen characterizes the entire affair as an "embarrassment," adding that "there was no proof that he [Pierce] did anything approaching treason," while John M. Taylor says only that the Hopkins letter was an obvious hoax and that "Seward had fallen for it." Frederick Bancroft, *The Life of William H. Seward* (New York: Harper & Brothers, 1900) 971; Glyndon G. Van Deusen, *William Henry Seward* (New York: Oxford University Press, 1967), 290; John M. Taylor, *William Henry Seward—Lincoln's Right Hand* (New York: HarperCollins, 1991), 170–71.

6

The Only Loyal Man in the Country

On the day of Franklin Pierce's triumph in the U.S. Senate, Nathaniel Hawthorne was only blocks away, wandering around the nation's capital and on the verge of greatly offending Yankee sensibilities.

On assignment by the decidedly pro-Lincoln *Atlantic Monthly* to record his impressions of the president and the war, Hawthorne was destined to disappoint: he shared Pierce's negative view of abolitionists, was indifferent to the president, and actually doubted that the war, from a Northern perspective, was worth fighting.

"I don't quite understand what we are fighting for, or what definite result can be expected," the author had confided to Horatio Bridge in May of 1861 as the towns of his native New England were awash in red, white, and blue bunting and endless military parades.

"If we pummel the South ever so hard, they will love us none the better for it," Hawthorne continued, before revealing that—unlike Pierce—he wasn't all that excited about maintaining the Union in the first place. "And even if we subjugate them [the South], our next stop should be to cut them adrift." 1

In New England, Hawthorne's indifference very obviously set him apart from majority thought. But unlike Pierce, Hawthorne was much too influential and esteemed in his field to have to suffer the kind of personal rancor that had become the former president's burden…

Yet even within his own family, Hawthorne was ever more the solitary man.

His wife Sophia stitched repairs to the uniforms of young soldiers and presented a gold piece to the first Union recruit in Concord. Her sister, Elizabeth, an ardent abolitionist, declared that there is a "time to every purpose" and lustily cheered every Northern victory. Even Hawthorne's son Julian, 14 years old when the war began, was caught up in the hoopla, excitedly practicing military drills for the day when he might be called into service. "I am too old to shoulder a musket myself," Hawthorne had also told Bridge, "and the joyful thing is, that Julian is too young." 2

Virtually all of Hawthorne's fellow writers in New England supported the war as a great moral cause. And the more they enthused about it, the more annoyed he became. When he heard of Ralph Waldo Emerson's latest pro-war missive, Hawthorne likened it to "breathing slaughter" and "theoretical nonsense." Listening to New England Transcendentalist Bronson Alcott one evening extolling the virtues of the Yankee cause, a paean that seemed to transfix Emerson, Hawthorne was unimpressed. "Let us to go dinner," was his abrupt response when Bronson concluded his remarks. 3

Yet Hawthorne also admitted that he found the quickened pulse of a nation at war undeniably exciting: "I never imagined what a happy state of mind a civil war produces," he told Henry Bright, a British friend, "and how it invigorates every man's whole being."

Watching young soldiers in Concord, Hawthorne remarked: "When I hear their drums beating, and see their banners flying, and witness their steady marching, I declare, were it not for certain silvery monitors hanging by my temples, suggesting prudence, I feel as if I could catch the infection, shoulder a musket, and be off to war myself." 4

It was perhaps inevitable, considering the multiplicity of feelings Hawthorne experienced—Pierce's attitude, by comparison was unwavering: the war was wrong and must end—that he would satisfy no one when he finally revealed his thoughts on the subject for publication.

"Chiefly About War Matters," appeared in the July 1862 edition of the *Atlantic Monthly* and nearly instantly aroused Northern readers who felt that Hawthorne had made fun of the military, abolitionism and even official Washington.

"It is pure intellect, without emotion, without sympathy, without principle," Charles Eliot Norton, the Boston literary critic, wrote in response to Hawthorne's article. "'A fig for your kindly feelings,' might the escaping fugitives say to him," William Lloyd Garrison's *Liberator* declared. 5

What his detractors might have said had Hawthorne not agreed, upon the suggestion of *Atlantic Monthly* editor James T. Fields, to delete several paragraphs on Lincoln, whom he described in one passage as "about the homeliest man I ever saw," can only be imagined. 6

Nor was it noted that Hawthorne actually resisted an easy target: George B. McClellan, recently relieved as general in chief of the Army, although he retained his position as commander of the Army of the Potomac, who seemed, in the winter of 1861–62, greatly adverse to advancing southward his huge force of more than 100,000 men.

As 1862 wore on, Northern politicians, first in a whisper and then somewhat louder than that, began to wonder just why the 34-year-old commander could not seem to move.

Hawthorne, visiting McClellan at camp in northern Virginia, took a different tack: noting that the general's men "received him with loud shouts," he declared "I shall not give up my faith in General McClellan's soldiership until he is defeated, nor in his courage and integrity even then." 7

By the time the *Atlantic Monthly* article appeared Hawthorne was trying to complete a series of sketches recalling his years in England that would be released under the title of *Our Old Home*. Throughout the rest of 1862 and the first half of the following year, Hawthorne worked.

Then, when the project finally reached its conclusion, Hawthorne had made a decision that was guaranteed to enrage his Northern audience: the book would be dedicated, he said, to Franklin Pierce.

James T. Fields, also Hawthorne's publisher, was horrified. The son of a ship's captain who had moved to Boston and slowly moved up the ranks in the famous Old Corner Bookstore—spiritual home to Emerson, Henry Wadsworth Longfellow and Harriet Beecher Stowe—Fields loved good writing, but he loved even more good writing that made money.

A large man given to Scotch tweeds, Fields prided himself on knowing his business. He was intimate friends with virtually all of the major booksellers on the East Coast as well as the literary critics for the major metro dailies, and also claimed to be able to guess the book-buying tastes of his customers entering the Old Corner Bookstore simply by looking at them.

Even though his opinions about the Civil War were undeniably shaped by the likes of Emerson, Longfellow and Stowe, Fields was much more interested in the business ramifications of the war, convinced that Southern victories would sap confidence in the North, damage the economy and hurt both book sales and *Atlantic Monthly* receipts. Postponing the publication of one work in 1861, Fields told its author that it would be best to wait, "til' we see how McClellan is doing." 8

And when, by mid-1862, it became obvious that the Civil War was not going to be won as easily as many of his friends had earlier assumed, Fields, characteristically, thought first of the regional book-buying market, telling one friend: "The Trade is in a state of apathy I never saw approached." 9

It was perhaps for that reason, as well as his fear that British readers would enjoy a mean harpooning of an American president, in this case Lincoln, that Fields had asked Hawthorne to "alter yr. phrases with reference to the President, to leave out descriptions of his awkwardness & general uncouth aspect." 10

Now Fields was convinced that dedicating *Our Old Home* to Pierce was a similarly bad idea, one that would have to hurt the book's sales, while also contaminating Hawthorne's work with a kind of politics that had become poison in New England.

His pessimism was bolstered after talking with a hardly unbiased group: Emerson, Longfellow and writer Ellery Channing, all strong abolitionists who quickly declared their opposition to the Pierce dedication.

Emerson, as usual, was the most upset, forced as he was to once more contemplate a Hawthorne-Pierce friendship he could neither understand nor participate in. Mulling things over in his journal, Emerson decided that Hawthorne had simply been "unlucky in having for a friend a man who cannot be befriended: whose miserable administration admits but one excuse, imbecility."

"Pierce," Emerson added, "was either the worst, or he was the weakest, of all our Presidents." 11

Meanwhile, trying to reason with Hawthorne, Fields candidly warned that a Pierce dedication "will ruin the sale of yr. book," adding that a "large dealer told me he shd. not order any copies, much as his customers admired your writing." Furthermore a "very knowing literary friend," added Fields, thought the dedication would be the "most damaging move you could possibly make." 12

Many others were saying the same thing, and for the most part Hawthorne listened to the complaints and warnings of his friends with good cheer, although he shortly began to wonder why it was anyone's business but his own. But when his sister-in-law Elizabeth also got into the act to voice her opposition, he finally had enough, taking issue with the notion that dedicating a book to such an unpopular man was a bad idea.

On the contrary, thought Hawthorne, it was more important to honor Pierce now, "at this moment, when all the administration and abolition papers are calling him a traitor."

It was a charge, to Hawthorne, that had been particularly repugnant.

It was the South that had seceded and abolitionist sympathizers like Emerson and Maria Lydia Child who were saying that the nation would be better off without it. Pierce, on the other hand, was the one who remained committed to the idea and reality of the Union.

"Why, he is the only loyal man in the country, North or South!" Hawthorne told Elizabeth. "Everybody else has outgrown the old faith in the Union, or got outside of it in one way or the other; but Pierce retains it in all the simplicity with which he inherited it from his father." 13

Elizabeth and Sophia gave up, as did Anne Fields, the wife of James, who undoubtedly shared the concerns of her husband that the Pierce dedication would drastically affect *Our Old Home*'s sales potential.

"Mr. P's politics at present shut him away from the faith of patriots, but Mr. Hawthorne has loved him since college days and he will not relent," Anne Fields recorded to herself, admitting that she secretly admired Hawthorne's intransigence, especially as she knew that the author was always in need of money: "Such adherence is indeed noble." 14

And it wasn't just the dedication that had everyone up in arms, but a much longer "dedication letter" in which Hawthorne planned to praise Pierce in greater and more specific detail beyond the book's title page.

"It would be a piece of poltroonery in me to withdraw either the dedication or dedicatory letter," Hawthorne told James Fields, adding: "I can only say that I would gladly sacrifice a thousand or two of dollars rather than retain the good will of such a herd of dolts and mean-spirited scoundrels." 15

Unfortunately for Hawthorne, Pierce was hardly making things easier. On the contrary, the former president seemed more determined than ever before to remain in the national debate, rejecting the obscurity that had shrouded other former presidents in favor of a loud and glaring publicity.

On July 4, at high noon, Pierce appeared before a massive crowd of Democrats in downtown Concord and delivered what was perhaps his greatest speech on the war and the administration's record on civil liberties.

With Hawthorne sitting behind him on the speaker's platform, Pierce reminded his audience of their common Revolutionary War heritage and how differently that war had been pursued: "Then we were the model republic of the world; honored, loved—or feared where we were not loved," Pierce said.

"No American citizen was then subject to be driven into exile for opinions sake, or arbitrarily arrested and incarcerated in military bastilles—even as he now may be—not for acts or words of imputed treason, but if he do but mourn in silent sorrow over the desolation of his country."

"No embattled hosts of Americans were then wasting their lives and resources in sanguinary civil strife," Pierce continued. "No suicidal and parricidal civil war then swept like a raging tempest of death over the stricken homesteads and wailing cities of the Union."

And who was to blame for this current state of affairs, which Pierce likened to a "smouldering ruin of conflagration and blood"?

Not flinching, Pierce said the war had been nearly entirely caused by the "vicious intermeddling of too many citizens of the Northern states with the constitutional rights of the Southern states." 16

The alarming erosion of civil liberties, on the other hand, could only be blamed on one source: the Lincoln administration, Pierce charged.

He then quoted from a recent letter written by Lincoln to Erastus Corning, a New York Democrat and businessman, in which the president tried to explain the difference between suspending the writ of habeas corpus in conventional criminal cases and in instances of suspected treason. 17

The former, Lincoln had written, addresses the "small percentage of ordinary and continuous perpetration of crime." The latter was directed towards those who would rise against their own government.

Then, with relish, Pierce added—still quoting Lincoln—"In the latter case arrests are made not so much for what has been done, as for what probably will be done."

The quote produced the result Pierce undoubtedly hoped it would as the large outdoor audience laughed and cheered. With a flourish reminiscent of his years as a country lawyer, Pierce concluded: "There is no doubt as to where the responsibilities for these unconstitutional acts of the last two years...properly resides."

But who, Pierce pushed on, gave Lincoln what he called the "power to dictate to any one of us when we must or when we may speak, or be silent upon any subject, and especially in the conduct of any public servant?"

If Pierce had concluded his remarks here he would be been on solid ground. Certainly the administration's almost-blanket suspension of the writ of habeas corpus had sparked enormous controversy across the country, engendering the kind of hostility, at least in certain parts of the North, that the president may have once thought possible only in the South.

Only two months before, in undoubtedly the most prominent arrest so far, former Ohio Representative Clement Vallandigham, who, like Pierce, thought the South had been wronged, was arrested and charged with treason. Uniquely, Lincoln decided that if Vallandigham liked the Confederacy so much he should live there, deporting the Peace Democrat behind enemy lines several weeks later.

But Pierce, delivering his first formal public speech since his lukewarm response to Lincoln's war declaration in April 1861, wanted also to talk about that war—and it was here that he got into the most trouble.

Reminding his listeners that he had warned in that 1861 address that the use of force was neither a "suitable or possible remedy for existing evils," Pierce now urged the Lincoln administration to enter into negotiations with the Confederate government. "My judgment impels me to rely upon moral force and not upon the coercive instrumentalities of military power," he remarked.

Only through "peaceful agencies, and peaceful agencies alone," added Pierce, could the conflict at long last finally be resolved. 18

But Pierce's argument was almost immediately undercut by events: Union soldiers, bloodily concluding a series of battles at Gettysburg, Pennsylvania, had successfully repelled an invasion force of 75,000 troops under the command of General Robert E. Lee in what would soon be regarded as the turning point of the war.

Not until July 4th was the news first transmitted by teletype to the nation's cities—Jefferson Davis would not learn the full details of the Confederate defeat for another two or three days—putting Pierce in the position of questioning the use of Union military force at the very moment of its greatest effectiveness.

Even worse, nine days later, New York City exploded in a riot that left many dead in response to the first drawing of names for the draft. It seemed that those who opposed Lincoln were barbarians, beating black people in the streets to death, ransacking and burning buildings. And those who supported him were only too happy to make the connection. Attacking the Peace Democrats, of who Pierce was now largely regarded as a leader, *Harper's Weekly* remarked: "They claim to be supporters of order and law, and anarchy rises and riots under their auspices."

But should Jefferson Davis triumph, the newspaper continued, "they would kneel before him," humbly begging for the "reward they have earned from him and from every other enemy of their country." 19

Long-time Pierce supporters, on the other hand, liked what he had to say.

Former Connecticut Governor Thomas Hart Seymour had served as Pierce's minister to Russia and, like Pierce, had been greatly critical of Lincoln, even publicly so. As a reward for his candor, lawmakers in Seymour's home state voted to remove his official gubernatorial portrait from the state capitol.

Now Seymour told Pierce that he had heard a "glowing account of the proceedings," and congratulated the former president for an address that is "mightily commended on all sides." 20

Describing the speech as "truthful, eloquent, and sincere," long-time New York newspaper publisher Elon Comstock added: "It is a real satisfaction for your old friends to hear from you in this public manner." 21

Sidney Webster, ever loyal, was quick to send in his praise as well, although his response may have left Pierce wondering if perhaps he had read another speech: "Your oration was admirable in thought and diction, and most admirably avoided the dangerous ground," he wrote on July 10. 22

In Montreal, George A. Magruder read Pierce's speech in the local papers and was impressed with what he regarded as a "patriotic address on the affairs of our wretched and bleeding country." Pierce's tortured response to recent events held a particularly poignant meaning for Magruder. In 1861, just days after the Confederate shelling of Fort Sumter, Magruder, then the chief of the Navy Ordnance, was troubled enough by the coming war to abruptly resign his post, inspiring in his wake a mass exodus of fellow officers.

But instead of joining the Confederate cause, as was usually the case with disenchanted military men in the North, Magruder moved to Montreal, where with dismay he watched his former country come apart. Now he wrote to Pierce: "It is refreshing to hear once more the voice of patriotism amidst the tempest of fanaticism, rapine blood and slaughter to which our poor country has been reduced." 23

Letter finished, Magruder then decided not to send it, at least for now, reasoning that the last thing Pierce needed was to be found in receipt of correspondence from an expatriate who had clearly been accused of cowardice and treason when he abruptly left the U.S.

Despite the best intentions of supporters near and far, the majority reaction to Pierce's speech was overwhelmingly negative, especially in the nation's press: "He wants to see the slaveholders, his old patrons, triumph," charged the *New York Evening Post*, which could not resist adding "Why did not General Pierce convert his friend Jefferson Davis to his new gospel before the order was given for battering down Sumter?" 24

"The speech of Franklin Pierce will excite the indignation and disgust of every loyal man," thought the *Providence Daily Journal*, which added that there was "no sadder spectacle" than that of an ex-president "spreading the polished periods of his graceful rhetoric over the sentiments of treason." 25

The *Boston Evening Transcript* also drew Davis into the controversy, remarking "Jefferson Davis was once the Secretary of Franklin Pierce. Franklin Pierce now seems to act as the Secretary of Jefferson Davis." 26

Horace Greeley's *New York Tribune*, meanwhile, attacked everyone who spoke at the Concord rally—including, of course, Pierce—charging that "every act and utterance was calculated to strengthen and aid the traitors." 27

Confining his thoughts to his diary, Benjamin Brown French angrily felt that the New York riots had to be blamed on "those who initiated them," and foremost on that list, thought French, "is my old friend Frank Pierce, late president of the U.S., who by his miserable, weak speech in Concord on the 4th inst. disgraced himself and the name that he bears."

"I thought better of him," French added, "but now I give him over to Secesh & Rebeldom." 28

Hawthorne, too, was inundated with complaints: "Some spiteful Abolitionist took the trouble to send me a compendium of abusive paragraphs from the newspapers in reference to you," he told Pierce on July 24, "and it seemed to me that the best method of disappointing his malice was to toss them aside without reading one of them—which I accordingly did." 29

The angry response clearly bothered Pierce, who characterized it to one correspondent as "an unusual outpouring of abuse." That Pierce felt that way after more than a decade of similar abuse from his opponents suggests that this time, because the speech was delivered in his home town, he must have also received a good deal of criticism to his face. 30

But despite the ferocity of the reaction, less than ten weeks later the furor over Pierce's speech had finally abated and *Our Old Home* was in bookstores. The response was perhaps predictable: Reviewers, as usual, extolled Hawthorne's writing, his extraordinary talent for character and description. But many had a hard time getting past the dedication to Pierce.

That anyone who knows the difference between "robbery and almsgiving" could call Pierce a patriot, "passes our comprehension," said the *Commonwealth* of Boston. The *New York Tribune* acknowledged that Hawthorne had a right to dedicate his book to whomever he pleased, "but gratuitous affirmation of the loyalty and patriotism of the ex-President is a gush of Quixotic enthusiasm which will expose Mr. Hawthorne to ridicule as mistaking a windmill for a giant." 31

Hawthorne's friends, or at least those who fancied they were, were no less unremitting. Critic Norton, amazed Hawthorne could do such a thing now, in the middle of the war, saw the Pierce dedication as the "bitterest of satires." 32

Harriet Beecher Stowe, writing to Fields, entered a state of disbelief when she asked "Do tell me if our friend Hawthorne praises that arch-traitor Pierce in his preface and your loyal firm publishes it."

"I never read the preface," Stowe continued, "and have not yet seen the book, but they say so here, and I can scarcely believe it or you, if I can of him…What! patronize such a traitor to our faces! I can scarcely believe it." 33

Emerson, opening our *Our Old Home* for the first time, was bewildered. He naturally treasured any book from Hawthorne, but this one could only be enjoyed through an exorcism: carefully, he cut the offending dedication from his copy.

But not all of the responses were as violent, and at least one was poignantly heart-felt.

Since she returned to the U.S. with her husband, Jane Pierce had made it her practice to avoid politics. Her only real friend from the political world was Varina Davis, wife of Jefferson, with whom she had earlier corresponded. But now the Civil War had made it impossible for the two women to actively maintain their friendship. Instead Jane spent most of her time with relatives in Andover and occasionally visited such New Hampshire vacation retreats as Hampton Beach Head, where she rediscovered what she called "an ardent love of the sight & sound of the ocean." 34

She had many reasons to be and remain reclusive, and now the war only gave her one more: she never enjoyed politics in the first place, had a distrust of political people, and usually could remember only sad things from her years as the nation's First Lady.

The denunciations of her husband—so much worse in New England than anywhere else—could not have been easy to bear either, only comfirming for her the pitfalls of public life. That Jane was also very often not physically well undoubtedly also detracted from her ability to endure that same life.

In the summer of 1863, a niece vacationing with Jane observed that no matter how sick she had been in the past, she always somehow seemed to recover. But this time, Harriet Lord would later note, "it seemed to me then that she was losing her hold upon the earth." 35

True to form, by September Jane seemed better, healthy enough to almost instantly read *Our Old Home* in its entirety. Exactly seven days after the release of the book, she—almost constitutionally incapable of overstatement—wrote Hawthorne to "acknowledge your pleasant book, which I have read from beginning to end."

"The added interest of the preface and the warm assurance of a friendship which has on both sides been so constant, so affectionate, and so true gives it a hold upon my regard of which even the 'Scarlet Letter' and 'Marble Faun' are destitute."

Then, after briefly pointing out several passages in Hawthorne's tales of his life in England that particularly delighted her, she closed, no doubt grateful to know that Franklin Pierce could always very obviously continue to count on the friendship of Nathaniel Hawthorne.

"I am, my dear sir, yours most sincerely, Jane M. Pierce." 36

CHAPTER SIX FOOTNOTES

1. Thomas Woodson, *Nathaniel Hawthorne—The Letters, 1857–1864* (Dayton: Ohio State University Press, 1987), Nathanial Hawthorne to Horatio Bridge, 26 May 1861, 130–31.

2. Louise Hall Tharp, *The Peabody Sisters of Salem* (Boston: Little, Brown and Company, 1950), 289–94; Woodson, *Nathaniel Hawthorne—The Letters, 1857–1864)* 130–31.

3. Edward Haviland Miller, *Salem Is My Dwelling Place—A Life of Nathaniel Hawthorne* (Iowa City: University of Iowa Press, 1991), 471; Edward Wagenknecht, *Nathaniel Hawthorne—Man and Writer* (New York: Oxford University Press, 1961), 127–28.

4. Woodson, *Nathaniel Hawthorne—The Letters, 1857–1864*, Nathaniel Hawthorne to Henry Bright, 14 November 1861, 420–21.

5. Brenda Wineapple, *Hawthorne: A Life* (New York: Random House Trade Paperbacks, 2003), 351.

6. James R. Mellow, *Nathaniel Hawthorne in His Times* (Baltimore: Johns Hopkins University Press, 1980), 556–58.

7. Nathaniel Hawthorne, "Chief About War Matters," *The Atlantic Monthly*, Volume X, No. LVIL, July 1862, 52.

8. W. S. Tryon, *Parnassus Corner—A Life of James T. Fields, Publisher to the Victorians* (Boston: Houghton Mifflin Company, 1963), 253–54.

9. Ibid.

10. Mellow, *Nathaniel Hawthorne in His Times*, 556–57.

11. Ibid., 564.

12. Nathaniel Hawthorne, *Our Old Home; A Series of English Sketches* (Dayton: Ohio State University Press, 1970), xxv.

13. Woodson, *Nathaniel Hawthorne—The Letters, 1857–1864*; Nathaniel Hawthorne to Elizabeth P. Peabody, 26, July 1863, 589–94.

14. Hawthorne, *Our Old Home*, xxvii-xxviii; Tharp, *The Peabody Sisters of Salem*, 295.

15. Woodson, *Nathaniel Hawthorne—The Letters, 1857–1864*, Nathaniel Hawthorne to James T. Fields, 18 July 1863, 586–88.

16. "Fourth of July in Concord, N.H.," *New York Times*, 12 July 1863, p. 2, col. 4.

17. Corning served on a resolutions committee with the Albany, New York Democratic Convention in June of 1863 which had officially denounced Lincoln for his stand on civil liberties.

18. "Fourth of July in Concord, N.H."

19. "A Transparent Mask," *Harper's Weekly*, 8 August 1863, p. 499, col. 1.

20. Thomas Hart Seymour to Franklin Pierce, 8 July 1863, Series 3, Reel 2, Franklin Pierce Papers.

21. Elon Comstock to Franklin Pierce, 10 July 1863, Series 3, Reel 2, Franklin Pierce Papers.

22. Sidney Webster to Franklin Pierce, 10 July 1863, Series 3, Reel 2, Franklin Pierce Papers.

23. "Highly Interesting in Washington," *New York Tribune*, 25 April 1861, p. 6, col. 2; G. A. Magruder to Franklin Pierce, 14 July 1863 and 2 August 1864, Series 3, Reel 6, Franklin Pierce Papers. That George Magruder was willing to write Pierce a note of admiration helped clear up one old mystery: in 1852 it was reported that Magruder's brother, John (who cut short a career in the U.S. military to join the Confederacy in 1861) had slapped Pierce while both served in the Mexican-American war. John Magruder never directly commented on the story, but did describe Pierce's service in the field as "faithful and gallant." The Magruders were a close family with a shared political perspective. It seems unlikely that George would have written the sort of letter he did if his brother, as the press had implied, thought Pierce was a coward. See Peter A. Wallner, *Franklin Pierce—New Hampshire's Favorite Son* (Conord: Plaindswede Publishing, 2004), 146, 147, 153, 224–

25; and Paul D. Casdorph, *Prince John Magruder—His Life and Campaigns* (New York: John Wiley & Songs, Incorporated, 1996), 79, 114.

24. "General Pierce to Generals Meade and Grant," *New York Evening Post*, 9 July 1863, p. 2, col. 1.

25. No title, *Providence Daily Journal*, 7 July 1863, p. 2, col. 1.

26. "Rebel Invasion of New Hampshire," *Boston Evening Transcript*, 6 July 1863, p. 2, col. 1.

27. "'Peace' in New Hampshire," *New York Semi-Weekly Tribune*, 10 July 1863, p. 3, col. 1.

28. Donald B. Cole, *Benjamin Brown French—Witness to the Young Republic, A Yankee's Journal, 1828–1870* (Hanover: University Press of New England, 1989), Diary entry, dated 17 July 1863, 427–28.

29. Woodson, *Nathaniel Hawthorne—The Letters, 1857–1864*, Nathaniel Hawthorne to Franklin Pierce, 24 July 1863, 595–96.

30. G. Kimball to Franklin Pierce, 27 July 1863, Series 3, Reel 6, Franklin Pierce Papers.

31. John L. Idol, *Nathaniel Hawthorne—The Contemporary Reviews* (Boston: Cambridge University Press, 1994), 281–83; Hawthorne, *Our Old House*, xxxiii.

32. Hawthorne, *Our Old House*, xxviii.

33. Philip McFarland, *Hawthorne in Concord* (New York: Grove Press, 2004), 285.

34. Norman F. Boas, *Jane M. Pierce (1806–1863)—The Pierce-Aiken Papers Supplement* (Mystic, Connecticut: Seaport Autographs, 1989), Jane Pierce to Anne W. Pierce, 15 August 1862, 57.

35. Norman F. Boas, *Jane M. Pierce (1806–1863)—The Pierce-Aiken Papers* (New London, Connecticut: New London Printers, 1983), Harriet Lord to Mary Aiken, no date, December 1863, 94–95.

36. Jane Pierce to Nathaniel Hawthorne, 30 September 1863, Series 3, Reel 2, Franklin Pierce Papers.

7

Private Information

When Jefferson Davis, in the early breathless weeks of 1861, was preparing to leave Washington and return home to Mississippi, he admitted to Franklin Pierce that he could not be certain of either his future or the future of what would be the new Confederacy, but was sure that "whatever circumstances demand shall be met as a duty." 1

Davis obviously hoped those circumstances would be military in nature. He yearned to be a commander in the field and had no doubt whatsoever of his ability in that regard. Delegates to the Confederate's provisional congress, however, had other ideas, electing him unanimously as the provisional president of the new nation.

That Davis picked Pierce to reveal his inner thoughts to was no accident: More than four years after Pierce had left the White House, Davis still had good memories of the collegial atmosphere Pierce had inspired among his cabinet. By selecting men of greatly varied geographical and political perspective, Pierce had shown himself to be a confident chief executive willing to listen to and contemplate viewpoints different from his own.

In return, by sticking with Pierce from the beginning to the end of his administration—by contrast almost all of Lincoln's cabinet was replaced two or three times over—Pierce's cabinet gave him a daily vote of confidence indicating that they enjoyed the open and free-wheeling atmosphere.

On the other hand, Davis, as president, was soon regularly attacked for adopting a rather different executive style that many regarded as too unilateral, with little or no input from either his cabinet or administrative assistants. "The President seems determined to respect the opinions of no one," General Josiah Gorgas, a Davis friend and director of the Confederacy's ordnance program, remarked. "He seems to be an indifferent judge of men, and is guided more by prejudice than sound discriminating judgment." 2

There could be no denying that Davis was deficient in political skills. Varina perhaps summed up the problem best when she said her husband "did not know the arts of the politician and would not practice them if understood." Yet it was also true that Davis faced an almost impossible task as the commander in chief of a nation that had not even existed the month before he became president. 3

Suddenly he was the head of a national government that had no existing or functioning bureaucracy, institutional memory, or executive precedents. And just to make his burden even more absurd, it was a government that was also at war with a far more powerful, rich, and populous opponent capable of recruiting more soldiers, producing far larger amounts of war materiel, and getting it to the front lines more efficiently on a vast expanse of rail lines twice as large as anything that existed in the Confederacy.

Even the constitutional structure of the new nation seemed to be designed to vex Davis. With an emphasis on state's rights, the Confederate constitution emboldened the governors of the Southern states to go their own way, regularly resisting the attempts of Davis to create a more centralized authority. This was, in a time of war, lethal, or so thought Secretary of State Judah P. Benjamin who, in late 1861, candidly remarked: "The difficulty lies with the governors, who are unwilling to trust the common defense to one common head." 4

Those same governors, in fact, were routinely shoring up their state militias at the expense of contributing to a Confederate army needed for the defense of the nation.

Davis was also given the hopeless task of trying to keep happy an astonishing and almost comical collection of fire-eaters and malcontents who could never be satisfied with anything he did. Prominent among this group was Robert Barnwell Rhett, who referred to Davis as "this little man," and questioned his every war decision through the pages of his paper, the *Charleston Mercury*, as early as February of 1862. 5

Robert Toombs of Georgia, undoubtedly sore that Davis had beat him out for the Confederate presidency, was soon calling him a "false and hypocritical wrench," while also complaining that Davis and his closest associates "conspire for the destruction of all who will not bend to them." Toombs' fellow Georgian Tom Cobb—who had always suspected that Davis was at heart not a true secessionist—called the president an "obstinate fool," at the head of a government that was also "imbecile and obstinate." 6

The Southern press was equally critical. "There is plenty of gloom resting upon the Confederacy and precious little sunshine," the *New Orleans Crescent* summed up the national mood in early 1862, at the same time that the *Charles-*

ton Mercury was publishing a list of complaints about Davis's performance as a war leader. "The discontents of our people with the management of the war are growing from day to day," the *Mobile Tribune* added. 7

The near-insubordination of two of Davis's top generals, P.G. T. Beauregard and Joseph E. Johnston, both prickly men easily offended who aired their complaints about the president freely, only added to the growing sense of dissatisfaction that Southerners, by 1863, generally felt towards their president. And matters were undeniably made worse that summer by two huge military defeats: Vicksburg, strategically important to the North because of its position on the Mississippi River; and Gettysburg, the site of General Robert E. Lee's failed invasion of the North.

But perhaps, for Davis, the cruelest blow—at least in a personal way—came in June when Union soldiers arrived at the Confederate president's beloved Brierfield plantation in Mississippi. Located downriver from the Hurricane plantation and home of Davis's elder brother, Joseph Emory—which was burned by Union forces the preceding summer—the Brierfield home was a one-story structure with eight spacious rooms, sixteen-foot ceilings and twelve-foot tall windows. 8

In glee, the Union soldiers defaced the property, destroyed furniture and rifled through letters found in the Davis library that they thought might shed light on the Confederate army's movements. Among the invaders was one Captain William H. Gibbs of the 15th Illinois infantry, 2nd brigade, who took for himself a gold-headed cane that had been given to Davis by Pierce, before finding a batch of letters sent to Davis from Pierce, the most recent of which was dated January 6, 1860. 9

An enthusiastic Republican from the state that had given the nation Lincoln and General Ulysses S. Grant, Gibbs later claimed that he never gave the letters a second thought until he saw an article in the fiercely anti-Pierce *Concord Independent Democrat*, which was, as he put it, "lying in camp." 10

Reporting on the capture of Brierfield, the paper wondered whether or not the soldiers had also found any correspondence between Pierce and Davis. It was not an idle speculation. Pierce would have been charged with treason if any evidence could be found of his being in contact with Davis or any other Confederate. Yet the opportunities for communication were obviously too great to assume that no such contact had ever been made.

Unique among Northern politicians, Pierce before the war enjoyed intimate and warm relationships with a wide variety of politicians and military leaders from the South, including nearly all of the men who would become members of the Davis cabinet. And clearly the secretaries, clerks and aides who worked for such men recognized in Pierce a man who was respected and admired by their bosses. From just this circle alone, it is possible that Pierce was kept up to date on the inner workings of the Confederacy.

The fact that the former president also maintained an active friendship with Northern Peace Democrats, some of whom did communicate with contacts in the South, only enhanced the opportunities.

How such communications may have been transmitted would never be ascertained through a search of dusty old letters in latter-day archives because such letters were dynamite, perhaps never written in the first place, and if so written, undoubtedly destroyed upon receipt.

Much more likely, Pierce's means for communicating with the Confederate government—again, if it ever occurred in the first place—was probably "word of mouth." Somehow, someone who knew someone else kept Pierce appraised of recent events, and may have even transmitted communications from Pierce back to the Confederacy. 11

Those most intrigued by a Pierce-Davis correspondence very obviously hoped to find a letter written since the beginning of the war—solid proof that the former president was communing with the enemy. But failing that, they would have been equally satisfied with anything that seemed to suggest that Pierce was in any way in sympathy with the enemy or supporting its cause.

Certainly the January 6, 1860 letter seemed to be that, or so Captain Gibbs must have thought as he sent a verbatim copy of the correspondence to the *Concord Independent Democrat*, instructing the editor: "You can make such use of it as you deem proper."

His goal in revealing the correspondence, Gibbs candidly admitted, was to "show up the doings, the feelings, and the sympathies of prominent men at the North who I fear are not as loyal as they might be." 12

If he also intended to wound Pierce politically, Gibbs did not say, although he obviously figured that the words of the president, written in 1860 but read in the substantively changed political context of 1863, would be damaging enough.

Sent from New York's Clarendon Hotel just days before the Pierces were set to begin their winter vacation in Nassau, Pierce began his letter contemplating the 1860 presidential race and his desire to see Davis win that year's Democratic nomination. But the correspondence quickly veered—as so many letters in 1860 did—to the question of secession, with Pierce observing: "I have never believed that actual disruption of the Union can occur without blood; and if through the madness of Northern abolitionists that dire calamity must come, the fighting will not be along Mason and Dixon's lines entirely."

On the contrary, predicted Pierce—wide of the mark—Yankees would shortly divide into two factions, those who "respect their political obligations," and those who would have "apparently no impelling power but that which fanatical passion on the subject of domestic slavery imparts." 13

To some, this could only mean one thing: Pierce not only thought that a mini-revolution would take place in the North if it went to war with the South, but that it should.

Published on September 17 in the *Concord Independent Democrat*, which was quick to note that the correspondence contained "not a word of remonstrance against the conspiracy of Jeff Davis and his followers, just ripening into rebellion," the Pierce letter was almost instantly reproduced in papers throughout the North—and in the South, too, (although generally without comment)—prompting editorialists to conclude that there could no longer be any doubt that Pierce was a traitor. 14

Describing the letter as "thoroughly saturated with treason," the *Albany Evening Journal* declared that Pierce's forecast of domestic division in the North was proof that his kind "must go down to posterity [as] liars as well as traitors." 15

"Everybody knows that Franklin Pierce is now a traitor," concluded the *Indianapolis Journal*, "but everyone may not know that he was a traitor in 1860." Abandoning the now-tired treason-traitor simile, the *New York Post* imaginatively likened Pierce instead to Satan, "contemplating the Eden he was about to ruin." 16

From Michigan, Robert McClelland read the Pierce-Davis letter and wondered what all the excitement was about, later telling Pierce that all he had really done, in assessing Northern sentiment for Davis, was place a "construction upon it which every upright and sensible man would." In that regard, McClelland added, he regarded the correspondence as entirely "unexceptionable." 17

The Pierce letter made the Boston papers almost immediately, appearing in the *Boston Post* on September 19, the *Boston Evening Transcript* two days later, and again in the *Post* on October 7. Running across the letter in the *Post*, Elizabeth Peabody was beside herself with delight. Still smarting over the sharply worded defense of Pierce her brother-in-law Nathaniel Hawthorne had sent her in July, Elizabeth could not wait to show the paper to her sister Sophia, who generally refused to hear anything bad about her husband's best friend. 18

Hawthorne himself—or so Elizabeth claimed many years later—made a point of never mentioning Pierce's name in front of his angry sister-in-law again after the Pierce-Davis correspondence was aired. Elizabeth's recollection could be true.

Certainly Hawthorne realized that Elizabeth would never let the matter rest, and so, if even for the sake of family harmony, may have been willing to suspend his pro-Pierce defenses, at least around Elizabeth.

But if Elizabeth also thought that Hawthorne shared her shock and outrage by what Pierce had written to Davis, she would have been mistaken—Pierce had long doubted both the morality of the Northern cause as well as it's ability to fight, and undoubtedly said as much to Hawthorne many times before.

Besides, Hawthorne had to listen to the complaints of detractors far more powerful than Elizabeth, most prominent of which was the *Harper's Weekly*, by 1863 one of the nation's most popular newsweeklies, which now demanded to know whether or not Hawthorne was aware of the Pierce-Davis correspondence before he dedicated *Our Old Home* to the former president.

"Mr. Hawthorne owes it to himself," the paper proclaimed, "to explain in a subsequent edition that the final proof of Pierce's infamy had not then been spoken or printed, and was unknown to him." 19

To no one's surprise, Hawthorne had no response to this suggestion, nor did Pierce to the many new broadsides against him. And even if either had been so inclined—and they weren't—they were both soon consumed with far more important matters. On December 2, Jane, a lifelong prisoner to illness and frequent depression, died.

Pierce had cared for her, felt mortally guilty when he thought about her, and loved her for more than three decades, so much so that one relative, Harriet Lord, wondered what his life would be like without her. "It seems to me that he will feel as tho' transplanted to another world, in the absence of those cares which have formed so large a part of his life," she wrote. 20

Jane was buried by the side of her children in Concord on December 5, a cold winter day. Noticing Hawthorne shivering at the gravesite, Pierce drew up the collar of his overcoat to protect him against the wind. Several weeks later, an obituary written by Jane's uncle, Alpheus Packard, appeared in the *Boston Recorder*. Pierce was particularly struck with one sentence because he knew it to be true: "She shrank with extreme sensitiveness from public observation." 21

Did Pierce, on the day of Jane's funeral, see something in Hawthorne, who rarely seemed weak, that alarmed him? Within weeks the 58 year-old writer was inexplicably tired, telling Pierce: "A little exertion fatigues me." 22

Pierce thought a long journey by carriage would revive him, but Hawthorne, who had surprised himself by feeling overcome at the site of Jane in her casket, told Sophia he was afraid to be alone just now with Pierce, afraid that the former president might be depressed with the passing of Jane, afraid perhaps of the death that hovered over them all.

Finally in early May he consented, meeting Pierce on the 10th in Boston. "It was apparent that he was much more feeble and more seriously diseased than I had supposed him to be," Pierce later wrote of his first impressions upon seeing Hawthorne. 23

By May 16, the two men had journeyed to Plymouth, New Hampshire, where they checked into a local inn. Adjoining rooms allowed Pierce to keep an eye on Hawthorne. Twice during the evening, Pierce left his room to check on him. The first time he saw Hawthorne sleeping on his side. The second, several hours later, Pierce placed his hand on the writer's forehead and realized he was dead.

"He must have passed from natural slumber to that from which there is no waking without the slightest movement," Pierce wrote in a telegram sent to James Fields later that morning. 24

Why Pierce felt compelled to write what would become a detailed account of Hawthorne's last night on earth would be a subject of speculation. Pierce perhaps anticipated as much. But he may have anticipated even more that those who thought he was an alcoholic would conclude that he and Hawthorne had probably been drunk the night the writer died, and that Hawthorne's passing would be used as yet one more reason to despise Franklin Pierce.

By compiling a moment-by-moment chronology of the two men's movements, composed just hours after Hawthorne's death, Pierce sought to prove that his head had been entirely his own throughout the long, sad evening.

Pierce accompanied Hawthorne's body back to Boston the following day. Newspapers at that very moment were publishing their accounts not only of Hawthorne's death, but of his long and important career. Surprisingly, the *New York Herald*, which never needed an excuse to ridicule Pierce, found a reason in Hawthorne's death to say something kind about him: "It is a singular and happy circumstance that friends who have lived so many years upon terms of unrestricted intimacy as Franklin Pierce and Nathaniel Hawthorne," the paper said, "should in the final hours of one still be so near to the other as to enable the survivor to hear, as it were, the last whisper of his friend as he entered the portals of eternity." 25

Other papers, reflecting an embittered and hardened Yankee resolve, were less charitable. "The regret and grief of the loyal people of the North is not and cannot be what it would have been had Mr. Hawthorne ever expressed a word of sympathy for the cause in which we are fighting," said the *Springfield Daily*

Republican, "or manifested any interest in the preservation of our national integrity." 26

Hawthorne's funeral put Pierce in an impossible situation. By all rights he should have been a pallbearer, but the presence of a solid phalanx of South-hating, Lincoln-loving abolitionists made any Pierce participation in the funeral explosive. They were all there: Ralph Waldo Emerson, Bronson Alcott, Elizabeth Peabody, Charles Eliot Norton, Henry Wadsworth Longfellow—New Englanders who despised Pierce for what they thought were all the just reasons, even as they did so in the most unjust ways.

Instead, Pierce sat quietly with the Hawthorne family, once again enraging Emerson who went home and not for the first time confided to his diary his abiding hatred of the former president. 27

In the weeks following Hawthorne's death, Pierce reached out to Julian Hawthorne, who would turn 18 one month after his father's passing. "Except my father, there was no man in whose company I liked to be as much as his," Julian later said of Pierce, admitting that he was impressed with everything the former president did: "His voice, his looks, his gestures, his gait, the spiritual sphere of him, were delightful to me."

In late August Pierce and Julian took a trip to Great Boar's Head on the New Hampshire coast. At one point during the journey, Pierce, driving the carriage, pulled up to the house of a man he described as "one of my bitterest foes in the presidential campaign."

To Julian's surprise, Pierce got down from his seat and approached his detractor, who by now had come out of his house and was scowling at the former president.

"Old foes make good friends when the fight is over," Pierce proclaimed as he offered the man his hand. "Buchanan and I have shaken hands, so must you and I."

"The old man grinned and melted," Julian observed, astonished. The man's sons, grim just moments before, were now transfixed. "None of them would ever forget that ten minutes under the shade of the butternut trees."

But just as memorable, at least from Julian's point of view, was what Pierce told him as they drove off: "Men are swayed less by political theories than by man-to-man." No statement more accurately described Pierce's true self or his utter inability to understand why the abolitionists—the angry Emersons, Peabodys and Stowes of the world—could possibly hate him so. 28

Pierce gave Julian his full attention during the journey, sharing in fond memories of Hawthorne, and later greatly alarming the young man when he suggested that someday he might want to hold down a regular job and get married.

But it would have been easy to be distracted by much larger events, far away.

In Chicago, during the final week of August, Democrats were convening to select a candidate to oppose Lincoln in the 1864 election. Friends of Pierce wanted him to run and planned to put his name in nomination. Throughout the spring and summer he listened to their enthusiasms, never committing himself.

It was true that he had, almost by sheer stubborn persistence, made himself a force in New Hampshire politics again, dominating the state's Democratic machinery through his allies beginning in 1862. And, as always, his presence proved to be something of a mix-blessing for those who shared his views: in early 1864 state Republicans sent out two circulars—one of which was titled *The Venom and the Antidote*—which received a wide distribution suggesting that if the Democrats won a majority in the state legislature, they might send a "defeatist" Pierce to the U.S. Senate. 29

While the anti-Pierce circulars may have held down Democratic victories in New Hampshire that year, they did little to diminish the respect that many national Democrats felt for Pierce as both a critic of the war and elder statesman.

In February Horatio Seymour, the governor of New York and a possible, though greatly reluctant, Democratic candidate for the presidency, hoped to number Pierce among his supporters and begged him to come to New York. "By doing so you would have the opportunity to meet a large number of leading men from the other states," Seymour said of the upcoming state Democratic convention, which would bring together his supporters as well as long-standing Pierce men. 30

On March 10, Jonah D. Hoover, the marshal of Washington, reported to Pierce: "Everyday I am inquired of by gentlemen from all sections of the country what you think of the future, and everyday someone suggests you as their preference for the nomination for President." 31

Two weeks later, George Hillard, about to embark upon a campaign biography of General George B. McClellan, who was also being put forth as a candidate for the Democratic presidential nomination, wrote to Pierce from Boston and asked for the "pleasure of seeing you for a few moments when you are next in town," undoubtedly to discuss Pierce's views on McClellan, national politics, and the rumors that Pierce himself might be interested in gaining the Democratic nod. 32

Sharing, in a private setting, his views on McClellan or any other political topic, was no problem for Pierce. But he steadfastly declined to make a public comment on the 1864 race, with the exception of saying that he hoped Lincoln would be defeated. And when friends and reporters tried to draw him out about his own plans for the year, and whether or not he would accept a draft for the nomination at the Democratic convention, they got nowhere.

In frustration, John J. Taylor, recently elected as a delegate from New York to the Democratic convention, wrote to Pierce, decrying the general condition of the nation, the war, and Lincoln, and wondering about "your views on these points." 33

Such letters, sent in the weeks leading up to a convention, oftentimes gave would-be candidates an opportunity to not only express their opinions on matters of the day but also to send a signal indicating a willingness to run.

Five days later, Pierce responded to Taylor, thanking him for the letter, agreeing with him that the country was on a perilous course and expressing no interest whatsoever in taking the fight to Lincoln personally.

That Pierce, at least to his supporters, just seemed to have a way of getting into trouble was seen in a letter he received on August 2 from George A. Magruder, the one-time head of the Navy Ordnance who abdicated and relocated in Montreal. One year ago, Magruder had read and greatly liked Pierce's controversial July 4th speech in Concord, and wrote the former president a letter of appreciation, saying, among other things, "Thank God there are some honest patriotic lovers of our dear old country left." 34

In this group Magruder also included Clement Vallandigham, Ohio Representative George H. Pendleton, and New York Mayor Fernando Wood—all prominent Peace Democrats—indicating not only his own political leanings, but where on the political spectrum he thought Pierce should be placed as well.

When Magruder wrote his original letter to Pierce, it was ten days after the former president had delivered his explosive July 4th speech in Concord. Ten days during which Pierce had been roundly castigated in the nation's press. Magruder, who had his own fair share of detractors, decided against sending Pierce the letter then, no doubt thinking that if it was somehow made public it would only cause more problems for the former president. "It might have involved you in trouble to get it," Magruder now said. "And as it could do no good for our poor bleeding country, I did not send it."

A year's passage, however, had left many in the Peace Democrat camp feeling that the political landscape in the country had changed, perhaps unalterably. The great Northern victories of 1863 seemed less significant in the more militarily stalemated climate of 1864. Lincoln, previously regarded by many as invincible, now suddenly seemed, on the contrary, vulnerable and anything but a sure bet for re-election.

Meanwhile the nation's newspapers were increasingly talking about negotiations, suggesting that a Civil War which seemingly could not be won on the battle field might find its end at a bargaining table.

Obviously Magruder felt it was just a safer thing all the way around to write to Pierce now. And as he did so, he enclosed his former correspondence with the note: "I am flattered with the hope that a brighter day approaches." 35

Exactly four weeks after Magruder sent his final letter to Pierce, as the delegates to the 1864 Democratic National Convention met in an atmosphere of great disorder, Charles Wickliffe, the former governor Kentucky, rose on the convention floor to officially put Pierce's name in nomination, a gesture that elicited a hail of cheers from older Democrats who fondly remembered the 1852 election and younger Democrats who had come to admire Pierce's stalwart defense of civil liberties.

But as soon as he did, Richard Spofford, an old Pierce devotee from Massachusetts, was given permission by the convention chairman to speak and dramatically announced that he had received both "written and verbal instructions" from Pierce asking that he not be considered for the nomination.

"He feels, sir, that he has received his full share of the honors of the party and that he has discharged his full share of the duty which it devolved upon him," Spofford explained. 36

In response, Wickliffe agreed to withdraw Pierce's name, explaining that his fellow Kentucky delegates "upon consultation among ourselves," remained convinced that Pierce was the best man to run for president because of what he called his "great purity of character."

The former president, added Wickliffe, remained in his mind "unstained as a politician and a man," a remark that elicited another round of cheers. 37

But even as he went out of his way to duck the spotlight, Pierce could not help but attract controversy. In his letter to Spofford, which was shortly made public, Pierce found it impossible to not make at least one reference to what he regarded as Lincoln's oppressive rule, saying that it was his hope that "no bayonets will attempt to control the judgment of the voters" during the upcoming election. 38

The jibe infuriated many, including the *New York Tribune*, which quickly rejoined: "Mr. Pierce ought to know that there is no danger of this whatsoever; and if he does not, he must be deeper in dotage than anybody supposed." 39

Of far greater interest to Pierce that summer was the strange gathering of Peace Democrats and Confederates in Windsor, Ontario.

In February, Davis, intrigued by the idea of insurrection in the North, an insurrection that would presumably be carried out by dedicated anti-Lincoln Northerners, sent a presidential order to Clement Clay, one-time U.S. Senator and now a member of the Confederate senate, always representing Alabama; and Jacob Thompson, a shadowy figure serving as an official Confederate commissioner.

"I hereby direct you to proceed at once to Canada," Davis had told the men, "to conduce to the furtherance of the interests of the Confederate States of America which have been entrusted to you." 40

The exact goal of the mission was never anything less than murky. Thompson believed that with an insurrection at his back and a continuing war at his front, Lincoln could be induced to enter into negotiations that would ultimately result in a permanent recognition of the Confederacy.

What Davis really thought about the mission remained unclear, but it is certain that he sent Thompson to keep an eye on developments and Clay to keep an eye on Thompson.

Eventually the two men met with Vallandigham, who had donned a fake beard sneaking out of the South that Lincoln had exiled him to, and now hoped for a triumphant political return by being elected governor of Ohio.

Together they mulled over the possibilities of an insurrection and negotiations—even Lincoln himself had recently said he was open to talks, contingent upon the "restoration of the Union and the abandonment of slavery"—but soon realized they had a problem with terms. 41

Vallandigham thought the war could and should only end in reunion. Clay and Thompson—in this case perfectly reflecting Davis's sentiments—wanted the war to end too, but only if it meant the existence of a permanent Confederacy.

Although the meeting between Vallandigham, Clay and Thompson was reported on in the press, what was said was supposed to be secret. Yet somehow Pierce got wind of what happened.

Now as he and Julian Hawthorne secured a small sailing boat on Rye Beach and put it in the direction of Appledore Island, home of the poet Celia Laighton Thaxton, Pierce encountered the historian James Parton, who joined them for the ride.

Almost as if on cue, Pierce told Parton that he was certain the war could be ended quickly if only the Lincoln administration would enter into negotiations with the Confederacy—the same line used by Vallindigham, Clay and Thompson.

Amazed, Parton several days later reported Pierce's remarks to General Benjamin F. Butler.

"He spoke darkly of private information that encouraged him to think so," wrote Parton of Pierce, who seemed inclined to believe that former president knew something and was capable of acting upon it.

"But what he would do in the case the negotiations should not succeed, I could not ascertain," Parton added, obviously wondering about the extent of Pierce's influence south of the border. 42

CHAPTER SEVEN FOOTNOTES

1. Lynda Lasswell Crist, *The Papers of Jefferson Davis, Volume 7, 1861* (Baton Rouge: Louisiana State University Press, 1992), Jefferson Davis to Franklin Pierce, 20 January 1861, 17–18.

2. Michael P. Riccards, *The Ferocious Engine of Democracy—A History of the American Presidency, Volume One* (New York: Madison Books, 1995), 253.

3. Varina Davis, *Jefferson Davis—Ex-President of the Confederate States of America—A Memoir by his Wife, Volume II* (New York: Belford Company Publishers, 1890), 12.

4. Riccards, *The Ferocious Engine of Democracy*, 258. For a good discussion analyzing the comparative leadership styles of Davis and Lincoln, see Ludwell H. Johnson, "Jefferson Davis and Abraham Lincoln as War Presidents: Nothing Succeeds Like Success," *Civil War History*, Volume XXVII, Number 1, Spring 1981, 49–63.

5. Laura A. White, *Robert Barnwell Rhett: Father of Secession* (New York: The Century Company, 1931), 224.

6. Thomas E. Schott, *Alexander H. Stephens—A Biography* (Baton Rouge: Louisiana State University Press, 1988), 371; William C. Davis, *The Union That Shaped the Confederacy—Robert Toombs & Alexander H. Stephen* (Lawrence: University Press of Kansas, 2001), 151.

7. "The Confederate Government and the Conduct of the Administration," *Charleston Mercury*, 28 February 1862, p. 1, col. 4; reproductions of the *New Orleans Crescent* and the *Mobile Tribune* articles also appeared in this edition of the *Mercury*.

8. Frank E. Everett, Jr., *Brierfield—Plantation Home of Jefferson Davis* (Hattiesburg: University and College Press of Mississippi, 1971), 77; Janet Sharp Hermann, *The Pursuit of a Dream*, (New York: Oxford University Press, 1981), 38–40; "President Davis's Plantation Destroyed," *Daily Picayune*, 12 June 1863, p. 1, col. 5.

9. Biographical information on Gibbs taken from the John W. Clinton Scrapbook, 19 August 1909, Polo Public Library, Polo, Illinois; *The History of Ogle County, Illinois* (Chicago: H. F. Kett & Company, 1878), 771–72.

10. Gibbs letter to the *Concord Independent Democrat*, reproduced in the *Boston Transcript*, 21 September 1863, p. 4, col. 5; "Franklin Pierce's Letter to Jeff. Davis," Series 3, Reel 6, Franklin Pierce Papers.

11. For an exploration on how secret correspondence traveled between the South and the North during the Civil War, see Adam Mayers, "Running the Gauntlet," *Civil War Times*, June 2001, 36–60.

12. "Ex-President Pierce's Letter to Jeff Davis," *Boston Transcript*, 21 September 1863, p. 4, col. 5; "Franklin Pierce's Letter to Jeff Davis," Franklin Pierce Papers, Series 3, Reel 6.

13. Franklin Pierce to Jefferson Davis, 7 January 1860, Franklin Pierce Papers, Series 3, Reel 2.

14. "Franklin Pierce's Letter to Jeff Davis," Franklin Pierce Papers, Series 3, Reel 6.

15. "Ex-President Pierce in Sympathy and Correspondence with Jeff. Davis," *Albany Evening Journal*, 18 September 1863, p. 2, col. 5.

16. "Ex-President Pierce to Jeff. Davis," *Indianapolis Journal*, 23 September 1863, p. 2, col. 4; "Ex-President Pierce on Secession," *New Orleans Bee*, 2 October 1863, p. 1, col. The quote from the *New York Evening Post* is republished in this edition of the *Bee*.

17. Robert McClelland to Franklin Pierce, 13 April 1864, Franklin Pierce Papers, Series 2, Reel 3.

18. Brenda Wineapple, *Hawthorne—A Life* (New York: Random House Trade Paperbacks, 2003), 357–58.

19. "Hawthorne's Letter to Pierce," *Harper's Weekly*, 3 October 1863, p. 626, col. 2.

20. Norman F. Boas, *Jane M. Pierce (1806–1863), The Pierce-Aiken Papers* (New London, Connecticut: New London Printer, 1983), Harriet A. Lord to Mary Aiken, no date, probably late December 1863, 94–95.

21. Pierce told author Laura C. Holloway, who was compiling a history of presidential wives, that he thought that sentence in the *Boston Recorder* obituary perfectly summed up Jane, adding "I cannot help being influenced by that very controlling trait of her character, and this, I am sure, is true of all of her relatives," Laura C. Holloway, *The Ladies of the White House* (Philadelphia: Bradley & Company, 1886), 494–95.

22. Thomas Woodson, *Nathaniel Hawthorne—The Letters, 1857–1864* (Dayton: Ohio State University Press, 1987), Nathaniel Hawthorne to Franklin Pierce, 9 March 1864, 646.

23. Ibid., 656.

24. Ibid.

25. "Obituary," *New York Herald*, 20 May 1864, p. 2, col. 3.

26. "Nathaniel Hawthorne," *Springfield Daily Republican*, 20 May 1864, p. 2, col. 1.

27. "Funeral of Mr. Hawthorne," *Boston Evening Transcript*, 25 May 1864, p. 2, col. 1; Linda Allardt, *The Journals and Miscellaneous Notebooks of Ralph Waldo Emerson* (Cambridge: The Belknap Press, 1982), 59–60.

28. Julian Hawthorne, *The Memoirs of Julian Hawthorne* (New York: The Mac-Millan Company, 1938), 187–96. Nathaniel Hawthorne worried that Julian's tastes were too expensive for a young boy and once admonished James Fields for giving Julian $10 to settle a clothing bill. "Please to record it against me," Hawthorne told Fields, "and don't let the little scamp have any more." With his father dead, Julian turned to Pierce, always an easy touch. After their trip to Great Boar's Head, Julian wrote Pierce a letter expressing his thanks for taking him along. He then added: "I received a bill of $22.00 from my tailor for several necessary articles," and wondered if Pierce would take care of it for him. Several days later, Pierce did, enclosing the money in a return letter to Julian. James R. Mellow, *Nathaniel Hawthorne in His Times* (Baltimore: Johns Hopkins University Press, 1980), 572; Julian Hawthorne

to Franklin Pierce, 1 and 11 September 1864, Franklin Pierce Papers, Series 3, Reel 6.

29. Lex Renda, "Credit and Culpability: New Hampshire State Politics During the Civil War," *Historical New Hampshire*, Volume 48, Number One, Spring 1993, 63–64.

30. Horatio Seymour to Franklin Pierce, 26 February 1864, Franklin Pierce Papers, Series 3, Reel 6.

31. Jonah D. Hoover to Franklin Pierce, 10 March 1864, Franklin Pierce Papers, Series 2, Reel 3.

32. George Hillard to Franklin Pierce, 21 March 1864, Franklin Pierce Papers, Series 2, Reel 3.

33. John J. Taylor to Franklin Pierce, 9 June 1864, Franklin Pierce Papers, Series 2, Reel 3.

34. George A. Magruder to Franklin Pierce, 14 July 1863, Franklin Pierce Papers, Series 3, Reel 3.

35. George A. Magruder to Franklin Pierce, 2 August 1864, Franklin Pierce Papers, Series 3, Reel 6.

36. *Official Proceedings of the 1864 Democratic National Convention* (Chicago: Democratic National Convention, 1864), 29–30, 36.

37. Ibid., 36.

38. "A Letter from Franklin Pierce," *New York Times*, 3 September 1864, p. 2, col. 3.

39. No title, *New York Tribune*, 9 September 1864, p. 3, col. 2.

40. John W. Headley, *Confederate Operations in Canada and New York* (New York: The Neale Publishing Company, 1906), 220–21.

41. Oscar A. Kinchen, *Confederate Operations in Canada and the North* (North Quincy, Massachusetts: The Christopher Publishing House, 1970), 82; see also Lynda Lasswell Crist, *The Papers of Jefferson Davis, Volume V, August*

1864-May 1865 (Baton Rouge: Louisiana State University Press, 2003), Jacob Thompson to Jefferson Davis, 12 September 1864, 24–35.

42. *Private and Official Correspondence of Gen. Benjamin F. Butler During the Period of the Civil War, Volume V, August 1864-March 1868* (Washington: Butler Family Publication, 1917), James Parton to Benjamin F. Butler, 19 August 1864, 79–80.

8

A Spirit of Domination and Partisan Rancor

Despite the important Union victories at Gettysburg and Vicksburg, victories that in hindsight foretold the ultimate collapse of the Confederacy two years later, both those who supported and opposed Abraham Lincoln entered 1864 believing he would be a one-term president.

It wasn't just that no incumbent had been re-elected since the massively popular Andrew Jackson had done the trick in 1832, but more a sense that too many things had gone wrong for Lincoln—a war which seemed endless, an uneven economy, an unpopular draft—for the nation to reward him with another term in office.

On February 22, in a move that created a sensation within Republican circles, Kansas Senator Samuel Pomeroy released a letter calling on Republicans to throw Lincoln over in favor of Secretary of the Treasury Samuel Chase, who was not at all adverse to the idea, noting "even were the re-election of Mr. Lincoln desirable, it is particularly impossible given the influences which will oppose him." 1

Perhaps remembering how Franklin Pierce had lost the pivotal support of the *New York Herald*—in 1860 Lincoln wisely said the paper's publisher "can do us much harm if hostile"—the president had worked assiduously to keep the unpredictable James Gordon Bennett satisfied, only to see his powerful paper on the day Pomeroy's letter was made public, declare: "It gives evidence that a very large number of the leaders of the Republican party strongly endorses the argument of the *Herald* against the re-election of Mr. Lincoln." 2

The strange Republican assault on Lincoln drew on many things. Some party leaders harbored no grudge against the president personally, but simply believed he would prove a drag on other Republicans in the states in November, perhaps even wiping out the thin 14-seat majority the party maintained in the House. In this group were many who possessed an inaccurate understanding of the North's growing advantage in the war and the fact that since 1863 the Confederacy had largely been reduced to essentially defending ground, not taking it.

For those who believed Lincoln was a loser, matters were only made worse by the president's Emancipation Proclamation; an act that many professional politicians—including Pierce on the Democratic side—were convinced was a mistake not just because it threatened to exacerbate not-very dormant racial anxieties across the country, but also because it changed the essential mission of the war from one of deciding whether or not a state or group of states could secede from the nation to one of freeing slaves.

Was that really the cause that young Northern boys were willing to fight and die for?

So pessimistic were the Republican state leaders, said party insider Thurlow Weed to the president, that his re-election had become "an impossibility."

Writing to Secretary of State William Seward, whose unsuccessful campaign for the Republican nomination in 1860 he had managed, Weed said of Lincoln going down to defeat: "Nobody here doubts it, nor do I see anybody from other states who authorize the slightest hope of success." 3

Perhaps Lincoln himself, normally politically astute, believed it too. Although he wondered how the Democrats, divided as they were between their peace and war factions, could realistically unite around one candidate and platform, he seemed to feel that somehow or other he would not be returned to the White House in November.

"This morning, as for some days past, it seems exceedingly probable that this Administration will not be re-elected," Lincoln wrote to himself several days before the 1864 Democratic convention was set to convene. 4

Strangely, Lincoln then asked each member of his cabinet to endorse his musings—which ultimately amounted to a pledge supporting whoever won the presidential election—on the reverse side of the paper, sight unseen.

All along, Lincoln had assumed that the Democrats would nominate General George B. McClellan, whom he had relieved of command in late 1863. And for most of the year leading up to the Democratic convention, McClellan undoubtedly assumed the same thing, dabbling in party affairs just enough to keep Democratic chieftains happy, but not enough to diminish the "above-politics" sheen he needed to carry into the general battle against Lincoln in the fall.

For many Democrats, McClellan just felt right: although large segments of the party were dedicated to the proposition that the war was morally wrong and that the North should simply withdraw from it, many Democrats also believed that they could win if only they could convince voters that it was not a matter of being afraid to fight, it was just that they chose not to do so in this particular battle. More than ever, the country needed a "skillful military man of disinterested devotion," former president Millard Fillmore told McClellan's wife Mary Ellen. "I believe General McClellan to be that man and hence my desire to see him as president." 5

Although McClellan's assets were obvious—he was young, handsome, articulate and solidly within the mainstream of the kind of conservative Democratic thinking embodied by Fillmore, Pierce, and James Buchanan—some Democrats worried that the general's recent performance in the field might be used against him.

Only 34 when he was named general in chief of the Army, McClellan proved to be an organizational wizard, taking firm control of an Army that would soon include more than 100,000 men. But he moved at a pace entirely too slow for Lincoln who wanted more victories, earlier; and constantly prodded his young commander to action.

"Have you determined, as yet, upon the contemplated movement we last talked of?" Lincoln wired him on February 8, 1862. "You now have over one hundred thousand troops," he wrote to McClellan two months later. "I think you better break the enemies' line from Yorktown to Warwick River, at once." 6

"You remember my speaking to you of what I called your over-cautiousness," the president, in despair, wired five months after that, when McClellan still declined to attack Richmond. "Are you not over-cautious when you assume that you can not do what the enemy is constantly doing? Should you not claim to be at least his equal in prowess, and act upon the claim?" 7

It was inevitable that McClellan would soon make himself as unpopular in Congress, where Republican leaders were even more obsessed with the notion of a quick Yankee victory, as he had in the White House. Yet the devotion that Nathaniel Hawthorne recorded for the general among his men appeared to be never-ending, giving tribute to something his enemies were incapable of seeing.

"I have more confidence in him than any living man," a young cavalry officer reported to his parents in early 1862. George Armstrong Custer, who only admired men who were brave, added: "I am willing to forsake everything and follow him to the ends of the earth and would lay down my life for him if necessary." 8

Like Lincoln, McClellan's most knotty problems as a presidential candidate came from within his own party. Peace Democrats represented by the ever-crusading Clement Vallandigham and Ohio Representative George Pendleton, pushed through a platform at the Chicago convention that amounted to a call for an unconditional armistice.

It was a platform, in the middle of a war, that offended many: "If Mr. Jeff Davis had been platform-maker in the Chicago convention, he could not have treated himself more tenderly," Horace Greeley's *New York Tribune* said in condemnation. 9

And George McClellan agreed.

"If those fools ruin the country, I won't help them," McClellan bluntly said of the Peace Democrats to William C. Prime, editor of the *Journal of Commerce,* on August 10, three weeks before the Democrats officially nominated him. 10

His views would only harden after the nomination, particularly when the Democrats named Pendleton as his running mate.

In an unprecedented move, in officially accepting the nomination on September 4, McClellan also effectively disassociated himself from the platform. He was hardly for peace at any price, he had said repeatedly, and thought the war—albeit under a different commander-in-chief—could and should be won, later telling Ohio Democrat Samuel S. Cox: "I could not have run on the platform as everybody interpreted it in this part of the world without violating all of my antecedents—which I would not do for a thousand presidencies." 11

The opposition naturally rejoiced over the obvious division within Democratic ranks, with Republican Representative Carl Schurz of Wisconsin summing up the General's career as a study in "how not to say it" in politics vs. "how not to do it" in war. 12

But in reality, the 1864 election turned less on the divergent nuances within the Democratic party on the how the war should or should not be pursued and much more on the war itself, particularly after both Atlanta and Mobile fell to Union forces in September; massive Union victories that Seward, for one, was certain "knocked the bottom out of the Chicago nominations." 13

For Pierce, the campaign had turned into a depressing affair of missed opportunities to remove from the White House the dreaded Lincoln.

He had originally hoped that Joseph Holt, secretary of war under Buchanan, might be persuaded to run. But Holt was now firmly in the opposition's camp. Agreeing to serve as the first Judge Advocate under Lincoln, Holt in 1863 almost single-handedly led the prosecution against Vallandigham, making his name anathema to Democrats in general and Peace Democrats in particular.

After Holt, Pierce may have preferred Horatio Seymour, but the New York governor displayed only a marginal interest in the nomination, perhaps recognizing—as Pierce did not—that the momentum toward McClellan was too great to be stopped.

Now, seeing that the Union victories in Georgia and Alabama had given Lincoln a new lease on life, Pierce watched with bewilderment as some fellow Democrats decided to cross party lines and vote for the president. Among them was George B. Loring of Massachusetts who described McClellan's campaign as "uncertain, indecisive, and halting," and told Pierce he just could not bring himself to vote for the Democrat. 14

The Democratic defections and Lincoln's obvious momentum gave Pierce a sense of the coming defeat even before it happened: "What have we to do but observe the march of events thus far beyond the control of human wisdom and wait for returning reason and patriotism?" Pierce asked former president Millard Fillmore. 15

Meanwhile another correspondent, jurist William Beach Lawrence of New York, told Pierce that he had "presumed from the beginning that the Army vote would secure Mr. Lincoln a re-election." And in the end, Lawrence was right. Some 33,000 soldiers voted for McClellan. But 116,000, many providing the margin of victory in states where the election was close, backed Lincoln, including Custer, who, admiration for McClellan notwithstanding, could not stomach the Democratic platform: "To me it seems like madness to think of *proposing* an armistice particularly at the present time when success is everywhere attending our armies and the rebel conspiracy is about to crumble to pieces," he declared. 16

In the end, Lincoln's victory was crushing. Even though Pierce still remained the record champion, at 254, for the most electoral votes ever won in a presidential election, Lincoln nevertheless won 55 percent of the popular vote, and all but three of the 25 states participating in the election, including, by a whisker, Pierce's New Hampshire.

Democrats around the nation, astonished that somehow Lincoln had managed to pull it off, just wanted to put it all behind them. "It is fortunate both for himself and the Democratic party that he was not elected," Buchanan, who unlike Pierce had made a point of never criticizing Lincoln in public, now said of McClellan. 17

Pierce entered the new year with what he described as a "heavy cold and searing cough," watching what now seemed to be an inevitable Union march toward victory. By January, the federals were in control of both Georgia and Tennessee. Then came the startling, swift sweep of William Tecumseh Sherman through the

Carolinas, with Columbia, Charleston, and most tellingly, Fort Sumter, all falling by mid-February. 18

Seeing the run of things, people throughout the Confederacy were shortly asking Davis a simple question: "Will we hold Richmond?" Davis himself was no longer certain and to some seemed not only beaten down by events, but unworldly in his calm. "Your Mother and the children are well and are anxious to have you back," he wrote to his son Jeff in mid-March, just days after Union soldiers had pushed deep into North Carolina. 19

Two weeks later, with time now clearly running out, Davis pressed into Varina's hand a small Colt pistol for protection. But even now his thoughts were with the Confederacy. When Varina said she hoped to secret out of Richmond several barrels of flour to feed their family, Davis was adamant: "You can't take anything in the shape of food from here," he said flatly, "for the people need it." 20

As the news worsened for the South, Pierce announced to friends that he wanted to take a trip down the East coast, purpose of which went unsaid. Jessie Fremont, the wife of General John C. Fremont, was excited. Although she and her husband opposed Pierce on almost all things politically, she could never forget how the former president had invited her father to stay at the White House after his Washington home burned in 1855.

"Few men in power ever did a more selfless and chivalrous act than I know of Mr. Pierce's doing," Jessie later recalled. Now she invited the former president to attend a dinner she was planning for the Belgium minister in New York. At the same time, from Philadelphia, General Robert Patterson, an old Pierce friend, offered him his residence.

To all invitations, Pierce was non-committal. "It is uncertain in what direction my steps may be turned when summer comes again," he told Patterson. 21

But before Pierce could go anywhere, the Confederacy collapsed. On April 3, Davis and a small band of loyalists were forced to flee Richmond. The following day, Lincoln, exhibiting a characteristic disregard for his personal safety, arrived there, surveying buildings that had been burnt by the rebels as they left, and to the cheers of Union soldiers, sitting in Davis's chair when he stopped off at the Confederate's executive mansion.

All across the North spontaneous celebrations erupted, with the largest taking place in New York where one speaker repeatedly shouting his desire to see Davis "hung at his door post," was repeatedly cheered. 22

The mood in Concord was no different as bells rang throughout the day and flags almost magically were posted on every downtown building. From the historic Depot Square came a 100-gun salute.

By night, the celebration, as it did in other cities, took on an ominous hue. Hundreds of boys flooded onto the streets, armed with what a reporter for the *Concord Monitor* described as "snap crackers, horns and Roman Candles." They filled the air with noise and seemed somehow vaguely angry and threatening to some onlookers. 23

Caught up in the joy of the moment, but yet filled with a curious rage, they would be heard from again.

Ten days later the same teletypes that clacked the reports of the fall of the Confederacy clacked news that, in its totality, affected far more people in Concord, the North and throughout the country: Lincoln, while attending a light comedy at Ford's Theatre in Washington with his wife, was shot in the back of the head and now lay dying in a nearby residence.

In seconds, the news got even stranger: Seward had been brutally and repeatedly stabbed in a separate incident that same evening. Rumors quickly flew that a general coup was underway and that the lives of both vice-president Andrew Johnson and Ulysses S. Grant, commander of the Union army, had been threatened.

Throughout the Saturday afternoon of April 15 crowds in every major and small city in America gathered around the nearest telegraph office for the latest news, praying that Lincoln would live, and cursing Jefferson Davis and his Confederate allies, of whom so many were certain must have played a nefarious part in the assaults.

In Concord, Pierce quietly mingled with a crowd outside the Eagle Hotel before retreating to his house on the west side of Thorndike and Concord streets. There he was resting when it was announced that Lincoln had died.

He was, in the end, Pierce's most important and prominent opponent, the man whose presidency, responding to extraordinary events, governed extraordinarily. Pierce, as president, ruled in and drew security from a tradition defined by limitations where the chief executive often deferred to Congress, made sure every budget was balanced and never even thought of proposing a program without first making certain it passed constitutional muster.

Jacksonian to his core, he perhaps would have been incapable of assuming the unprecedented powers that Lincoln felt he needed in order to lead a troubled nation in the middle of a great war. But that assumption, bringing with it an assault on the constitution and the nation's cherished tradition of protecting civil liberties, was in many ways a riveting and exciting latter-day challenge for Franklin Pierce, giving him a new life as a public figure, and firing him with a kind of passion and implacable purpose that many thought had been missing from his years in the White House.

In a strange way, Abraham Lincoln was the best thing that had ever happened to Franklin Pierce.

And now the great Lincoln was dead. With him went not only an understandable conflict of emotions on the part of Pierce, but a gallantry of spirit marking a president whose only goal, he repeatedly told Southern secessionists as well as northern abolitionists, was to bring the country back together.

In Lincoln's wake something dark and forbidding swept over the country.

At Fort Jefferson, Florida, soldiers turned on one of their own who said he was glad Lincoln had been shot and hung him. "I honestly confess that I have *very* little *sympathy* for him or any man who is not punished for similar expressions," a fellow soldier remarked. 24

Enraged crowds seeking to avenge the president's murder ransacked the offices of the *San Francisco Union* and *San Francisco American*, both of which papers had been generally anti-administration. In Maryland, the editor of the *Westminister Democrat* was killed for unwisely running a column critical of the deceased president. 25.

In New York, Peter Britton, visiting from England, heard the news of Lincoln's death, got drunk, and judged his journey a success if it meant the president was gone. A New York policeman quickly arrested Britton, and had he not, said a reporter for the *New York Herald*, "he would have been severely punished and perhaps killed by a highly excitable crowd of persons who were collecting about him." 26

But in capture, Britton fared little better: a district judge sentenced him to six months in jail for inciting a riot, the same sentence he gave to at least two other men on the same day for the same thing.

Politicians who had been known to oppose Lincoln, or were simply prominent members of the opposition party, were suddenly suspect, in particular the nation's three surviving ex-presidents, all of whom were Democrats.

In Washington, journalist William Finn sent a quick note to Buchanan: "The streets and corners are thick with citizens expressing their wrath and vengeance upon the assassins." He then advised Buchanan to "write a few lines on the death of Mr. Lincoln, which will soothe the bitter extremists of the Lincoln party against you and your friends." Buchanan, sometimes maddeningly reticent, declined, but the fact that Finn thought such a statement was even needed spoke volumes. 27

In Buffalo, crowds began to wonder about Fillmore, noting that his house was devoid of both American flags and black bunting, all of a sudden that afternoon proof of loyalty to the country and tribute to Lincoln.

To think that Fillmore was anything less than a patriot was absurd. While he had gently criticized Lincoln, it had never gotten to the Pierce level. On the contrary, he had many times publicly expressed his support for the war, swinging his hat and leading the cheers in a pro-Union rally just hours after the fall of Fort Sumter, and later serving on a local committee for the promotion of defense.

But he was now bunched in with the opposition, an opposition that—or so it was thought on April 15, 1865—had done everything it could to hurt and destroy a beloved, martyred president. Who were these old men anyway, protested one letter writer to a Buffalo newspaper. If Pierce, Fillmore and Buchanan hated it so much in America, maybe they should move to Europe: "Let them leave a land which they no longer love and no longer loves them." 28

A local man named Paran Stevens only further reflected the new mood. Noting that he had once admired Fillmore enough to name his son after him, he now said the fact that the former president had failed to memorialize Lincoln by decorating his home in black made him want to find another name for his offspring.

Startled by the vituperation of his neighbors, Fillmore appeared at his front door and said that because he had been inside taking care of his invalid wife, he had not yet heard the news about Lincoln. Because many people in Buffalo knew Mrs. Fillmore was in fact a sick woman, the former president's explanation seemed to satisfy the crowd, but not enough to stop someone from heaving a pitcher of black ink onto the Fillmore porch.

In Concord, it was raining. By early evening a gathering composed of several dozen men was soon joined by hundreds of boys; undoubtedly many of the same boys who had seemed so menacing during the recent celebrations marking the end of the war.

Perhaps acting on their own, but more than likely encouraged by adults in Concord who hated Pierce, the boys walked en masse down the wet cobblestone streets yelling threats to the occupants of any home not bearing either an American flag or black bunting. Destination: the home of Franklin Pierce.

What began as a jeer—"Hang out a flag! Hang out a flag!"—soon turned into a menacing taunt, as onlookers watched in wonder and fear.

Now numbering more than 400, the boys gathered in front of the Pierce residence, forming an arc around the old mansion. Inside, Pierce had been resting in his study, but was alerted to the coming of the mob by a young boy who often did errands for him.

In the early evening darkness, came the demand: "Hang out a flag! Hang out a flag!"

Whatever Pierce thought at the moment, he quickly rose to his feet and peered outside as a young newsboy named Charles Nichols scurried onto the porch and rang the front door bell.

If the boys had expected to encounter a cowering figure, they were soon disappointed. Throwing open the doors of the house, his profile dramatically illuminated by the light cast from a single burner behind him, Pierce asked, in what may have seemed more like a demand: "What is your desire?"

The force of his words and military presence seemed to momentarily throw the boys, one of whom, rather meekly, said that they only wished to hear a speech by the former president.

James Lyford, a writer who many years later would compile an extensive history of Concord and as he did, would also listen to Nichols' recollection of the unreal night, later declared of Pierce's remarks: "Never were words more fitly spoken. Never was the charm of that persuasive voice more potent."

Recalling in another part of his narrative that Pierce as a lawyer had many times transfixed local jurors by what seemed his simple presence alone, Lyford added: "Never was that winning personality which had gotten so many victories more completely imparted to his hearers." 29

Pierce began quietly: "If your hearts are oppressed by events more calculated to awaken profound sorrow and regret than any which have hitherto occurred in our history, mine mingles its deepest regrets and sorrow with you."

He felt a personal sadness, he said, for Lincoln and Seward, as well as the "hearts and homes of the two most conspicuous families of the republic," and gave to them his complete sympathy, "as I am sure all persons within the hearing of my voice must do."

But he challenged the boys to remember that they, too, were citizens of the same republic, and as such must always be "obedient to law, revering the Constitution, holding fast to the Union...loving, with the devotion of true and faithful children, all that belongs to the advancement and glory of the nation..."

The boys fell into silence, not certain what to say or do next. But then a voice rose from the back of the crowd—was it an adult who hoped to see Pierce attacked?—reminding everyone of why they were there in the first place: "Where is your flag?"

Undeniably the question newly emboldened the boys. But now Pierce became angry, and his anger stunned his young listeners.

"It is not necessary for me to show my devotion to the stars and stripes by any special exhibition or upon the demand of any man or body of men," he replied bitterly.

He was 60 years old, and had endured the taunts and torments of his neighbors, colleagues, and one-time friends longer than anyone could remember. For almost a decade, since the calamitous end of his presidency, people had gone out of their way to hurt him, to try and make him angry, to make him think that somehow everything that had gone wrong in the country since then had happened because of him.

And now he stood on a wet night before a mob composed of boys old enough to know anger, but too young to understand much of anything else, and had to defend who he was—which for an incredible moment he was even willing to do, recalling his family's service to the country and his own in the Mexican-American war.

But then came the clincher: if, after all of this, "the question of my devotion to the flag, the Constitution and the union is in doubt, it is too late now to remove it by any such exhibition as the inquiry suggests."

"Besides, to remove such doubts from minds where they may have been cultivated by a spirit of domination and partisan rancor—if such a thing were possible—would be of no consequence to you and it certainly is none to me. The malicious questionings would return to reassert their supremacy and pursue their work of injustice."

His was more tired now than angry. And the boys may well have sensed his resignation.

"I have never felt or found that violence or passion was ultimately productive of beneficient results," Pierce added, almost to himself.

And then, taking the boys to a place where they in reality had not yet visited, he summed up: "It is gratifying to perceive your observation, briefer than mine, has led your minds to the same conclusion."

Suddenly what had been only a drizzle turned into a downpour. The boys, getting soaked, moved to leave. "I thank you for the silent attention with which you have listened to me," Pierce concluded, reminding them all that they remained his neighbors. 30

The boys, lost in purpose, then cheered the former president, before silently walking away.

Too many things were happening all at once for too many people to be concerned about what happened to Pierce in Concord on the night of April 15. The country was preoccupied with the coming funeral of Lincoln; who the new president, Andrew Johnson, was and what his program would be; and the hunt to capture Lincoln's assassin, now widely identified in the papers as the popular actor John Wilkes Booth.

But what happened in front of the Pierce home was not quickly forgotten by everyone. The *Concord Monitor* condemned what it described as a "boot-black brigade," of which the "great mass of our citizens did not identify themselves with," while the *New Hampshire Patriot* wondered about "the mob spirit that still exists here," which it was certain was "encouraged by men of influence and property." 31

A Pierce nephew, Charles Aiken, read of what happened to his uncle in the newspapers, and frankly admitted that he was "fearful that some fanatic or company of fanatics might have molested you."

But after reading an account of the speech Pierce gave to the boys, Aiken continued: "That you spoke so ably and strongly is like yourself. One could not expect anything else of you." 32

Stephen Healey, a long-time Pierce supporter from Brooklyn, wrote to laud Pierce for what he said was a "manly, patriotic, and dignified address." 33

But as comforting as such remarks may have been, Pierce remained troubled. He had been eagerly scouring the newspapers and listening to the speculations of friends concerning the whereabouts of Jefferson and Varina Davis, and the only things he knew for sure was that they had both left Richmond in the panic of the Confederacy's collapse and that seemingly the entire Union was now looking for them.

Even worse, Edwin Stanton, the secretary of war, was appointing commissioners who would be assigned to conduct the trial of those accused of conspiring to assassinate Lincoln, and among those named was Joseph Holt, who was convinced beyond a doubt that Davis was the principal inspiration behind the murder.

In a time when the loudest voices in the North were calling for Davis's head, Pierce would remain loyal to him, quietly determined to do everything and anything he could for his old friend. And if the people in Concord or anywhere else in the Davis-hating North were shocked or outraged by Pierce's sympathies, it was clear he didn't care.

CHAPTER EIGHT FOOTNOTES

1. "The Presidential Campaign," *New York Herald*, 22 February 1864, p. 5., col. 1.

2. James L. Crouthamel, *Bennett's New York Herald and the Rise of the Popular Press* (Syracuse: Syracuse University Press, 1989), 79, 138–54; "News from Washington," *New York Herald*, 22 February 1864, p. 4, col. 1.

3. Thurlow Weed to William Seward, 22 August 1864 Series One, General Correspondence, 1833–1916, Abraham Lincoln Papers.

4. Stephen W. Oates, *With Malice Towards None—The Life of Abraham Lincoln* (New York: New American Library, 1977), 429.

5. Harold M. Dudley, "The Election of 1864," *The Mississippi Valley Historical Review*, Volume XVII, June 1931 to March 1932, 506.

6. Roy P. Basler, *The Collected Works of Abraham Lincoln, V* (New Brunswick: Rutgers University Press, 1953), Abraham Lincoln to George B. McClellan, 8 February and 6 April, 1862; 130, 182.

7. Ibid., Abraham Lincoln to George B. McClellan, 13 October 1862, 460.

8. George A. Custer to Emmanuel and Maria Custer, 17 March 1862, Reel 2, Images 417–423, Elizabeth B. Custer Microfilm Collection, Monroe County Library System.

9. "The Union and Democratic Platforms Contrasted," *New York Semi-Weekly Tribune*, 6 September 1864, p. 8, col. 1.

10. Stephen W. Sears, *The Civil War Papers of George B. McClellan—Selected Correspondence, 1860–1865* (New York: Ticknor & Fields, 1989), George B. McClellan to William C. Prime, 10 August 1864, 586.

11. Ibid.; George B. McClellan to Samuel S. Cox, 15 September 1864, 598; see also Stephen W. Sears, "McClellan and the Peace Plank of 1864: A Reappraisal," *Civil War History*, Volume XXXVI, Number 1, March 1990, 57–64.

12. Carl Sandburg, *Abraham Lincoln—The War Years, Volume III* (New York: Harcourt and Brace, 1939), 258.

13. Ibid., 237.

14. George B. Loring to Franklin Pierce, 2 November 1864, Series 2, Reel 3, Franklin Pierce Papers.

15. Franklin Pierce to Millard Fillmore, 2 November 1864, Millard Fillmore Papers, Special Collections, Penfield Library, Oswego State University.

16. William Beach Lawrence to Franklin Pierce, 17 October 1864, Series 2, Reel 3, Franklin Pierce Papers; Jeffrey Wert, *The Controversial Life of George Armstrong Custer* (New York: Simon & Schuster, 1996), 179.

17. John Bassett Moore, *The Works of James Buchanan, Volume XI, 1860–1868* (New York: Antiquarian Press, 1960), James Buchanan to Nahum Capen, 28 December 1864, 378–79.

18. Franklin Pierce to Robert Patterson, 16 February 1865, Series 2, Reel 3, Franklin Pierce Papers.

19. Hudson Strode, *Jefferson Davis—Tragic Hero, The Last Twenty-Five Years, 1864–1889* (New York: Harcourt, Brace & World, 1964), 157.

20. Ibid., 161.

21. Jessie B. Fremont to Franklin Pierce, undated, but most probably early March 1865, Series 3, Reel 6; Franklin Pierce to Robert Patterson, 16 February 1865, Series 2, Reel 3, Franklin Pierce Papers; Pamela Herr and Mary Lee Spence, *The Letters of Jessie Benton Fremont* (Urbana: University of Illinois Press, 1993), Jessie Benton Fremont to Elizabeth Palmer Peabody, 20 March 1864.

22. Franklin Pierce to Robert Patterson, 16 February 1865, Series 2, Reel 3, Franklin Pierce Papers.

23. "The Glorious News," *New York Times*, 4 April 1865, p. 1, col. 6.

24. "Patriotic Demonstrations," *Concord Daily Monitor*, 11 April 1865, p. 2, col. 1.

25. Michael W. Kauffman, *American Brutus—John Wilkes Booth and the Lincoln Conspiracies* (New York: Random House, 2004), 236.

26. "Onslaught of Newspaper Offices," *New York Herald*, 20 April 1865, p. 3, col. 4; Lloyd Lewis, *Myths After Lincoln* (New York: The Press of the Readers Club, 1941), 58.

27. "Arrests by Police," *New York Herald*, 17 April 1865, p. 3, col. 2.

28. Moore, *The Works of James Buchanan*, Willam Flinn to James Buchanan, 15 April 1865, 381.

29. Robert J. Scarry, *Millard Fillmore* (Jefferson, North Carolina: McFarland & Company, 2001), 320–21, 400; "An Insult to an Ex-President," *New Orleans Bee*, 2 May 1865, p. 1, col. 2.

30. James O. Lyford, *History of Concord, New Hampshire, Volume II* (Concord: City of Conocrd, 1896), 1195–97; "Mob Demonstrations—Speech by Gen. Pierce," *New Hampshire Patriot*, 19 April 1865, p. 2, col. 4.

31. No title, *Concord Monitor*, 18 April 1865, p. 2, col. 2; "Mob Demonstrations—Speech by Gen. Pierce," *New Hampshire Patriot*.

32. Charles Aiken to Franklin Pierce, 18 April 1865, Series 2, Reel 3, Franklin Pierce Papers.

33. Stephen W. Healey to Franklin Pierce, 28 April 1865, Series 2, Reel #, Franklin Pierce Papers.

9

The Beloved Friend and Ever-Honored Chief

As soon as he learned of the attacks on Lincoln and Seward, Joseph Holt was convinced that somehow or other Jefferson Davis and other leaders of the Confederacy were involved.

And he quickly shared that view with the much-harassed Secretary of War, Edwin Stanton, who several hours after Lincoln's death said he was in possession of evidence showing that "these horrible crimes were committed in execution of a conspiracy deliberately planned and set on foot by rebels, under pretense of avenging the South and aiding the rebel cause." 1

It was understandable that Stanton would be reassured by Holt's conspiratorial visions.

Throughout the nightmarish evening of April 14 Stanton took virtual control of the federal government, holing up in the back room of the Petersen house, across the street from Ford's theatre, where Lincoln lay dying, bucking up vice-president Johnson, and almost single-handedly spearheading what would prove to be a massive search for the assailants of both Lincoln and Seward.

For hours he had tried to make sense of dozens of reports given to him by aides, the local police, the president's guard and eye witnesses from Ford's theatre, and finally was certain of only one thing: the famous actor John Wilkes Booth had shot Lincoln.

At 3:55 a.m. Stanton issued an order to Brigadier General W. A. Morris calling for the arrest of Booth, whom he now called "the murderer of President Lincoln." 2

Everything else in a sea of names, faces, and theories remained murky, especially the part about who else may have helped Booth.

But this was where Holt, almost naturally suspicious and obsessed with punishing the leaders of the Confederacy, stepped in, telling Stanton that he had evidence that Booth had conducted his deadly deed upon the orders of Jefferson Davis.

For Holt, the jump between the assassination and the Confederacy was easily made. During the preceding four years, he had come to detest the men of the Confederate leadership, whom he characterized in disgust as "Iscariots of the human race." 3

Surely, these were men who were capable of anything—upholding slavery, maintaining barbarous prison camps, and trying to destroy the United States of America. That they might also plot and act to assassinate Lincoln was, from Holt's view, perfectly in keeping with the general low character of their nature.

Outraged by the Southern secession, Holt had jumped into the thick of things as early as 1861 when he urged his fellow Kentuckians to remain loyal to the Union. If his voice could "reach every dwelling" of his native state, he said, he would implore his neighbors to "fly to the rescue of their country before it is everylastingly too late."

"Man should appeal to man, and neighborhood to neighborhood," continued Holt,"until the electric fires of patriotism shall flash from heart to heart in one unbroken current throughout the land."

Did the people of his state really understand the danger they faced? "The howl of the storm is in our ears and the lightning's red glare is painting hell on the sky," Holt added, sounding his own bugle call to battle. 4

Such passion only naturally brought Holt to the attention of Lincoln who desperately wanted to make certain that Kentucky did not join the Confederacy. A border state Democrat, the former secretary of war in the Buchanan administration, and a long-time friend of Franklin Pierce (although that friendship would be clearly strained by the war), Holt was symbolically powerful to Lincoln who very much liked the idea of making him a part of his administration. Creating the office of the judge advocate, the president also happily made Holt its first occupant.

In office, Holt quickly emerged as a crusader, a man greatly inclined to see things starkly in black and white, with no mitigating gray in between. He also maintained a flair for dramatic overstatement that colored nearly all of his wordy written decisions and was perhaps most conspicuously on display in 1864 when he submitted a report to Stanton on the largely non-existent Knights of the Golden Circle.

"Judea produced but one Judas Iscariot; and Rome, from the sinks of her demoralization, produced but one Cataline," Holt wrote in the introduction to his report. "And yet, as events prove, there has risen together in our land an entire brood of such traitors, all animated by the same parricidal spirit, and all struggling with the same relentless malignity for the dismemberment of our Union." 5

Unfortunately for those who ended up in Holt's courtroom, his actions in every way proved to be the equal of his words.

Responsible for reviewing the case records of all courts-martial, he did so with a stunning efficiency that saw him make final and oftentimes deadly decisions in more than 34,000 cases just between 1863 and 1865 alone, almost always affirming earlier convictions, even if it meant the execution of a Union soldier for desertion.

Holt's final words: "Application denied and sentence approved," would appear on the case files of thousands of soldiers who saw him as their last hope. Assigned to serve as the prosecutor before a tribunal drawn up to hear a court-martial case against General Fitz John Porter of New Hampshire, Holt would later be criticized not so much for the way he performed his duties before the body, but for the rather one-sided summation of the hearings that he sent to Lincoln. 6

But if critics thought Holt was too severe and unbending, it didn't really matter. He only had to please one person, and that person was the president. And Lincoln was very happy with him, particularly after suspending the writ of habeas corpus and giving to Holt the responsibility—for the first time in U.S. history—of conducting military trials for civilian political prisoners.

It was in this capacity that Holt oversaw the treason conviction of Pierce ally Clement Vallandigham as well as Indiana peace activist Lambdin P.Mulligan, who was sentenced to death; convictions that Lincoln himself reviewed and signed off on. 7

Thriving at the center of an intricate web of War Department agents and anonymous tippers, many of whom were certain the Confederate leadership was plotting to kill the president, even though there appeared to be little actual proof of it, Holt nonetheless on the morning after Lincoln's assassination thought he had enough evidence to link John Wilkes Booth with Jefferson Davis.

And by the last week of April he had shared his findings with Stanton, who may have also let what he wanted to believe color his otherwise unsympathetic judgment, prompting the Secretary of War to dramatically announce: "This department has information that the president's murder was organized in Canada and approved at Richmond." 8

One week later, on May 2, many things happened quickly. President Johnson told Stanton that if there was evidence of a conspiracy to kill Lincoln, he wanted the conspirators to be named and evidence of their guilt presented to him. Stanton, in turn, not certain about Johnson's intentions, quickly penned a note to Holt, asking for "a list of the persons," about whom "there is evidence of complicity or procurement in the murder of the late President."

"You will please furnish a report of the names to this Department this morning." Stanton added. 9

Hastily, Holt sent over to Stanton what he had, specifically naming Davis, Clement C. Clay, Jacob Thompson and three other Confederates as the men who were "in complicity with the assassins and their accomplices who committed the crimes referred to." 10

Stanton then had a proclamation drawn up calling for the conspirators' arrest and trial. The Secretary handed the paper to President Johnson, who saw that a reward of $100,000 was being offered for the capture of Davis, and after some hesitation, put his signature on it.

The problem was, of course, that no one was really sure where Davis was. Traveling with a small group of aides and troops by rail and finally on horseback in a generally southeastern direction, Davis had temporarily set up headquarters first in Danville and then Greensborough, North Carolina, before reuniting with Varina—who had left the chaos of Richmond ahead of him—in Dublin, Georgia.

Almost alone in his belief, Davis still harbored notions that somehow all was not lost for the Confederacy.

Finally, on May 10, Davis saw an approaching cavalryman and tried to quietly walk away from him in a dark forest at Irwinville, Georgia. But when the corporal from the Fourth Michigan Cavalry confronted him and indicated that he was about to be arrested, Davis resisted the urge to upend the soldier off his horse and instead agreed to go quietly. "God's will be done," Davis remarked, almost in a whisper. 11

Not until May 19, after a numbing journey on land and water, would Davis be certain of his destination. Transported to the steamer *William P. Clyde*, Davis watched as virtually all of the remaining friends still in his company were sent to other Union facilities until he and Clement Clay were nearly the only ones left.

Three days later, Davis and Clay were escorted to Fort Monroe, a forbidding fortification built during the War of 1812 that was now serving as a Union prison. Guided into a single damp cell, Davis was also immobilized by his Union guards when they clamped irons around his legs.

Almost instantly Varina Davis and Virginia Clay, the wife of Clement, began a vigorous campaign to lobby prominent men they knew would be sympathetic to their husbands' plight, and the name of Franklin Pierce was at, or very near, the top of their list.

Meanwhile Davis supporters began to craft what they hoped would be a formidable defense team. Not surprisingly, Davis himself had his own ideas: Dr. John Craven, the physician assigned to watch over Davis at Fort Monroe, heard him praise Pierce as a "public man who had studied constitutional law." In his diary, Craven thought that if it were up to Davis to select his own counsel, "Mr. Pierce would be one of those whose advice he would think the most reliable." 12

But friends of the Confederate president turned instead to Charles O'Conor, a prominent New York defense attorney who disdained politics and politicians even as he rose in political circles.

A man with a quiet wit, O'Conor had won the loyalty of the women of New York when he successfully represented the actress Catherine Sinclair in her divorce proceedings against her famous husband, the great Shakespearean Edwin Forrest. Winning five judgments in a row against Forrest, O'Conor later joked that his wins were defined by "the peculiar effect of compound interest." That same year O'Conor also served as a New York elector for Pierce, although the two men would eventually part over patronage issues in New York. 13

The Civil War, however, had a funny way of creating the most interesting bedfellows. By 1863, O'Conor, Pierce, and even Forrest were all Peace Democrats, making the selection of O'Conor as lead counsel for Davis almost a natural. 14

Representing Davis, however, would be no easy thing. Stanton initially prohibited any personal contact between O'Conor and his famous client, and even made it difficult for the attorney to correspond with Davis.

Undoubtedly annoyed, O'Conor reached out to Pierce, asking for his advice and help on the case. "I know not precisely what you saw in the papers, and therefore will briefly state the facts," O'Conor wrote to Pierce from New York on July 5, telling him that he had, indeed, agreed to represent Davis but that the government seemed determined to make his job more difficult by denying him access to Davis. "My application for a personal interview with him is deemed inadmissible at present," O'Conor reported. 15

On the same day that O'Conor wrote to Pierce, Holt presented to an ailing Johnson the sealed verdicts of the military court he had presided over in Washington trying seven men and one woman accused of co-conspiracy with Booth in the murder of Lincoln. All of the defendants were found guilty, with four sentenced to death by hanging.

Throughout Washington and across the country, efforts had been made to spare the life of one of the defendants, Mary Surratt, because she was a woman and the evidence against her was less than compelling. Senator James McDougall of California was one among many who urged Johnson to pardon Surratt: "Extend to her *your grace*. I presume you have done it. If you have not, then do it. It will be a noble Christian act—whatever the sin." 16

But far more important was a petition signed by a majority of the commissioners that had tried Surratt asking that she not be killed. Tragically for Surratt, Johnson never saw the petition, or so he later claimed. Holt, just as steadfastly, insisted that he had attached the petition to the official findings and sentences that he had personally carried to the White House.

Two days later, Surratt and three male co-conspirators were hung. What effect the swift sentences, and the sudden public distaste for the execution of Surratt, would have on the movement to try Davis was not immediately known. But the air was rife with speculation.

On July 18, O'Conor warned Pierce of what he called the "various and conflicting rumors" swirling around the Davis case, adding that he had not yet decided what tack he would take and was hesitant to proceed based upon "any opinion one might form as to what would be a proper course." 17

On his way to Saratoga Springs in central New York, O'Conor invited Pierce to join him, noting that he had recently learned the ex-president was ill. "Perhaps a few days spent in that region might have a beneficial effect on your own health," he suggested. 18

Pierce declined, even though he would be sick for most of the summer and well into the fall of 1865. Once again he was laid low by the bronchitis that had plagued him since he was young, a condition that was only made worse when he drank.

Yet Pierce remained busy. In September he set out to read all of Nathaniel Hawthorne's major works one more time, an exercise that once against left him in awe of his long-time friend, but also made more glaring the void in his life that had remained unfilled since Hawthorne had died.

"Have been more than ever impressed by the amazing intuition, the wonderful insight, and the peculiar power all his own," Pierce said of Hawthorne in a letter to their old Bowdoin classmate Horatio Bridge. 19

By then news of Pierce's illness had made the papers, causing concern. Samuel Cooper, the former adjutant general for the U.S. Army who had resigned in 1861 to serve as a senior general in the Confederate cause, sent him a quick note: "Do not be surprised at finding these few lines emanating from a 'so-called traitor.'

They are intended only to convey to you the honest sympathy in your recent illness." 20

George William Brown, former mayor of Baltimore who had himself been imprisoned on charges of treason during the Civil War, wrote to express his desire that Pierce would be "spared for many years of honor and usefulness."

"I believe that no one has a larger circle of warm personal friends than yourself," Brown continued, before candidly adding: "Your country, I know, does not now do you justice." 21

Feeling better, Pierce sought to reassure friends that he was, in fact, fine: "I suppose my condition was very critical at one stage of the disease," he told Bridge. "But the worst is now over. The disease is apparently mastered and within the last few days I have been gaining strength as rapidly, probably, as is desireable." 22

On December 2 it would be two years since Jane's death, and Pierce dreaded marking the date, asking Mary Aiken—Jane's sister—and her husband John to stay with him in Concord for the weekend. "I thought there would be a subdued satisfaction in having you and Mary with me, on, to me, the saddest of all anniversaries," he wrote to John Aiken on December 1.

But a sudden New England snowstorm, Pierce conceded, made such a visit unlikely. Perhaps he was taking about his heart when he told Aiken: "The clouds are dense, the morning very dark, and appearances seem to me to portend a storm of some duration." 23

Yet he was not, he insisted, low. On the contrary, Pierce had reason for renewed optimism: on Sunday, December 3, he was going to be baptized at St. Paul's Episcopal Church in downtown Concord, finally finding in religious faith a comfort that had eluded him his entire life, certainly since his days as president when the pastors of so many of the churches he visited wanted only to lecture him about the evils of slavery.

The rector of St. Paul's, the Reverend James Eames, appeared to be more concerned with Pierce's soul. After initially resisting Eames' overtures, Pierce gradually warmed to both his theology and the inviting idea of at long last finding a spiritual home.

"I have turned, I hope," Pierce told Aiken, "with a submission of spirit to Him who is 'the resurrection & the life.'" 24

Pierce's baptism, carried in the nation's religious press, delighted many. "It gladdened my heart, as it must the hearts of all Christians," James M. Mac-Donald, clergyman and Bibilical scholar in Princeton, New Jersey, told him. At

Fort Monroe, Davis, who had little reason for good cheer, received the news that Pierce had found religion, a visitor reported, with "sincere gratification." 25

If his new-found religion gave him solace, Pierce would need it as he continued his campaign to somehow free Davis, realizing that that release would more than likely be a matter of months and not days.

Pierce's friends thought Davis's cause—and, indeed, the cause of the Democratic party—would only be enhanced if Pierce returned in a prominent way to the national stage. As early as the month after Lincoln's assassination, Clement Vallandigham had urged Pierce to become more politically active. "The time has come for us to move and let us do it strongly & earnestly, at least where we are clear," Vallandigham had told the ex-president. Former New York Mayor Fernando Wood suggested the same thing, asking Pierce to "impart to this country your counsel and advise—the people have a right to know what are the views of our eminent statesmen." 26

James Guthrie, Pierce's former secretary of the treasury, wrote to warn that time would not wait for the Democrats, particularly as the Radical Republicans, who were becoming increasingly confrontational with President Johnson, "have consolidated their ranks in both Houses and are consolidating their party in all states." 27

But Pierce knew that he remained a controversial and divisive figure in many circles and could end up doing Davis more harm than good if he became too identified with the public effort to free the first and only Confederate president.

Besides, Pierce also knew that Davis's freedom could be most easily attained at the stroke of a pen if Johnson could be persuaded to simply drop the charges against Davis. The president had, in fact, told Varina he would probably grant a pardon if Davis would only apply for one. But Varina knew her husband would never make such an application for the simple reason that he remained convinced that he had done nothing for which he needed to be pardoned.

Pierce also knew that Johnson was under tremendous political pressure to do something about Davis. "He is no better than Booth," Massachusetts Senator Charles Sumner said of Davis in a private correspondence. "He is an assassin. The evidence against him seems to increase." 28

Other Radical Republicans in Congress said as much in public, revealing a passionate desire to see Davis imprisoned or killed. It was a theme that was also latched onto by lesser Republican officeholders who wrote to Johnson: "Hang the very worst of them," Albert Williams, Michigan's attorney general, said of the Confederate leadership, specifically mentioning Davis. 29

"New Jersey supports your administration, and loyal men call for the execution of Jeff Davis as the reward for his *treason*," William Lewis, a corporate attorney, and Henry Greene, a postmaster, wrote to Johnson. 30

"I think now that the immediate trials, conviction and execution of Jeff. Davis…would have the effect of restoring a hearty respect for the Government," suggested Alex N. Wilson, tax collector. 31

Pierce studied Johnson, trying to decipher the new president's views on a variety of issues, from releasing Davis from prison to welcoming the South back into the Union and granting black Americans the right to vote.

Pierce could even feel somewhat reassured recalling that Johnson had once regarded himself as the ex-president's supporter. In 1852 Johnson had campaigned for Pierce in Tennessee and angrily sought to slap down those who called Pierce's bravery into question.

"He spoke harshly of those accusing Gen. Pierce of cowardice by fainting," a correspondent for the *Nashville American* reported of one Johnson speech, "and gave his hearers to understand that in nine cases out of ten the accusers of Pierce had not the courage to volunteer in the Mexican war, so as to give themselves the opportunity of fainting." 32

After that election, Johnson grumbled that Pierce was associating with too many New Englanders, but he still could not help but admire the way Pierce ignored the Washington power establishment when it came to forming his own cabinet, keeping his own counsel as he went along. "A very good trait in an executive officer," Johnson thought. 33

Even as late as 1855, when Johnson was the governor of Tennessee, he gamely defended the Pierce administration and its patronage policies, policies that had not been particularly favorable to the one Southern state that had failed to vote for Pierce in 1852.

But during the Civil War, the two men had gone their own ways. Johnson, like Pierce, was a dedicated Union man. But unlike Pierce, he had no sympathy for the Confederacy, and detested Davis personally, whom he regarded as the sort of typical Southern aristocrat who had promoted secession and caused the war to begin in the first place.

Still, after all of this, Johnson and Pierce had much in common: they were both Jacksonian Democrats who grew misty talking of their association with the seventh president; they both abhorred the Radical Republicans who were now determined to punish the South at any costs; and both were generally wary of molding federal policy along the lines of black suffrage.

Pierce may have even felt that the abuse he had suffered for so long at the same hands that now threatened to strangle Johnson might make him a sympathetic figure from the perspective of the White House. And that may have been the case had it not been for a sensational speech delivered on the floor of the Senate on December 18 by Sumner, who had just finished reading a brief message delivered by Johnson on current conditions in the South.

Sumner had proven himself to be one of Pierce's most consistent foes during the historic Kansas-Nebraska debate of 1854. Although he was less personal in his remarks against then-President Pierce than many other Northern Republicans, Sumner's outrage could be heard throughout the Capital when he charged that Pierce had purposely downplayed violent conditions in Kansas.

Now, eleven years later, it was all coming back for Sumner as he read the machinations of another president and determined that Johnson was purposely ignoring violent conditions in the South.

"We have a message from the President which is like the whitewashing message of Franklin Pierce with regard to the enormities in Kansas," Sumner declared as he held a copy of Johnson's message in his hand. 34

That simple remark set off a two-day skirmish among Sumner's colleagues, particularly the Democratic members, who thought his remarks offensive. In the end, the Massachusetts senator denied that he had ever meant to insult anyone, but still he refused to retreat from his original statement, even to the point of once more comparing Johnson with Pierce and, again, rolling out the phrase "whitewashing." 35

The effect of Sumner's remarks was clear: to large segments of the 1865 Washington political establishment, memories of Franklin Pierce and his administration were memories of something bad; parallels to the man and his time always and perhaps forever made when someone else was found wanting.

If Sumner's remarks bothered Pierce, he did not say. But he was now more convinced than ever that not only were the Radical Republicans being unfair to Johnson, but that Johnson—in an almost impossible situation, trying to bring together a country still deeply divided—was proving himself to be a good president.

"You need no expression of the thanks, which my heart readily acknowledges, for your brave devotion to the Constitution and the Union and for the unanswered & unanswerable arguments with which you have dumbfounded the enemies of both," Pierce wrote to Johnson on April 13, 1866, in a brief note. 36

Pierce's allies were similarly impressed with the new president: "He is as firm as a rock, and right or wrong, cannot be easily moved," Robert McClelland,

Pierce's former secretary of the interior, told Pierce. "As to bullying him, it is out of the question." 37

But as much as Pierce yearned to see Johnson succeed, his first concern remained getting Jefferson Davis out of prison. In June he endorsed a letter sent to Johnson by O'Conor protesting the conditions at Fort Monroe, characterized by the New York attorney as "detrimental, and probably dangerous to his life." 38

One month later, former Mayor Brown of Baltimore visited Fort Monroe and reported to Pierce: "The long continual imprisonment and cruel treatment to which he has been subjected have told severely upon him. He is very thin and feeble and suffers from neuralgia and indigestion."

But Davis remained defiant, as convinced of his course as ever before. And on the subject of Franklin Pierce, this man with so many enemies talked warmly of his friend. He "spoke of you in terms of the greatest affection and respect and said he would have written to you if he wrote to anyone besides his immediate family," Brown continued. 39

In September, Pierce found himself drawn to the cause of yet one more man whom he felt had been badly served during the Civil War: General Porter, who was hoping to reverse the court-martial prosecuted by Holt and clear his name.

Circulating a petition to be endorsed by what he described as "persons of influence and prominence" asking Johnson to revoke Holt's verdict, Porter on September 15 wrote asking for Pierce's support. 40

The ex-president responded immediately. He had read the transcripts of the proceedings against Porter with what he described as "indignant regret," adding: "I thought then and I think now that upon the whole case you were entitled not only to an honorable acquittal but that you should have been thanked for your conduct."

He would do anything he could to help, Pierce vowed as he angrily wondered: "Is this great wrong to stand? Is such a sentence upon such testimony to pass down into history without reversal?"

"For the sake of justice, for the honor of our country," as well as for Porter's blemished name, Pierce added, "I hope not." 41

On September 21, an ecstatic Porter, particularly short of powerful friends at the moment, wrote Pierce back, saying he took "great pleasure in expressing my heart-felt acknowledgement for your generous assistance and kindly expressions of interest." 42 By the late spring of 1866, Pierce was pleased to see the government's resolve against Davis begin to crumble, even though Holt to the very end continued to make the case for trying Davis as a co-conspirator in Lincoln's murder. On April 17 Clement Clay, who, like Davis, had been charged with complicity in the assassination, was suddenly released; all charges against him just as swiftly dropped.

That same month the government in a huge blow to Holt announced it's intention to focus only on a treason case against Davis, dropping altogether any effort to connect Davis with John Wilkes Booth and the assassination.

In mid-summer, Dr. Craven published a sensational book entitled *The Prison Life of Jefferson Davis*, which detailed the oppressive conditions at Fort Monroe as well as the stoic manner in which Davis responded to those conditions.

Davis himself dismissed Craven's book as excessively melodramatic, sardonically labeling major portions of it as "fiction distorting fact." But there could be no doubt of it's impact. Readers in both the North and South expressed outrage over the treatment Davis received at the hands of his jailers and the government's ongoing prosecution of him, perhaps indicating that at the grass roots level, beyond the machinations of the Radical Republicans, the nation was beginning to move on. 43

In the now-growing crusade to free Davis came a powerful voice: Horace Greeley, the publisher of the *New York Tribune* and a long-time abolitionist. That no one in the government—with the obvious exception of a fuming Joseph Holt—seemed to know what to do with Davis was not lost on Greeley, who regarded that case as thoroughly muddled.

But on a higher plane, Greeley thought the release of Davis would be good for not only the South, but the North and the nation in general, a first and greatly significant "step toward a beneficent and perfect reconciliation." 44

Within the powerful New York press, Greeley was supported only by the pro-Pierce and pro-Johnson *New York World*, which condemned the "wanton and wicked torture of an invalid lying a helpless prisoner in the strongest fortress of the Union." 45

Several months later, in Baltimore, Varina Davis received a tip that a man named John W. Garrett, the president of the Baltimore & Ohio Railroad, was interested in seeing her husband released.

What made this news particularly important was that Garrett was also a close friend of Stanton, who had repeatedly insisted to Johnson that Davis should remain behind bars.

Meeting with Garrett, Varina was abrupt, telling him her husband was "slowly dying in prison." Could he really use his influence with Stanton to help? 46

Garrett promised to do what he could and several days later met with an ill Stanton at his Washington residence, pointedly telling his old friend that if Davis was to die in prison it would be the very worst thing that could happen from the perspective of Washington, making Davis a martyr to the entire South.

Garrett added that two other members of the president's cabinet were for releasing Davis, and that Johnson himself was ambiguous and only waiting for Stanton's approval in the matter. Either seeing the logic of Garret's argument, or weakened from his recent illness, Stanton finally agreed to approve Davis's release.

Upon hearing what had happened, Charles O'Conor in New York helped to arrange bail with the support of Greeley and several others, traveled down to Washington, and had a writ of habeas corpus sent to Richmond…

Pierce, meanwhile, was growing impatient. Whether or not Davis was released, Pierce knew, he would still face trial on the treason charge, set for May 11. And although he had great confidence in O'Conor's legal abilities, Pierce wanted to make certain that Davis got as much advice as possible. Moreover, he thought it important that such advice be delivered in person.

On May 8, Pierce arrived at Fort Monroe via steamer from Baltimore. For some reason he had failed to ask for President Johnson's permission to visit Davis. For a man almost obsessed with protocol, Pierce's failing was odd and may have simply reflected a desire not to bother the president any more than necessary, or perhaps more than likely a belief that he, of all people, would not need a pass to get into Fort Monroe.

After all, what guard would be brave enough to deny entry to a former president of the United States?

Pierce soon enough got his answer as he neared the front gates of the fort, only to be prevented from entering the structure by a soldier on guard duty. "In vain the ex-president expostulated," a wire reporter who happened to be on the scene observed with some astonishment. But still, "the sentinel refused him."

Undoubtedly put out, Pierce asked the guard to inform the commander at Fort Monroe, Brigadier General Henry S. Burton, that he wanted to see Davis and would be found waiting for an answer at the nearby Hygeia Hotel, a one-time popular haunt for both Confederate leaders and soldiers.

In the lobby of the hotel, Pierce found a place to sit and began to read the morning papers. Several minutes later the Reverend Charles Minnegerode, the rector of Davis's church in Richmond, was introduced to him.

A German immigrant and expert in Greek and Roman archaeology, Minnegerode regularly visited with Davis in prison, usually praying with him and offering communion. He had, in fact, done just that the day before and was anxious to talk to Pierce about his most recent visit.

Soon Pierce and Minnegerode fell into a warm conversation and decided to go outside.

"For more than an hour the two personages, with locked arms, walked up and down the wharf," the reporter noted, "creating considerable attention and interest among the crowd, which had gathered around the steamboat landing." 47

Those onlookers could only speculate: certainly the sudden and dramatic appearance of Franklin Pierce must have something to do with Fort Monroe's most famous prisoner? With rumors running rampant that Davis was on the verge of being released, maybe Pierce himself was here to escort his old friend to freedom?

Finally General Burton appeared. Without President Johnson's approval, but obviously unwilling to do battle with an ex-president, Burton told Pierce he could see Davis and then led him back to the fort.

Pierce, clutching at his side a small cloth bag which undoubtedly contained his written strategy for the Davis defense, saw the giant doors to Fort Monroe open before him.

Inside it was cool and dark. Burton led Pierce to a large room on the second floor of the fort where Davis, his military posture unbowed by the ravages of the past two years, warmly greeted the man he always called his "commander-in-chief."

Over the course of eight hours the two old friends talked. Pierce made a mental note of how thin and tired Davis looked. He had always been a slender and fit man, but now, for the first time, he seemed frail and old, his face partially hidden behind a thick white beard.

Davis, at the same time, sized up a man more gray and fleshy than the dashing, dark one he remembered, perhaps noticing how Pierce was struggling against the advance of a receding hairline to maintain his famous pompadour.

Both men were admittedly old before their time and had known more than their share of tragedies and defeat. Yet both were strangely resigned to the vicissitudes of life. Davis had long ago decided that he would calmly accept any card that was dealt to him by the courts, even if it meant death. .

Pierce, meanwhile, remained buoyant at heart, his optimism perhaps infectious as he declared that the government would never actually bring Davis into a courtroom because surely it knew that no jury in Richmond would ever return a guilty verdict against him.

And an acquittal, Pierce continued, would in essence prove that Davis had been correct all along—secession was legal and permitted, or at least not expressly forbidden, by the Constitution.

It went without saying that such an acquittal would also mean that Davis's imprisonment had been a gross miscarriage of justice. Was the federal government really ready to risk and lose so much?

Listening, Davis could only hope that Pierce was correct.

Besides contemplating a bad ending, Davis had also pondered what he would do if acquitted, telling Pierce that he had already promised Varina he would go directly to Canada where his older children were in school and he could escape, at least for awhile, the passions and memories of the Civil War.

Not until early evening did Pierce leave Fort Monroe. More than a dozen years ago, the people of Virginia had lustily cheered a banner fireworks display that spelled out the names of Franklin Pierce and Jefferson Davis in the night sky above the fort. Now all was quite and dark as Pierce caught a steamer that would return him to Baltimore. 48

Arriving back in Concord five days later, Pierce found a telegram announcing the news: the government, for now, was not pressing its case against Davis. It looked like Pierce had been right all along.

Represented by O'Conor and a battery of other lawyers, Davis appeared in the U.S. District Court in Richmond on May 13. Greeley and a group of other supporters put their signatures on a surety bond for $100,000, allowing Davis to walk out of the court room a free man to the great cheers of a large crowd that had gathered outside the building. 49

Pierce immediately penned a quick note to Varina: "I would not influence your husband with regard to his movements, but I am strongly impressed with the conviction that his state of health, if no other consideration, should settle the question of his remaining at the North during the summer months now at hand," Pierce wrote.

He was in the process of building a small cottage at Little Boar's Head and hoped the Davis family would feel free to stay there upon its completion in August. "The latter part of the month and the whole of September is unusually delightful there," Pierce added. "The place will be as quiet as could be desired—and I need not express to you how much pleasure I should find in trying to make everything agreeable to you." 50

It was a mark of Jefferson Davis's eternal affection for Pierce that he declined the invitation, undoubtedly certain that his presence in New Hampshire would only cause more grief for Pierce. But it was also yet another mark of Pierce's complete disregard for what his New England neighbors might think that he made the offer to Mr. and Mrs. Davis in the first place.

Jefferson Davis was truly Franklin Pierce's last great friend. Davis said as much when he arrived in Richmond for his court date and generally refused to talk to reporters about anything else: "He said little about his imprisonment, but spoke in terms of the warmest affection of Ex-President Franklin Pierce, who visited him on Thursday last," a reporter for the *New York Times* recorded. "He said there was no man living for whom he entertained a higher regard." 51

Now, alone once more in Concord, Pierce sorted through the mail and shortly came upon a small envelope bearing a Fort Monroe postmark. Opening it, Pierce read: "8 May 1867…this day made bright by a visit of my beloved friend and ever-honored chief."

In still-elegant handwriting, the note was signed: "Jefferson Davis. To Presdt. Franklin Pierce." 52

CHAPTER NINE FOOTNOTES

1. *The War of Rebellion—A Compilation of the Official Records of the Union and Confederate Armies* (Washington: Government Printing Office, 1894), Edwin M. Stanton to Charles Francis Adams, 15, April 1865, 784–85.

2. Michael W. Kauffman, *American Brutus—John Wilkes Booth and the Lincoln Conspiracies* (New York: Random House, 2004) 68.

3. William Hanchett, *The Lincoln Murder Conspiracies* (Urbana: University of Illinois Press, 1983), 62–63. For a balanced, yet critical, exploration of the role Holt played in tying Jefferson Davis to John Wilkes Booth, see Elizabeth D. Leonard, *Lincoln's Avengers—Justice, Revenge, and Reunion After the Civil War* (New York: W. W. Norton & Company, 2004).

4. "Major Holt Dead," *New York Times,* 2 August 1894, p. 9, col. 7.

5. John A. Logan, *The Great Conspiracy—It's Origins and History* New York: A. R. Hart & Company, 1886). The Holt report was entitled "Masked Treason Exposed" and was sent to Stanton on October 8, 1864. In his introduction, Holt likened the existence of groups like the Knights of the Golden Circle in the North to "the horrible criminality of a son stabbing the bosom of his own mother while impressing kisses on his cheeks." 778–79.

6. Almost every narrative of the Porter court-martial is critical of Holt, particularly for the official review of the court-martial tribunal's findings that he prepared. Among the most recent scholarship is Michael D. Haydock's "The Court-Martial of Fitz John Porter," *American History Magazine,* Volume XXXIII, Number 6, February 1999, 48–57. Haydock charges that Holt "sent a heavily slanted review of the case to President Lincoln," 52. In Curt Anders' *Injustice on Trial—Second Bull Run, General Fitz John Porter's Court-Martial, and the Schofield Board Investigation That Restored His Good Name* (Zionsville, Indiana: Guild Press, 2002), the author says that Holt "prepared a summary of the case that may have misled Lincoln, and he was active for years in resisting Porter's attempts to clear his reputation," 99.

7. Leonard, *Lincoln's Avengers*, 29.

8. "The Assassins," *New York Herald*, 24 April 1865, p. 4, col. 5; Seymour J.Frank, "The Conspiracy to Implicate the Confederate Leaders in Lincoln's

Assassination," *The Mississippi Valley Historical Review*, Volume 40, Number 4, March 1954, 629–32.

9. Edwin Stanton to Joseph Holt, 2 May 1865, Andrew Johnson Papers, Series 1, Reel 13.

10. Joseph Holt to Edwin Stanton, 2 May 1865, Andrew Johnson Papers, Series 1, Reel 13.

11. Hudson Strode, *Jefferson Davis—Tragic Hero; The Last Twenty-Five Years, 1864–1889* (New York: Harcourt, Brace & World, 1964), 221.

12. John Craven, *The Prison Life of Jefferson Davis* (Scituate, Massachusetts: DSI Digital Reproduction, 2001), 164–65.

13. "Death of Charles O'Conor," *New York Times* 18 May 1885, p. 5, col. 1; William Rounseville Alger, *Life of Edwin Forrest—The American Tragedian* (Philadelphia: J. B. Lippincott & Co., 1877), 489.

14. Edwin Forrest to James Lawson, 9 July 1863, Edwin Forrest Papers, Early Americana Collection, William L. Clements Library, University of Michigan.

15. Charles O'Conor to Franklin Pierce, 5 July 1865, Franklin Pierce Papers, Series 2, Reel 3.

16. James A. McDougall to Andrew Johnson, 6 July 1865, Andrew Johnson Papers, Series 1, Reel 16. Historians would never be able to agree over who was telling the truth in the matter of the "lost" document recommending clemency for Surratt: Holt or Johnson. But as Holt had a history of manipulating evidence, and Johnson—whatever his other faults—was generally known for being honest, perhaps too much so for his own good, it would seem that the Judge Advocate probably had more to answer for in the matter.

17. Charles O'Conor to Franklin Pierce, 18 July 1865, Franklin Pierce Papers, Series 2, Reel 3.

18. Ibid.

19. Franklin Pierce to Horatio Bridge, 27 November 1865, Horatio Bridge Papers, Bowdoin College Library.

20. Samuel Cooper to Franklin Pierce, 2 December 1865, Franklin Pierce Papers, Series 2, Reel 3.

21. George William Brown to Franklin Pierce, 10 January 1866, Franklin Pierce Papers, Series 2, Reel 3.

22. Franklin Pierce to Horatio Bridge, 27 November 1865, Horatio Bridge Papers, Bowdoin College Library.

23. Franklin Pierce to John Aiken, 1 December 1865, Franklin Pierce Papers, Series 4, Reel 6.

24. Ibid.

25. James MacDonald to Franklin Pierce, 20 March 1866, Franklin Pierce Papers, Series 2, Reel 3; Felicity Allen, *Jefferson Davis—Unconquerable Heart* (Columbia: University of Missouri Press, 1991), 481.

26. Clement Vallandigham to Franklin Pierce 20 May 1865, Franklin Pierce Papers, Series 3, Reel 6; Fernando Wood to Franklin Pierce, 26 March 1866, Franklin Pierce Papers, Series 2, Reel 3.

27. James Guthrie to Franklin Pierce, 2 February 1866, Franklin Pierce Papers, Series 2, Reel 3.

28. Beverly Wilson Palmer, *The Selected Letters of Charles Sumner, Volume Two* (Boston: Northeastern University Press, 1990), Charles Sumner to John Bright, 5 June 1865, 303–04.

29. Albert Williams to Andrew Johnson, 21 April 1865, Andrew Johnson Papers, Series 1, Reel 13.

30. William A. Lewis and Henry A. Greene to Andrew Johnson, 8 November 1865, Andrew Johnson Papers, Series 1, Reel 19.

31. Alexander N. Wilson to Andrew Johnson, 25 November 1865, Andrew Johnson Papers, Series 1, Reel 19.

32. Leroy P. Graf, *The Papers of Andrew Johnson, Volume 2, 1852–1857* (Knoxville: University of Tennessee Press, 1970), 86–88.

33. Ibid.; Andrew Johnson to Blackston McDannel, 1 December 1852, 90–91.

34. *Congressional Globe, Debates and Proceedings, 39th Congress* (Washington: Congressional Globe Office, 1866), 78–80; *Charles Sumner—His Complete Works, Volume XIII* (Boston: Lee and Sheppard, 1900), 47–55.

35. *Congressional Globe, Debates and Proceedings, 39th Congress*, 78–80.

36. Franklin Pierce to Andrew Johnson, 13 April 1866, Andrew Johnson Papers, Series 1, Reel 22.

37. Robert McClelland to Franklin Pierce, 5 August 1866, Franklin Pierce Papers, Series 2, Reel 3.

38. Paul H. Bergeron, *The Papers of Andrew Johnson, Volume 10, February-July 1866* (Knoxville: University of Tennessee Press, 1992), Charles O'Conor and Thomas G. Pratt to Andrew Johnson, 13 June 1866, 583–84.

39. George William Brown to Franklin Pierce, 14 July 1866, Franklin Pierce Papers, Series 2, Reel 3.

40. Fitz John Porter to Franklin Pierce, 15 September 1866, Franklin Pierce Papers, Series 2, Reel 3.

41. Franklin Pierce to Fitz John Porter, 18 September 1866, Andrew Johnson Papers, Series 1, Reel 24.

42. Fitz John Porter to Franklin Pierce, 21 September 1866, Franklin Pierce Papers, Series 2, Reel 3. Despite his efforts, Porter would not see his name cleared until 1879 when an army review board judged him totally blameless for his actions at Second Bull Run. In 1886, President Grover Cleveland restored Porter to the regular rank of colonel.

43. For more on Dr. Craven's *Prison Life of Jefferson Davis* and Davis's response to it, see Edward C. Eckert, *Fiction Distorting Fact: The Prison Life* (Macon: Mercer University Press, 1987).

44. Glyndon G. Van Deusen, *Horace Greeley—Nineteenth-Century Crusader* (New York: Hill and Wang, 1964), 353; "Mr. Greeley and Jeff. Davis," *New York Times*, 13 August 1866, p. 8, col. 4; "Why Mr. Chase Does Not Want to Try Mr. Davis," *Richmond Dispatch*, 15 May 1866, p. 2, col. 1.

45. *The War of Rebellion*, 915–17.

46. Strode, *Jefferson Davis—Tragic Hero, The Last Twenty-Five Years, 1864–1889*, 304.

47. "The Visit of Ex-President Pierce to Jefferson Davis," *Richmond Dispatch*, 13 May 1867, p. 3, col. 2.

48. Virginia Clay-Clopton, *A Belle of the Fifties—Memoirs of Mrs. Clay of Alabama* (Tuscaloosa: University of Alabama Press, 1999), 68.

49. Upon Davis's release, William Lloyd Garrison's *National Anti-Slavery Standard* came to the same conclusion that Pierce had arrived at, though from an entirely different perspective, when it noted: "The government cannot afford to try him; for if the indictment fail, or the verdict be in his favor, then the rebellion was not a crime." But that did not stop the paper from taking one last shot at Pierce: "And so, amid the men that were his [Davis's] advisers and supporters during the rebellion, with his cunning talents stirring up mischief henceforward, with all the lackeys of the North, with Franklin Pierce at their head and Horace Greeley at the tail, paying court to his person, he will live unmolested," "Exit the 'State Prisoner,'" *National Anti-Slavery Standard*," 1 June 1867, p. 1, col. 4.

50. Robert McElroy, *Jefferson Davis—The Unreal and the Real* (New York: Harper & Brothers Publishers, 1937), 591–92.

51. "To the Associated Press," *New York Times,* 12 May 1867, p. 5, col. 2.

52. Jefferson Davis to Franklin Pierce, 8 May 1867, Franklin Pierce Papers, Series 3, Reel 6.

10

Opinions Honestly Entertained and Firmly Supported

When Franklin Pierce pledged his support to the cashiered General Fitz John Porter, he expressed confidence that President Johnson would do the same thing by clearing Porter of all wrong-doing.

"I believe it will be his pleasure to correct the grevious error and right the wrong," Pierce predicted. But that correction would only come, the ex-president had earlier warned, if Johnson could find the time to review Porter's case "in the midst of his multiple and multiplying labors." 1

With a sense of the president's workload that could only be fully appreciated by one who had already been there, Pierce knew that Johnson by the fall of 1866 was a besieged man. The Radical Republican opposition would be greatly bolstered by gains in the mid-term elections seeing them replace mostly conservative fellow Republicans who had been less inclined towards confrontation with the president.

Their numbers, in fact, would become so great and their confidence so unwavering, that they even envisioned a fundamental shifting in the constitutional separation of powers in favor of Congress, enough so to make an extremely unwilling Johnson—or so the Radical Republicans hoped—submissive to their demands. "No government official, from the President and Chief Justice down, can do any act which is not prescribed and directed by legislative power," an exultant Thaddeus Stevens, Radical Republican House leader from Pennsylvania, declared in the election's wake. 2

Throughout the coming year, relations between the president and Congress would become alarmingly vitriolic: In January 1867 Johnson vetoed a bill granting the vote to the black residents of the District of Columbia, arguing that such matters could only be determined at the state and local level. In response, Congress quickly overrode the veto.

Just weeks later, the Radical Republicans triumphantly passed the first of a series of hallmark legislation called the First Reconstruction Act which divided nearly all of the South into a series of military districts, a bill that Johnson, astonished, characterized as "absolute despotism" and vetoed in late February. On March 2, Congress overrode this veto too. 3

Finally, as spring dawned in Washington, the Radical Republicans at long last moved to chip away at the president's actual power, passing the Army Appropriations Act, which included a provision stating that Ulysses S. Grant could not be assigned duty outside of Washington without his agreement—a move designed to prevent Johnson from using the popular general, or so it was said, for his own political purposes.

Then, in an act inspired by Secretary of War Edwin Stanton, who was convinced that Johnson wanted to fire him, Congress—with Stevens' prodding—passed the Tenure of Office Act. The legislation denied the president the power to remove anyone from office whose appointment may have been originally approved by Congress. Johnson only naturally vetoed this legislation as well, with Congress, now almost sensationally, voting to override.

More legislation, more vetoes, more overrides: not since Pierce's last year in office had the atmosphere between the two branches of government been as poisoned.

In the context of the moment what happened next was almost inevitable: Stanton, in a cabinet meeting, in a manner that the president found offensive, told Johnson that the new military governors in the South were answerable only to Congress and not the president. Johnson, just then also learning that Joseph Holt had kept from him the petition of clemency to save Mary Surratt's life, sent a quick note to Stanton in response: "Public considerations of a high character constrain me to say that your resignation as Secretary of War will be accepted." 4

Even more remarkable, Stanton refused to go, ushering in a series of complicated maneuvers between the president and the secretary. In Congress, the cries for Johnson's impeachment were deafening: "I'll take that man's record—his speeches and his acts, before any impartial jury you can get together," an obviously excited Stevens declared, "and I'll make them pronounce him either a knave or a fool, without the least trouble." 5

Old Pierce foes were ready to act: "It is a great calamity that A. J. was not impeached a year ago," Charles Sumner of Massachusetts declared. Zachariah Chandler of Michigan, who had tried to connect Pierce with the Knights of the Golden Circle in 1862, wanted to see Johnson impeached, convicted and removed from office too—he only hoped that it was done quickly. 6

But just then the voters sent an unexpected message of support for Johnson with a series of Democratic wins in elections held in Vermont, Pennsylvania, Ohio, Montana, and California, among other places. For Pierce, the elections, nearly none of which decided major races, were hugely significant, a sign that the voters were at long last coming to their senses and throwing off the Lincoln Republicans who had governed the nation since 1860.

And he said as much in a rambling election night address in Concord: "It has been so long your part and mine, my friends and neighbors," Pierce began, "to breast and smile back defiance at what we have believed to be the torrent of evil, that one hardly knows how to receive notes of triumph."

But Pierce would try, hailing Vermont as "Mantagne Verde," Montana as "far-off Montana...over the mountains...'Wave Munich, all thy banners wave,'" and California, "booming over cape and ocean to assure us that the Pacific has recovered its feet." 7

If Pierce was drinking again, he could be excused for celebrating even the most minor Democratic victories in what clearly had seemed to be a Republican era. But his speech only opened him to ridicule with the *New York Times* wondering "what claims Montana has upon Munich," and "what cape and what ocean California boomed over."

"It seems that the object of this booming was to 'assure us that the Pacific has recovered its feet,'" the paper went on. "We hasten to congratulate that venerable body of water on the achievement." 8

Far more effective, in early January 1868, was an address Pierce wrote for the annual celebration of the Battle of New Orleans, a celebration that provided Democrats with a chance to not only pay tribute to Andrew Jackson, but also to air their grievances against the Radical Republicans and the effort to remove Johnson from the White House.

Meeting at the elegant Metropolitan Hotel in New York with Johnson sitting prominently at a dais overlooking some 300 people, the Democrats listened as a letter written by Pierce was read to the energetic gathering, convening during the same week that the Radical Republicans had voted to reject Johnson's dismissal of Stanton.

"No one can sit at your banquet table without contrasting with painful emotions the condition of our country now with what it was during the eight years that the great defender of the Crescent City was at the head of the government," Pierce declared.

The condition that induced those painful memories, Pierce said, was obviously created by the Radical Republicans—although he did not mention them by name—forcing a "humiliating reign of absolutism," in Jackson's Tennessee as well as throughout the entire South.

But still glowing from the Democratic victories of the previous fall, Pierce encouraged his listeners to be brave, noting: "There are, it seems to me, marked and sheering indications that the people are rising in their majesty with united strength to deliver from misrule their country and themselves." 9

That deliverance, however, did not apparently extend to New Hampshire which voted in support of a Radical Republican slate in March. Gideon Welles, a Lincoln Republican now serving as Secretary of the Navy, was particularly delighted, figuring that the Republican victory meant that Pierce's long-time but waning influence in his state was finally at an end.

Calling Pierce a "vain, showy and plaint man," Welles confided to his diary on March 11 a conviction that Pierce "by his errors and weakness" had destroyed the modern Democratic party, undoubtedly for many years to come. "How could such a man and his associates impart strength and vigor to any party anywhere?" 10

As Welles wrote his remarks, the fifty-four members of the 1868 Senate were meeting to consider eleven articles of impeachment that had been passed under Stevens' relentless prodding in the House. Despite the atmosphere of anger and the fact that those who detested the president seemed to occupy most of the air, the Radical Republicans knew it might be close: 36 votes were needed for conviction and all twelve of the Senate's Democrats were already pledged to acquit.

That meant that only six senators would determine Johnson's fate, and one of them, James W. Grimes of Iowa, who disagreed with the president on most things, had already declared his intention to vote for acquittal, worried that if the Radical Republicans, "with their revolutionary and repudiating ideas," became ascendant, "the government would not last 12 mos." 11

For his effort, Grimes was instantly vilified by his fellow Republicans. Near the end of the trial, he suffered a paralyzing stroke and had to be carried to his seat. Yet he insisted on standing on his own when it came time to vote and in a clear voice cried out "Not guilty."

That vote, along with the ballots of six other Republican dissidents who either felt that the case against Johnson had not been made or that his impeachment was a dangerous folly, saved the day for the president.

But despite Johnson's dramatic triumph, many Democrats felt he was a ruined man politically and began to search around for another nominee for the summer convention. Johnson, naturally, was bewildered, wondering "Why should they not take me up?" 12

Even Pierce was doubtful. In April Democratic insider C. W. Wooley wrote to ask the ex-president's thoughts on the coming convention, receiving a letter from Pierce several days later in which he said he had heard good things about George H. Pendleton's "ability, attainments and true manhood." 13

That Pierce was passing along such positive reviews about the 1864 vice-presidential nominee reflected how much his thinking had changed as a result of the Civil War. Before, he was primarily a conservative Jackson Democrat, suspicious of passion and idealism in politics. Now, like Pendleton, he was firmly committed to the party's peace wing, even three years after the war between the states had ended.

And that designation did little to dampen the enthusiasms of those who continued to devote themselves to Pierce. In May he was feted by the incoming governor of Connecticut, James E. English, also a Pendleton supporter. Two months later, the *Norfolk Journal*, in an article that was reprinted in the New York press, lauded Pierce as not only "one of the soundest Democrats in the country," but "one of the best men."

"The affection evinced toward him by his friends has been remarkable and this has been without regard to party," the paper continued, "for all know him to be an honest man."

Concluding, the *Journal* added: "May so noble and true a man long be spared to his state, the Union and his friends, of whom he has legions in the South." 14

As the Democrats prepared to convene in New York, a Johnson supporter, William W. Warden, candidly warned the president that he was well short of the two-thirds needed for nomination, but added that Johnson was, at least, "the second choice of more delegates than any other." 15

Warden was also frank about the Democrats' chances for success in the fall, noting that the party no longer seemed to be an incubator of new ideas.

Ultimately rejecting both Johnson and Pendleton, as well as Pierce, who received exactly one vote from the convention floor, the Democrats nominated the extremely reluctant Horatio Seymour, former governor of New York.

But party enthusiasm was at a low ebb. The Republicans in May had nominated the widely popular Grant for president, almost guaranteeing a sweeping win in November.

And as they entered the fall race, many Republicans determined that simply having Grant as their standard-bearer was not enough. They needed to remind the voters of how the Democrats acted and thought leading up to the Civil War. Accordingly, Henry Wilson, Republican senator from Massachusetts and national party leader, told a huge gathering in Maine, as the fall campaign was launched, that Jefferson Davis "held the written assurance of ex-president Pierce, who believed that the disruption of the Union would not occur without blood…Did not this assurance of Franklin Pierce, that the fighting would be in our streets, between our citizens, give aid and comfort to the rebel president?" 16

Raw meat indeed. But it was not the way Grant, who never had anything bad to say about Pierce, intended to run his campaign.

In return, Pierce refrained from campaigning very much against Grant. And after the General's predicted landslide win became a reality, Pierce even told Horatio Bridge that he indulged a "pretty decided hope that Gen. Grant will exert his best powers to bring our country back to cordial Union, reduce the public debt and make integrity and economy the general rule, instead of the exception." 17

As Pierce wrote his letter to Bridge, sensational news was heard from Richmond: the government's case against Jefferson Davis charging him with treason had imploded. In one of his last acts as president, Johnson had issued a proclamation of general amnesty for all the leaders of the now-deceased Confederacy.

From Pierce's perspective, the Civil War was now at long last over; Davis was free and soon would be returning to the South a hero; while Grant, sworn in on March 4, called for a new era of national harmony and unity devoid of any measures to punish the South, but made distinct by legislation to establish the "security of person, property, and free religious and politician opinion in every part of our common country." 18

Grant said nothing about the continued presence of Northern troops and administrators in the Reconstruction South, but it was clear to anyone south of the Mason-Dixon line who read his words that he did not harbor a grudge against the old Confederacy and was far removed, in terms of his emotional outlook, from the revenge attitudes of Sumner, Chandler and Stevens.

What very much appeared to be a softening of regional tensions under Grant should have made Pierce, in the spring of 1869, a happy man, and to a certain extent it did. But something continued to nag him, a disquieting sense that somehow he was no longer a part of the country, or that the country he so deeply loved had simply left him behind.

He had been accused of treason enough times to know that many people thought he really was guilty of the charge; that he was somehow *against* the United States, and a patriot only for the other side, which in the Civil War meant the Confederacy.

And even worse, when those same people talked about his time in the White House, they did so in a manner that suggested it was an era shrouded in shame, and that Pierce as commander-in-chief had inflicted a wound on the nation for which he should never be forgiven.

Somehow, Pierce wanted to have the last word, even if no one was listening, and regarded an invitation to speak before the Society of the Cincinnati in Baltimore on May 19 as his best and perhaps even last opportunity to do so.

Meeting at Barnum's Hotel, from which he and Jefferson Davis once spoke to the cheering masses by balcony, Pierce wore a gold badge with an image of an eagle on one side and a field of diamonds on the other—the official insignia of the Society.

In the great parlor of the old hotel, he encountered other members of the Society from across the country, including the new Secretary of State Hamilton Fish, who invited him to the White House.

But Pierce was incapable of flaunting the principles of protocol: ex-presidents should never be in Washington unless they had a public-spirited reason to do so. Having none, Pierce politely declined the Fish invitation.

The Society on this evening was dominated by men with impressive titles: generals, colonels, commodores and reverends. Pierce had known some of the men for years. Others he had never met before now.

Rising in the grand ballroom of the hotel, a hall made distinctive by its thick drapes and impressive chandeliers, Pierce began his address with the usual pleasantries, paying tribute to the legends of Baltimore, which included John Eager Howard, a colonel in the Revolutionary War, of whom George Washington, Pierce noted, was once asked: "Have you not noticed that Colonel Howard is sometimes rather late with his regiment in the fight?"

That question, Pierce reminded his audience, inspired a classic response from the Father of the Country, who asked in return: "Have you not always observed that he is the last out of it?"

During the Civil War, Pierce continued, the Howard family still served their country. Only this time, the Colonel's grandson, Frank Key Howard, the editor of the *Baltimore Exchange*, ran afoul of federal authorities for criticizing the Lincoln administration and spent more than a year at Fort Lafayette, "a prison house," said Pierce, "in which to incarcerate for months, without trial and in flagrant violation of all laws, the descendent of the man who always remained upon the field to see the last blow struck."

This was what Abraham Lincoln, with his incessant domestic arrests, had wrought, and Franklin Pierce would go to his grave convinced that it had all been wrong, and that he had been forever right to fight it: "If the Howards were disloyal, I was disloyal, too," Pierce declared, "though I do not believe that I ever saw a day when I would not have made any possible sacrifice to maintain the constitution and the Union based upon it."

"The opinions or perhaps it would be better to say, the convictions, which have controlled me, may have been matters neither of merit or demerit," Pierce continued, telling his audience that what he did, he did because it was, for him, almost instinctual.

Then he added a sentence that could have, in the end, served as an epitaph for his entire career, but most certainly for his years as a lone voice of dissent in Lincoln's America: "Some men are so constituted," Pierce said, "that they do not incline to bow before a storm." 19

Pierce returned to New Hampshire a tired man. In the fall of 1868 he had been seriously ill and surprised that he no longer seemed to possess the energy that he had called his own his entire life. "I do not spring up readily from my serious illness," Pierce told Bridge, before adding: "Does it ever occur to you, Bridge, that we are rightly classed among the old men now?" 20

Resting at his cottage during the summer of 1869, he was visited by friends, particularly the members of his old, mysterious network: people in legal trouble, former Confederates, and controversial Peace Democrats. The summer before, even Senator Grimes, one of the handful of men who had prevented Johnson from being removed from office, stopped in. Although he was in failing health himself, Pierce could not do enough for Grimes, prompting Elizabeth, the Senator's wife, to marvel over the ex-president's "many attentions & constant kindness." 21

Now, a year later, Pierce was staring at the sea when Bridge came by and noticed that Pierce was "too weak to leave his bad," and "was sadly emaciated."

But when it came time for Bridge to leave, he later recalled, Pierce "raised himself from his pillow and embraced me like a brother." 22

By September, Pierce was back in Concord and attended to by his family physician, Dr. Charles P. Gage, who determined that he was suffering from what he called "abdominal dropsy." When, by the end of the month, Pierce was no longer responding to medication, Dr. Gage knew the life expectancy of his famous patient could be measured in days instead of months.

Yet even towards the end, Pierce would rally: "He talked freely of the public men with whom he had been associated in political life," Dr. Gage would soon recall, "and spoke freely of his former Cabinet members," as well as the many others he had known in his life.

The names would come and go, but surely his memories of Nathaniel Hawthorne and Jefferson Davis were predominant to the end. Yet, there were so many others: Andrew Jackson, Henry Wadsworth Longfellow, Abraham Lincoln, even Ralph Waldo Emerson. It had been a life rich in legendary personalities and events.

Finally, near sunrise on the morning of October 8, Franklin Pierce died, "as calmly and as sweetly as a child would sink to its rest," thought Dr. Gage. 23

Pierce's death presented Concord with a dilemma: how to honor their most important resident, a man so many of the best people of the city despised?

The challenge was met when members of the local bar took over the active arrangements of the funeral. Lying in state in an open casket decorated with a large American flag, Pierce's remains would be seen by hundreds before he was buried three days later.

Reluctantly, Concord ceased commerce, if only for a few hours, to pay Pierce tribute. In Boston, a city where he had few friends, bells tolled. In Baltimore, flags waved at half-mast. In New York, a 21-gun salute was fired from the Naval Yard in Brooklyn and Fort Hamilton. In Washington, the Supreme Court suspended its work, undoubtedly taking its cue from President Grant who issued a statement calling Pierce one of his "honored predecessors."

"Eminent in the public councils and universally beloved in private life, his death will be mourned with a sorrow befitting the loss which the country sustains by his decease," Grant added. 24

The tributes may have been more heartfelt inside the Old Confederacy: "He was strongly suspected of sympathizing with the southern people," recalled the *Richmond Dispatch* and for that was "harshly judged by the Northern people." At the executive mansion in Richmond once used by Jefferson Davis, as well as all of the city's public facilities, flags were lowered for Pierce. In New Orleans, the busy downtown Custom House, the home to so many former Confederate leaders who were now confining their activities to making money, closed its doors. 25

Davis himself, just returned from a trip to Europe with Varina, "seemed much pained," upon learning of the news, noted a reporter for the *Baltimore Sun*, but made no official statement. Sidney Webster, in the *New York World*, perhaps the only major metropolitan paper that remained loyal to Pierce, penned a long tribute to his former boss, in which he took issue with those who said the former president was a pliable and yielding man. 26

That mistaken perception, said Webster, came largely "from the gentleness of his bearing and the quickness of his sympathies."

"His affectionate interest in all who were worthy of it was not an artificial thing, assumed for effect and practiced from habit," added Webster. "It was innate. It had its source deep in a liberal, generous, catholic, noble nature, and to the day of his death it never lost its freshness and charm." 27

Pierce's old friend Richard Spofford wrote a poem that began: "Him no more shall malice wrong, Hate nor envy's shaft come nigh him; Sorrow that he borne so long, Nevermore it's pangs shall try him." 28

The pastor of the Concord Unitarian Society, the Reverend J. R. Lovering, undoubtedly trying to reconcile the New England hatred of Pierce with what he thought should be a proper sympathy over his passing, urged his parishioners to forgive Pierce's mistakes: "Let us cast a vail over his frailties," Lovering suggested.

Like so many of those who defended Pierce, Lovering reminded his listeners that the virtue of Pierce as a man was without question. He could never forget, he said, "the dignified form, the graceful manner, the benignant smile, the courteous sympathy of Franklin Pierce." 29

But there the positive remarks mostly came to an end and something altogether different appeared in their stead; something malignant and venomous that seemed to confirm what Pierce had so long feared, that he really was a hated and despised man, expatriated from his own country by those who would consign him forever to the outposts of memory: "Mr. Pierce was a small man, "Horace Greeley's *New York Tribune* remarked in its official notice of his death, "placed by a succession of accidents at the head of the Government when events too great for his control, or even his comprehension, were in progress." 30

The paper was particularly critical of the role Pierce had played in the Civil War, noting that although he had made a speech in April of 1861, "in favor of the Union and against the Southern Rebels," everything he did since then was "in opposition to those professions, and he, by voice and vote, encouraged those who would drive peace from a distracted country." 31

"He was essentially a weak man," agreed the *New York Times,* "who left office with little credit to himself." 32

"His political vision was limited," said James Bennett Cooper's *New York Herald*, which, incredibly, on the day that Pierce died, continued to refer to him as "Poor Pierce." 33

The establishment Eastern press could just not let it go: *Harper's Weekly* derided Pierce's entire careers as one that had "outraged humanity, liberty and the better sense of the country." The "official conduct of Mr. Pierce inflicted deep and terrible wounds upon the country," the magazine added. 34

Only four years old, but already reflecting an elite readership, *The Nation* declared that Pierce's death was "neither a public calamity or loss, nor will it much touch the popular heart, for of late years more than the usual obscurity that is the lot of presidents out of place had fallen on him."35

Some regional papers were equally harsh: "He was a man of mediocre talents, in every respect," said the *Albany Argus*; a man "execrated or despised for his political sins," thought the *Springfield Daily Republican.* 36

Abolitionists who remained convinced to the end that Pierce was pro-slavery seemed happy that he was finally gone: "A more pliant and submissive servant the slave power never had than Franklin Pierce," said the *National Anti-Slavery Standard*. And even in his native New Hampshire, press sympathy for Pierce was found wanting: "His administration was one of the most deplorable failures ever recorded," said the *Granite State Free Press.* 37

The print press memorials, such as they were, only presaged a historical verdict condemning Pierce as one of the worst presidents ever—if not *the* worst. In the decades to come, Jefferson and Varina Davis, Virginia Clay, Sidney Webster, Julian Hawthorne, Horatio Bridge, and even Ulysses S. Grant, among others, would publish memoirs that would contain accounts detailing various aspects of Pierce's career, defending him and remarking upon his humanity. His devotion to the Constitution was frequently mentioned, as was his fearless defense of civil liberties during the Civil War, a time when those liberties were clearly most at risk.

But not until 1895, more than a quarter of a century after Pierce's death, and nearly four decades since he had left the White House, did anyone change their mind about him. And that was when John Sherman sat down to document his more than four decades as a public servant.

Elected to the House of Representatives from Ohio as part of the anti-slavery revolt of 1854, Sherman was only 31 years old when he entered Congress, restless, and so good at absorbing the arcane nuances of states rights and fiscal policy that he almost overnight emerged as a sharp-edged spokesman for the Republican opposition, early on leading an investigation into border troubles in Kansas and verbally carving up any and all opponents who got in his way.

His sharp skills as a debater were perhaps never on better display than in December 1856 after Pierce had sent his final message to Congress, a message that enraged many because it not only seemed to downplay events in Kansas but blamed his political opponents for stirring up the slavery issue.

Outraged, Sherman rose in the House to respond to Pierce's message, but by doing so quickly ended up attacking the president personally: "The ghost of his defeated hopes haunt him at every step, and he seeks to allay the phantom by ceaseless clamor," Sherman said of Pierce as his fellow lawmakers sat in transfixed silence, realizing they were listening to a young master at work.

"How vivid the imagination of the President," Sherman exclaimed at another point in his address as he attacked Pierce's contention that it was the abolitionists who were causing most of the chaos in Kansas. "It is a pity to deny the innuendo, for it is like taking the ghost from the play of Hamlet," Sherman said.

Events in Kansas, Sherman declared firmly, had been proven to be a disaster for everyone, those who lived there, those who wanted to live there, pro and anti-slavery advocates, and slaves themselves, because of one man—Franklin Pierce—and his poorly thought-out strategy.

"He was reckless and bold in producing the storm," Sherman added as he neared the end of his excited remarks, "and when it came upon him, and actual strife and discord were the result, he was weak, inefficient, timid and partial." 38

Between the time that Sherman gave this speech and wrote his memoirs, a lot would happen to the young firebrand. But it was the things that never happened that seemed to define his long career: denied as Speaker of the House in a historic and protracted battle in 1859, Sherman moved on to the Senate just as Lincoln was moving to make the executive branch the dominant branch of government.

Contributing to Sherman's eclipse was the very real ascent of his younger brother, General William Tecumseh Sherman, whose leadership with Grant at Vicksburg in 1863 and the path that he blazed through Georgia and the Carolinas in 1865 made him a name known to every Northern household.

Throughout the 1860s and 70s, John Sherman was more of a second lieutenant, ushering through the Senate legislation sponsored by Lincoln and Grant. Yet those who admired him, and there were many, pointed out that he was still a young man, only 57 in 1880, and surely on the verge of presidential glory.

But that glory proved maddeningly elusive: in 1880, 1884 and 1888 delegates to the Republican convention came in regarding Sherman as a major front-runner and left after nominating someone else.

Although by the 1890s Sherman owned a resplendent mansion on K Street in Washington as well as several other tracts of land in the nation's capital, he was clearly a man whose promise had never been realized through subsequent events, a state of affairs that may have given him pause and allowed him to view the various personalities and events of his career with a certain detached perspective.

That perspective would make his two-volume *Recollection of Forty Years in the House, Senate and Cabinet,* published in 1895, a valuable exploration of how government works; a sober appraisal of some of the most epic legislative battles, all recounted with a remarkably small degree of personal rancor.

In compiling his book, Sherman read everything he could get his hands on, and one day came across the well-known campaign biography of Pierce that Nathanial Hawthorne had written in 1852. Everyone who had read the book—and indeed, Hawthorne himself—regarded it as a brief for a candidate, biased, of only a little value historically, and, in the end, a tribute from one famous old friend to another.

But something in the book got to Sherman, who began to think about Pierce and the things he had said about him, prompting him to apologize on paper for what he described as "the tone and temper" of his anti-Pierce remarks in the 1850s, admitting that he was "strongly prejudiced against him."

Sherman now wrote: "A more careful study of the motives and conduct of public men during this period has changed my opinion of many of them, and especially of President Pierce."

"That he was a genial, social and agreeable companion is affirmed by all who were familiar with him," Sherman continued. "That his opinions were honestly entertained, and firmly supported, is shown by his adherence to them without change or shadow of turning."

"In this respect, he compares favorably with many leading men of his party, who stifled their opinions to meet the currents of the day," Sherman added.

All things being equal, Sherman concluded, Franklin Pierce was a far better man and politician than he had ever been given credit for. "He had been a general of distinction in the Mexican War and a member of both the Senate and House or Representatives," Sherman wrote. "His messages to Congress, considered in a literary view, were able state papers, clearly and strongly expressed."

Looking back, Sherman could only have wished that somehow, someway, Pierce had done better.

But it was not to be. Not then and not four decades later when a worthy opponent reexamined the things that had gone wrong for Pierce and walked away from it feeling only a sense of sadness and missed opportunities for a man who, Sherman greatly suggested, deserved better.

"I can appreciate his ability, integrity and agreeable social qualities," Sherman finally concluded of a man he rarely socialized with in the 1850s, adding: "and only regret that he was President of the United States at a time when the sagacity of a Jefferson, the determined courage of a Jackson, or the shrewdness and wisdom of a Lincoln were needed to meet the difficulties and dangers which he had to encounter." 39

It was, in the end, a thought that perhaps even Franklin Pierce's most buoyant supporters would have found little to quarrel with.

CHAPTER TEN FOOTNOTES

1. Franklin Pierce to Fitz John Porter, 18 September 1866, Franklin Pierce Papers, Series 1, Reel 24.

2. Arthur M. Schlesinger, Jr. *The Almanac of American Politics* (New York: G. P. Putnam's Sons, 1983), 306.

3. Michael P. Riccards, *The Ferocious Engine of Democracy—A History of the American Presidency, Volume One* (New York: Madison Books, 1995), 292.

4. Andrew Johnson to Edwin Stanton, 5 August 1867, Andrew Johnson Papers, Series 1, Reel 28; "Washington—Secretary Stanton Requested by the President to Vacate his Office," *New York Herald,* 6 August 1867, p. 5, col. 5.

5. Fawn M. Brodie, *Thaddeus Stevens—Scourge of the South* (New York: A. A. Norton & Company, 1959), 326.

6. Beverly Wilson Palmer, *The Selected Letters of Charles Sumner—Volume Two* (Boston: Northeastern University Press, 1990), Charles Sumner to Edward Atkinson, 27 February 1868, 420; *Zachariah Chandler—An Outline Sketch of His Public Life and Public Services by the Detroit Post and Tribune* (Detroit: Post and Tribune Company, 1880), 294–96.

7. "The Elections," *New York Herald,* 9 October 1867, p. 3, col.1; "Ex-President Pierce on the Elections," *New York Times,* 12 October 1867, p. 1, col. 6.

8. "Minor Topics," *New York Times,* 14 October 1867, p. 4, col. 5.

9. "Battle of New Orleans," *New York Times,* 9 January 1868, p. 1, col. 4.

10. Howard K. Beale, *Diary of Gideon Welles, Secretary of the Navy Under Lincoln and Johnson, Volume III* (New York: W. W. Norton & Company, 1960), 309–10.

11. Michael Les Benedict, *The Impeachment and Trial of Andrew Johnson* (New York: W. W. Norton & Company, 1973), 67.

12. Riccards, *The Ferocious Engine of Democracy*, 298; Andrew Johnson to Democratic party leaders, 2 July 1868, Andrew Johnson Papers, Series 1, Reel 33.

13. Franklin Pierce to C. W. Wooley, 2 April 1868, Franklin Pierce Papers, Series 4, Reel 6.

14. "Ex-President Pierce—An Extremely Rare Instance of Self-Sacrifice," *New York Times*, 3 July 1868, p. 8, col. 3.

15. William W. Warden to Andrew Johnson, 28 June 1868, Andrew Johnson Papers, Series 1, Reel 33.

16. "Political Affairs," *New York Times*, 28 August 1868, p. 1, col. 1.

17. Franklin Pierce to Horatio Bridge, 16 February 1869, Horatio Bridge Papers, Bowdoin College Library.

18. Inaugural address of Ulysses S. Grant, 4 March 1869, Ulysses S. Grant Papers, Series 3, Reel 4.

19. "Speech before the Society of the Cincinnati," 19 May 1869, Franklin Pierce Papers, Series 4, Reel 6; "Society of the Cincinnati," *Baltimore American and Commercial*, 20 May 1869, p. 4, col. 5.

20. Franklin Pierce to Horatio Bridge, 11 October 1868, Horatio Bridge Papers, Bowdoin College Library.

21. Elizabeth Grimes to Franklin Pierce, 11 March 1869, Franklin Pierce Papers, Series 3, Reel 4.

22. Horatio Bridge, *Personal Recollections of Nathaniel Hawthorne* (New York: Harper & Brothers Publishers, 1893), 181.

23. "The Last Illness of Ex-President Pierce," *New York Times*, 11 October 1869, p. 1, col. 3.

24. "Official Announcement," *New York Tribune*, 9 October 1868, p. 7, col. 4.

25. "The Death of Ex-President Pierce," *Richmond Dispatch*, 9 October 1869, p. 2, col. 1; "Local Matters," *Richmond Dispatch,* 12 October 1869, p. 1, col. 4; no title, *Daily Picayune*, 12 October 1869, p. 9, col. 1.

26. "The Return of Jefferson Davis," *New York Times*, 14 October 1869, p. 5, col. 7.

27. Sidney Webster, *Franklin Pierce and His Administration* (New York: D. Appleton and Company, 1892), 38.

28. "Franklin Pierce," by Richard Spofford, 11 October 1869, Franklin Pierce Papers, Series 3, Reel 6.

29. "Clerical Tributes to Gen. Pierce," *New Hampshire Patriot*, 13 October 1869, p. 2, col. 4.

30. No title, *New York Tribune*, 9 October 1869, p. 6, col. 2.

31. "Obituary," *New York Tribune*, 9 October 1869, p. 7, col. 3.

32. "Political Accidents—Franklin Pierce," *New York Times*, 9 October 1869, p. 6, col. 6.

33. "Death of Ex-President Pierce," *New York Herald*, 9 October 1869, p. 6, col. 4.

34. "Franklin Pierce," *Harper's Weekly*, 30 October 1869, p. 690, col. 3.

35. No title, *The Nation*, Volume IX, Number 224, 14 October 1869, p. 306, col. 1.

36. "Franklin Pierce," *Albany Argus*, 9 October 1869, p. 2, col. 3; "Death of Ex-President Pierce," *Springfield Daily Republican* 9 October 1869, p. 4, col. 4.

37. No title, *National Anti-Slavery Standard*, 16 October 1869, p. 2, col. 5; "Death of Franklin Pierce," *Granite State Free Press*, 16 October 1869, p. 2, col. 1.

38. *Congressional Globe, 3rd Session, 34th Congress* (Washington: John C. Rives Publishing, 1857), 53–55.

39. John Sherman, *Recollections of Forty Years in the House, Senate and Cabinet, Volume 1* (Chicago: The Werner Company, 1895), 140–43.

Index

978-0-595-40367-7
0-595-40367-0

Printed in Great Britain
by Amazon

65509909R00123